The Short Oxford History of France

Modern France

D1344044

The Short Oxford History of France

General Editor: William Doyle

The Short Oxford History of France

General Editor: William Doyle

Modern France

1880–2002

Edited by James McMillan

OXFORD
UNIVERSITY PRESS

OXFORD
UNIVERSITY PRESS

Great Clarendon Street, Oxford OX2 6DP

Oxford University Press is a department of the University of Oxford.
It furthers the University's objective of excellence in research, scholarship,
and education by publishing worldwide in

Oxford New York

Auckland Bangkok Buenos Aires Cape Town Chennai
Dar es Salaam Delhi Hong Kong Istanbul Karachi Kolkata
Kuala Lumpur Madrid Melbourne Mexico City Mumbai Nairobi
São Paulo Shanghai Taipei Tokyo Toronto

Oxford is a registered trade mark of Oxford University Press
in the UK and in certain other countries

Published in the United States
by Oxford University Press Inc., New York

© Oxford University Press, 2003

British Library Cataloguing in Publication Data

Data available

Library of Congress Cataloging in Publication Data

Data available

ISBN 0–19–870059 8 (pbk)
ISBN 0–19–870058 X (hbk)

10 9 8 7 6 5 4 3 2 1

Typeset in Minion
by RefineCatch Limited, Bungay, Suffolk
Printed in Great Britain by
T.J. International Ltd., Padstow, Cornwall

General Editor's Preface

During the twentieth century, French historians revolutionized the study of history itself, opening up countless new subjects, problems, and approaches to the past. Much of this imaginative energy was focused on the history of their own country—its economy, its society, its culture, its memories. In the century's later years this exciting atmosphere inspired increasing numbers of outsiders to work on French themes, so that, more than for any other country, writing the history of France has become an international enterprise.

This series seeks to reflect these developments. Each volume is coordinated by an editor widely recognized as a historian of France. Each editor in turn has brought together a group of contributors to present particular aspects of French history, identifying the major themes and features in the light of the most recent scholarship. All the teams are international, reflecting the fact that there are now probably more university historians of France outside the country than in it. Nor is the outside world neglected in the content of each volume, where French activity abroad receives special coverage. Apart from this, however, the team responsible for each volume has chosen its own priorities, presenting what it sees as the salient characteristics of its own period. Some have chosen to offer stimulating reinterpretations of established themes; others have preferred to explore long-neglected or entirely new topics which they believe now deserve emphasis. All the volumes have an introduction and conclusion by their editor, and include an outline chronology, plentiful maps, and a succinct guide to further reading in English.

Running from Clovis to Chirac, the seven volumes in the series offer a lively, concise, and authoritative guide to the history of a country and a culture which have been central to the whole development of Europe, and often widely influential in the world beyond.

William Doyle

University of Bristol

Contents

List of contributors

JOHN HORNE is Professor in the Department of Modern History at Trinity College Dublin. With Alan Kramer, he co-authored the prize-winning monograph *German Atrocities 1914: A History of Denial* (New Haven, 2001). He is also the author of *Labour at War: France and Britain, 1914–1918* (Oxford, 1991), editor of *State, Society and Mobilization in Europe during the First World War* (Cambridge, 1997), and co-editor (with Hugh Gough) of *De Gaulle and Twentieth-Century France* (London, 1994).

MAURICE LARKIN is Professor Emeritus at the University of Edinburgh. He is the author of *France since the Popular Front, 1936–1996* (2nd edn., Oxford 1997), *Religion, Politics and Preferment in France since 1890: La Belle Epoque and Its Legacy* (Cambridge, 1995), and *Church and State after the Dreyfus Affair: The Separation Issue in France* (London, 1974).

JAMES MCMILLAN is Richard Pares Professor of History at the University of Edinburgh. Among his books are *Napoleon III* (London, 1991), *Twentieth-Century France: Politics and Society 1898–1991* (London, 1992), and *France and Women 1789–1914: Gender, Society and Politics* (London, 2000).

KEVIN PASSMORE is Lecturer in History at Cardiff University. He is the author of *From Liberalism to Fascism: The Right in a French Province* (Cambridge, 1997) and of *Fascism: A Very Short Introduction* (Oxford, 2002). He has co-edited *Writing National Histories: Western Europe since 1800* (London, 1999) and *Women, Gender and Fascism in Europe, 1919–1945* (Manchester, forthcoming).

SIÂN REYNOLDS is Professor of French at the University of Stirling. She is the author of *France between the Wars: Gender and Politics* (London, 1996), editor of *Women, State and Revolution: Essays on Power and Gender in Europe since 1789* (London, 1986), and translator of Fernand Braudel's *The Identity of France* (London, 1988).

ROBERT TOMBS is a fellow of St John's College, Cambridge. He has written *The Paris Commune, 1871* (London, 1999), *France 1814–1914*

(London, 1996), *The War against Paris, 1871* (Cambridge, 1981), and (with J. P. T. Bury) *Thiers, 1797–1877: A Political Life* (London, 1986), and is editor of *Nationhood and Nationalism in France from Boulangism to the Great War, 1889–1918* (London, 1991).

RICHARD VINEN is Reader in History at King's College, London. He is the author of *The Politics of French Business, 1936–1945* (Cambridge, 1991), *Bourgeois Politics in France 1945–1951* (Cambridge, 1995), *France 1934–1970* (London, 1996), and *A History in Fragments: Europe in the Twentieth Century* (London, 2000).

DAVID WATSON taught history at the University of Dundee between 1961 and 1997. He has published many articles on French and European history as well as *George Clemenceau: A Political Biography* (London, 1974).

List of abbreviations

ALP	Action Libérale Populaire
AD	Alliance Démocratique
ARS	Action Républicaine et Sociale
CFDT	Confédération Française Démocratique du Travail
CFLN	Comité Français de Libération National
CGPME	Confédération Générale des Petites et Moyennes Entreprises
CGT	Conféderation Générale du Travail
CNIP	Centre National des Indépendants et Paysans
CNR	Conseil National de la Résistance
CRS	Compagnies Républicaines de Sécurité
EDC	European Defence Community
EEC	European Economic Community
EMS	European Monetary System
ENA	École Nationale d'Administration
FFI	Forces Françaises de l'Intérieur
FLN	Front de Libération Nationale
FN	Front National
FNC	Fédération Nationale Catholique
FNSEA	Fédération Nationale des Syndicats des Exploitants Agricoles
FR	Fédération Républicaine
GDP	gross domestic product
GNP	gross national product
JAC	Jeunesse Agricole Chrétienne
JEC	Jeunesse Étudiante Chrétienne
JOC	Jeunesse Ouvrière Chrétienne
MLF	Mouvement de Libération des Femmes
MRP	Mouvement Républicain Populaire
NATO	North Atlantic Treaty Organization
NHS	National Health Service
PCF	Parti Communiste Français
PDP	Parti Démocrate Populaire
POW	prisoner of war
PPF	Parti Populaire Français

PRL	Parti Républicain de la Liberté
PS	Parti Socialiste
PSF	Parti Socialiste Français
RGR	Rassemblement des Gauches Républicains
RPF	Rassemblement du Peuple Français
RPF	Rassemblement pour la France
RPR	Rassemblement pour la République
SNCF	Société Nationale des Chemins de Fer
SFIO	Section Francaise de l'Internationale Ouvrière
STO	Service du Travail Obligatoire
UDF	Union pour la Démocratie Française
UDR	Union des Démocrates pour la République
UJFF	Union des Jeunes Filles de France
UNR	Union pour la Nouvelle République

Introduction: Republic and nation in the *belle époque*

James McMillan

In 1880 the French Third Republic had been in existence for ten years. That it was destined to fulfil the revolutionary dream of creating a viable democratic polity and go on to become the longest-surviving regime since 1789 was, however, far from self-evident. French national life had been fractured by conflicting ideas of the nation since 1789, and if anything the advent of the Republic in 1870 served only to deepen the ideological divide. Apologists for the regime remained obsessed with the threats posed by enemies on both the left and the right of the political spectrum. In 1871, the government headed by the veteran Orleanist politician Adolphe Thiers had ruthlessly put down the revolutionary uprising known as the Paris Commune. Some 20,000 Communards were killed, many by summary execution, and thousands more transported into penal servitude or exiled. Immediately afterwards, the Republic had been obliged to see off a serious challenge from the monarchist right, which was bent on a restoration of the Bourbons. Survival could never be taken for granted, and never was.

Nevertheless, by 1880 republicans could feel that they were at last masters in their own house, having gained definitive control of the Chamber of Deputies in 1877 and of the Senate in 1879. Two events in 1880 symbolically marked the triumph of the new order. One was an amnesty for the Communards, strongly urged by Léon Gambetta on the grounds that it would draw a line under republican divisions and rally the nation to the Republic. The other was the decision to make 14 July—Bastille Day—a public holiday. A new tradition was invented, and as the bands struck up the stirring strains of the once proscribed 'Marseillaise', a new national anthem likewise rapidly established itself as a favourite with the French public. But what exactly did the Republic stand for?

The republican project

Out of the struggles to establish the Republic between 1848 and 1879 there had gradually emerged a new republican *mystique* which glorified the Revolution of 1789 but was not itself a direct product of it. For republicans, the Republic was both a *lieu de mémoire*, a 'site of memory', and a future project, a vision of a new fraternal, egalitarian, and democratic order founded on the principle of popular sovereignty. Political democracy was the only acceptable institutional form in which democracy could be incarnated and the Republic was the only legitimate political regime. Fired by historical memories of 1789, 1793, 1848 and resistance to the Second Empire, republicans believed as ardently as any Whig or Marxist that History was on their side and that the triumph of the Republic was inevitable. The Republic was to be more than a regime: it was deliberately represented as a new 'civic religion'—precisely the kind of 'spiritual principle' which the prominent republican intellectual Ernest Renan would identify as central to the creation of national unity in a celebrated lecture of 1882 on the idea of the nation. For Renan, a nation was the product of neither language nor race but of consent and of political will, 'a plebiscite of every day'.

The republican leadership's aim was to bring about the moral unity of the nation. The distinguishing hallmark of the French republican tradition was its claim to universalism: republican values were French values, and French values were those of humanity itself, as was fit and proper for the nation which had most clearly committed itself to the Enlightenment project, proclaimed the Rights of Man, and given birth to the Revolution. In the republican vision, the true Republic had to be seen to be 'one and indivisible': in pursuit of equality for all, there could be no accommodation of particular interests. 'Society' mattered more than the individual and a strong, centralized, 'Jacobin' state was the only guarantee of national unity. The failure of the newly enfranchised peasant masses to rally to the Second Republic had convinced republican leaders of the need to school the electorate in republican values: hence education, always a major preoccupation of republicans, acquired added importance under the Empire, as the agency of Enlightenment which would guarantee victory in the battle for minds with the Catholic Church. For too long, the moralization of the masses had been entrusted to the clergy. The time had come for the Republic to confer this task to secular schoolteachers zealous to regenerate society in accordance with the positivist philosophy expounded by the likes of Auguste Comte and Emile Littré, who looked to science and reason rather than religion to deliver unprecedented progress. The new republican order was to be rigorously materialist and secular, organized without kings and without God, and dedicated to the *idée laïque*, a belief in the creation of a secularized state and society.

This republican vision was incarnated in a new generation of leaders who had emerged in the 1860s. Outstanding among them were Léon Gambetta and Jules Ferry. The bohemian Gambetta, the son of an Italian immigrant, was himself a classic example of the 'new social strata' (*nouvelles couches sociales*) which the Republic was supposed to represent, a self-made man of petty-bourgeois origins from the south of France who owed his rise to his oratorical skills. Although reputed to be a radical firebrand, he was essentially a man of government, passionately committed to the idea that the Republic should be identified with order, not the utopian dreams of 1848. Jules Ferry came from a very different background, that of the upper-class notables, who included many families with strong republican connections (those of Georges Clemenceau and René Waldeck-Rousseau among them). Like Gambetta, however (and indeed the entire republican leadership), Ferry came to power determined to fulfil the republican programme, particularly with regard to *laïcité* and the secularization of the state and the social order. Hence the bitter 'culture war' between republicans and the Catholic Church which was the dominant feature of politics after 1880 and which was much more intense and protracted than the *Kulturkampf* which set Bismarck and the German Liberals against German Catholics in the new Second Reich.

Between 1880 and 1914 the Third Republic endowed France with a democratic political culture that was as distinctive as it was durable. In a conscious effort at nation building, republicans tried to unite the French people behind the ideals of liberty, equality, and fraternity, institutionalizing and commemorating the Revolution in devices such as the tricolour flag, the 'Marseillaise', 14 July parades, the erection of statues of Marianne (the peasant girl who symbolized the Revolution), and the naming of streets. State funerals provided another opportunity for the regime to honour its luminaries, spectacularly so in the case of Victor Hugo, whose death in 1885 was followed by an elaborate funeral ceremony designed to allow the regime to bask in his reflected glory and to equate the Republic with the nation. His body was allowed to lie in state under the Arc de Triomphe, where possibly a million people filed past to pay their respects, and the ritual culminated in his committal to the Pantheon, the former church of Sainte-Geneviève transformed by the French revolutionaries into a 'temple of the fatherland' and a monument to the illustrious dead.

The centenary of the Revolution in 1889 likewise gave rise to innumerable acts of commemoration, including the erection of statues, such as that of Danton commissioned by the municipal council of Paris for the place de l'Odéon and the various effigies of the Republic commissioned in provincial centres such as Bordeaux, Lyon, and Toulouse. Whatever the means adopted in its politics of symbolic representation, the Republic's message was invariably the same: it sided with the people and identified with their long, heroic, and ultimately successful struggle against despotism and privilege. The regime was the incarnation of the democratic myth and the fulfilment of the dreams of the revolutionaries of 1789.

The radical agenda of the republicans in the matter of cultural politics, however, should not obscure the fact that their real long-term goal was to build an essentially conservative Republic which would be acceptable as much to the seriously wealthy—the great landowners, bankers, and captains of industry—as to Gambetta's *nouvelles couches*—the peasants and petty bourgeoisie—who loomed so large in republican propaganda. Moderate republicans, especially, were determined to live down the Republic's former associations with violence and bloodshed and to create a durable political edifice which would be synonymous with order and good government. The new

Republic was to be a bourgeois Republic: it would not repeat the errors of the *démoc-socs* of 1848, who had dreamed of a 'social' Republic. To imagine that government held the solution to the 'social question', Ferry told the Chamber of Deputies in 1884, was a dangerous illusion. Even when the 'radical' Republic replaced the 'opportunist' Republic at the turn of the century, the lurch to the left was expressed in the politics of anticlericalism, not in any new commitment to social or gender equality. By then, the republican ruling elite had largely succeeded in its task of creating a viable conservative state and of establishing the political stability which had eluded its predecessors of 1792 and 1848. This was the key political development of the period before 1914, even if it has sometimes been overshadowed in accounts which emphasize the scandals and crises which rocked the republican boat, and persuaded contemporary republican leaders that their regime was forever condemned to live dangerously.

Alternative visions: the right, religion, and national identity

The major problem for the republicans was that, for all their universalist rhetoric, they had no monopoly over the idea of the nation. The right never accepted the notion that the Revolution had invented the nation and instead pointed to the long work of centralization carried out by the Capetian monarchy as the main begetter of a sense of national identity that was focused on the king. It mattered, too, that the king was a Catholic king, *le roi très chrétien*. Catholics and conservatives therefore imagined France as 'the eldest daughter of the Church' and represented the Revolution as a catastrophic rupture with the nation's religious and monarchical traditions. As a result, nineteenth-century France was rent by an ongoing Franco-French war which, though not a civil war in more than a figurative sense except in 1871, was characterized by bitter ideological conflicts and identification with antagonistic cultural references and symbols. For the right, Marianne, the symbol of the Republic, was *la gueuse*, the slut. The right's icons were Joan of Arc, rediscovered and reappropriated by Catholics and conservatives in the late nineteenth century as a martyr and candidate for sainthood, and the Sacred Heart of Jesus, whose cult, spread by the Jesuit Order, evoked memories of the Vendée uprising against the First Republic in 1793. The building of the massive neo-Byzantine basilica of Sacré-Cœur as a votive church on the hill of Montmartre in Paris after the Commune was hailed as an act of reparation by Catholics (who did not easily forget that the Communards had shot the archbishop of Paris and other hostages from the ranks of the clergy) but denounced by radical republicans as a provocation.

Contemporary commentators frequently spoke of a war between the 'two Frances', the France of the Revolution and Catholic and conservative France. The prominent republican intellectual, Charles Renouvier, writing in 1872, claimed that 'There are two Frances in France, that of the clericals and that of the liberals . . . there are no longer virtually any ideas or sentiments in common between the two groups, between these two people obliged none the less to live under the same civil law.' The Catholic monk and historian Dom Besse agreed, claiming in 1904 that there was a struggle to the death between 'royalist and Catholic France and revolutionary and atheist France'. Following the failure of the attempt to restore the monarchy in the 1870s, it was the religious issue which increasingly marked the dividing line between the two Frances. At stake was the place of religion in public life. For republicans, religion was essentially a private matter: after 1880 they wanted it to play no role in the public sphere. Catholics, on the other hand, refused to allow religion to be relegated to the margins of public life and argued for the maintenance of the historic links between the Catholic Church and the French nation.

Some historians dismiss the idea of a war of the two Frances as an exaggeration, and it is certainly true that on both sides it was a conflict maintained by extremists. There were many Frenchmen, republicans and Catholics, who wanted to find common ground in the centre, notably at the time of the *ralliement*, or rallying of French Catholics to the Republic in the 1890s. The fact remains, however, that it was the extremists who tended to prevail and the violence of their rhetoric prevented any real reconciliation between republican France and apologists for the Catholic idea of the nation. Furthermore, the culture war also had a local dynamic and was much more than an intra-bourgeois quarrel within the ranks of the French intelligentsia. In the countryside, especially in strongly Catholic regions such as the west, the culture war was fought out on the ground, between parish priests and villagers. The *guerre scolaire*, or 'battle of the schools', in Brittany in the 1890s, for instance, showed that the culture war was all too real and no figment of the imagination of contemporary intellectuals.

The 1890s also witnessed the rise of a new, nationalist right which provided the Republic with yet another challenge to its legitimacy. Rejecting the republicans' abstract and essentially political conception of the nation, this *droite révolutionnaire*, or revolutionary right, envisaged the nation not in terms of the one and indivisible secular Republic but as an ethnic, racial, and cultural entity. Paul Déroulède, founder of the League of Patriots in 1882 and apostle of a war of *revanche* against Germany, was a prominent convert from republican nationalism during the Boulangist crisis of the late 1880s. The *fin-de-siècle* nationalism championed by the likes of Maurice Barrès and Charles Maurras had much in common with the *völkisch* nationalist tradition in Germany and affirmed an identity rooted in the blood and soil of France—the cult of *la terre et les morts*, in the phrase of Barrès. Maurras, the moving spirit of the neo-monarchist league Action Française, founded in 1898 during the Dreyfus Affair, idealized 'true France', the *pays réel*, which he distinguished from the *pays légal*, the corrupt republican regime. A French manifestation of a general European intellectual reaction against reason, liberalism, and the entire Enlightenment project, this new 'integral' nationalism was anti-Semitic and xenophobic as well as anti-liberal and anti-democratic. Preaching a doctrine of 'France for the French', it excoriated both the enemy without—the foreigner, especially the German—and, even more important, the enemy within—the Jew, the Protestant, the naturalized Frenchman—all of whom allegedly lacked the psychic awareness of what it meant to be 100 per cent French.

The new nationalism was never more than a minority tradition. It proved, however, to be a persistent one, and even when the Republic triumphed over it, as during the Boulanger and Dreyfus crises, it continued to exercise a powerful cultural influence on the life of the nation. Maurras may have lacked a mass following, but his *Action Française* newspaper had plenty of admirers among educated public opinion, both before and after the First World War. The new right was a harbinger of unpleasant things to come—the fascist leagues of the 1930s and Vichy—but in the years before 1914 it was unable to dislodge a republican regime which seemed to offer peace, prosperity, and tangible material progress.

The state, society, and culture

It helped greatly that the republican project was developed in a society which underwent only gradual change and which had been spared the ravages of a full-blown industrial revolution. In the 1880s, France was still recognizably a peasant society, and would remain so until the 1950s. Though productivity was high and some sectors of the economy were buoyant at the turn of the century—France was a market leader in the new automobile industry, for instance—agriculture was backward and population growth had already slowed to a point where concerned voices had begun to be raised about the implications for French prosperity and security by comparison with the high birth rate and industrial might of Germany. Yet the Republic succeeded in identifying itself with material progress. The 'universal expositions' or world's fairs of 1889 and 1900 far outdid their predecessor of 1878, not to mention those of the Second Empire, as gigantic spectacles, which, in addition to providing extravagant entertainment for millions of Parisians and tourists, served as a showcase for the marvels of French technology and engineering. The wonder of the 1889 exhibition was the Eiffel Tower, at the time the tallest structure in the world and an affront to conservative taste. Also hugely impressive was the Galerie des Machines, a site of some 16,000 machines spread over nearly 15 acres from which people went away 'stupefied and ravished' in the words of the writer J.-K. Huysmans. The centrepiece of the 1900 exhibition was the Palace of Electricity, where dazzling light shows enchanted a public fascinated with the new and the spectacular.

The Republic likewise benefited from its successful restoration of French prestige and standing in international affairs after the disaster of the Franco-Prussian War. *Revanche*—the dream of a war of revenge against Germany—was abandoned by all but a minority of zealous patriots such as Déroulède and his disciples but the moderate leaders of the Republic pursued a policy of French aggrandizement by other means, notably by the construction of a vast overseas empire to rival that of Britain. At the same time, they worked to bring France out of twenty years of diplomatic isolation in Europe by forming a military alliance with Russia in the 1890s. The signing of the Entente Cordiale with Britain in 1904—a remarkable reversal of the situation in which the two countries had almost come to war in 1898— completed the diplomatic revolution. In a world increasingly fraught with danger and beset by international tensions, it was considered essential to have powerful friends—which is why France was ready to go to war in 1914 in order to uphold the Franco-Russian alliance in the face of German attempts to destabilize it.

The *belle époque*—the 'good old days' before 1914, as they would seem in retrospect from the vantage point of the 1920s, after the experience of the horrors of the First World War—was also a time of extraordinary intellectual vitality and cultural creativity. Paris was the uncontested cultural capital of the world, above all for the artistic avant-garde. Painters such as Picasso and Miró, Modigliani and Chagall were drawn to the home of Cézanne and Matisse. Poets like Mallarmé, Rimbaud, and Verlaine broke the poetic mould with their 'symbolist' verse. The revolution in music announced in 1894 by Claude Debussy's *Prélude de l'après-midi d'un faune* (*Prelude to the afternoon of a faun*), an ethereal musical evocation of a celebrated Mallarmé poem about a Roman god who in the guise of a satyr falls in love with a young wood nymph, was continued by the visits of Diaghilev's Ballets Russes from 1909. The sensation of the 1912 season was their ballet version of the *Après-midi*, in which the dancer Nijinsky's movements in the role of the satyr were denounced by the editor of *Le Figaro* as 'filthy and bestial in their eroticism'. Still more sensational was the première in May 1913 of the Stravinsky/Nijinsky ballet *Le Sacre du printemps* (*The Rite of Spring*), whose primitive savagery of music and choreography shocked both the conventional critics and the bourgeois audience. That same year Proust published *Du côté de chez Swann*, the first volume of his *A la recherche du temps perdu*, which arguably stands with James Joyce's *Ulysses* as the greatest product of the modernist literary imagination. The scientist Marie Curie, Polish by birth and French by marriage, twice won the Nobel Prize. A society in which the life of the mind flourished to such a prodigious extent clearly had a great deal going for it.

Nevertheless, the *belle époque* was no pre-war golden age. Schools, the completion of the communications network, and the introduction of compulsory military service may have converted many peasants into Frenchmen, sensitized, for the first time, to their relationship with the imagined national community that was the French nation, but rural France remained beset with problems of peasant indebtedness, subsistence farming, and the flight of rural labour from the land. Many of the country's 4.5 million industrial workers experienced a strong sense of alienation both from the workplace and from the wider society and parliamentary politics, and expressed their disenchantment in sympathy with revolutionary syndicalism, the creed of class war articulated by the militants who headed the CGT (General Confederation of Labour). Strikes were numerous, and almost always political, either overtly or implicitly. The substantial presence of immigrant workers—Belgians in the north, Italians in the east and south-east—was far from welcome to indigenous workers and did nothing to improve industrial relations. Women workers—an important element in the industrial workforce in textiles and the clothing industry—were likewise resented by male proletarians who were convinced that they took away jobs from men and depressed male wages.

Women in general had plenty of cause to feel aggrieved with the way in which society was ordered. In French law married women were required to obey their husbands and accorded the same status as children. The Penal Code upheld a double standard of morality by which the adultery of a wife was treated as a much more serious offence than that of a husband. No woman was allowed the right to vote: in the traditions of the Jacobin Republic, women could and should be the mothers and educators of citizens but citizenship itself was an exclusively masculine prerogative. A notable political development in the *belle époque* was the emergence of a women's movement, committed to the removal of gender discrimination and the achievement of equal rights, including, above all, the right to the suffrage. France may have lacked suffragettes of the Pankhurst variety but it was not short of suffragists. As we shall see, however, they had a hard struggle on their hands to defeat the entrenched forces of male chauvinism. French women would only obtain the right to vote in 1944. The Republic was as anti-feminist as it was anti-Catholic— indeed, the two causes were linked in the minds of the republican leadership on the grounds that women were allegedly more susceptible to clerical influence than men and were thus more likely to support the parties of the Right than the progressive adepts of republicanism.

Republican political culture, therefore, was not free from a bias against workers and women as well as against the Catholic religion. If this last could be justified on the grounds that it was necessary to break the political power of the Church, it nevertheless guaranteed the prolongation of the war of the two Frances well into the twentieth century, while the rise of the new, nationalist right (with which many Catholics openly sympathized, at least until the condemnation of Action Française by Pope Pius XI in 1926) represented for some an attractive alternative to the republican consensus. The attacks of the right were all the more effective because lofty republican principles seemed to be too often at odds with the shoddy practicalities of everyday political life. Yet the ideals of the Republic *were* high, even noble, and while they were articulated mainly by intellectuals and politicians, through universal schooling, they impacted on the masses too. Millions would be prepared to fight and die for the republican idea of France, both in 1914 and again in 1939. What Thiers had said in 1875 was true: the Republic was the regime which divided Frenchmen least.

1

Consolidating the Republic: politics 1880–1914

James McMillan

The new republican leadership was immediately confronted with the problem of how to translate its ideals into tangible political realities. Apart from inevitable clashes of personality and temperament, it was divided over the question of the pace of progress towards a fully democratic order, and in particular on how rapidly to proceed with the implementation of the secularization programme which would create the *état laïc*. 'Radicals', claiming to be the custodians of the flame of republican purity, called for immediate and sweeping anti-clerical measures: moderates were more cautious, mindful of the influence the Church still exercised in many rural areas, and advocated only such reforms as were 'opportune' (thus earning themselves the sobriquet of 'opportunists').

Disagreements also arose over the issue of state intervention in economic and social matters. Whereas opportunist republicans remained sensitive to the interests of big business and the financial oligarchy, radicals presented themselves as the champion of the small producer—be he peasant, artisan, or small businessman—and sympathetic to progressive legislation designed to address the 'social question' and to alleviate the plight of the worker through the introduction of measures such as old-age pensions, a graduated income tax, and a programme of nationalization, though by the turn of the century radicals themselves were split over these issues. Opportunists, too, shared the preoccupation of liberals with constitutional issues, the rule of law and proper parliamentary control over the executive power. For some twenty years after 1879, it was these political moderates who were entrusted with the charge of fashioning a regime in their own likeness. They did so by means of a democratic instrument which was admirably suited to their purpose.

The political system

For many observers, the very nature of the political system itself reinforced the impression of the regime's vulnerability. Its most obvious feature was the weakness of the executive by comparison with the legislature. Presidents were elected by the two houses of Parliament (the Chamber of Deputies and the Senate) sitting as a National Assembly and, though the constitution of 1875 gave the president considerable theoretical powers, in practice presidents chose not to exercise them after 1877. Fearful that a strong president could use his position to subvert republican institutions from above—there were, after all, the precedents of MacMahon in 1877 and Louis Napoleon in 1851–2—republicans normally preferred to assign the presidential office to harmless figureheads, who were supposed to be content to open the proverbial flower show rather than seek to play any active role in government. Appearances, however, could be deceptive. Presidents were not always the ciphers they were made out to be. They appointed the prime minister (the 'President of the Council'), which meant that they could often keep out someone they disliked, as Grévy demonstrated in the case of Gambetta. They also signed international treaties, which ensured that presidents had a role in the conduct of foreign policy. In practice, the role of the president depended largely on the personality of the incumbent and varied according to the political circumstances in which he found himself, which is why an able and prominent politician such as Raymond Poincaré, with a particular interest in maintaining the interests of France as a major power, was willing to take on the job in the period of high international tensions which resulted in the outbreak of the First World War.

The key political institution was the Chamber of Deputies, elected by universal male suffrage through *scrutin d'arrondissement*, a single-member electoral system which favoured the individual deputy with a strong local power base. In the absence of a disciplined party system—constituents expected favours rather than adherence to a party line from their representatives—the deputy was king. *Interpellation*—the right to grill ministers for hours on end—allowed reputations to be established at the podium. The formidable debating skills of a Clemenceau, for instance, brought down more than one ministry. Equally, talented individuals could make a name for themselves by serving as *rapporteurs* of parliamentary bills, chairing the commissions which scrutinized draft legislation and assuming responsibility in the Chamber for acts of parliament which might eventually bear their name. The second house, the Senate, was a home for retired politicians and civil servants. Elected by indirect suffrage, it vastly over-represented rural and provincial France at the expense of the urban population and was intended to act as a check on any tendency to radicalism on the part of the Chamber—a role which it fulfilled with relish on a number of important issues, including the introduction of a graduated income tax and women's suffrage.

A direct consequence of this political system was the instability of ministries. The Third Republic had sixty governments between 1870 and 1914. On average, they lasted eight months: some fell after only a few weeks, or even days. It is true that this instability was something of an optical illusion: in the many ministerial reshuffles, it was the same faces of those deputies who had marked themselves out as *ministrables* which tended to reappear, albeit with responsibility for a different portfolio. In a long career which stretched from the *fin de siècle* to the late 1920s, Aristide Briand would be a minister in twenty-five governments and hold office for over sixteen years. The need for continuity at certain ministries, like foreign affairs, was also understood: thus Delcassé served continuously at the Quai d'Orsay between 1898 and 1905. Clemenceau, when accused of being a serial destroyer of governments, riposted: 'I have overthrown only one. They are all the same.' Even so, the constant coming and going of ministries gave the impression that politics was largely a game played by a professional *classe politique* whose principal preoccupation was manoeuvring for the spoils of office rather than working for the good of the *patrie*.

The Republic of Grévy and Ferry, 1880–1885

The epitome of the moderate Republic was its president, Jules Grévy, a man who could be relied on never to attempt to thwart the will of the electorate or to challenge the authority of parliament. Indeed, he had made a name for himself by opposing the creation of the office which he now held, on the grounds that it was a relic of the royalist past. Profoundly conservative by instinct, he wanted to see the country run by moderates of whom he approved—men like the wealthy Protestants Waddington and Freycinet, and that other pillar of bourgeois republican respectability, Jules Ferry. As long as possible he dispensed with the services of the flamboyant Gambetta, who for Grévy remained too much of a rabble-rouser. Only after Gambetta had led the republicans to victory in the legislative elections of 1881 was Grévy finally compelled to give him a crack at government. In the event, however, the much anticipated 'great ministry' of Gambetta lasted a mere seventy-three days, weakened from the outset by the refusal of other top republicans to join his cabinet. A year later, following a mysterious illness, Gambetta was dead at the early age of 45, leaving the way open for Ferry to become the dominant figure on the political scene.

Ferry was a political moderate, but, as a freemason and an adept of the positivist philosophy which characterized the outlook of so many of his generation of republicans, he adhered unswervingly to the view that the Republic stood for the triumph of liberty, progress, and science over the forces of reaction and obscurantism. The triumph of the Republic needed to be accompanied by the establishment of 'republican liberties'—laws which removed restrictions on individual freedom, such as the legislation in 1881 to permit the opening of new bars and cafés (widely appreciated in republican circles not merely as convivial watering holes, but as places conducive to the spread of republican ideas). Other laws of the same year authorized the organization of public meetings and provided for freedom of the press, while legislation of 1884 legalized trade unions.

At the top of Ferry's agenda, however, was the objective of creating the *état laïc*—a secular state in a secular society. The key area here was education and already in 1879, as minister of education, in article 7 of a law on secondary education, he had declared war on unauthorized religious orders (the Jesuits being the main target) and banned them from teaching. Laws of 1881 and 1882 made primary schooling free, compulsory, and non-denominational to age 13 for both sexes. A subsequent law of 1886 sought to republicanize the teaching profession, removing the religious orders from the classrooms in state schools and requiring teachers to hold a qualification from a state training school (*école normale*). Girls' education was a special target, since republicans believed that, in the battle for the minds of future generations, it was necessary to woo women away from their traditional prejudices and superstitions—in other words from their religious beliefs. The law of 1879 provided for the creation of at least one female training school for women teachers in each department, while another law of 1880 established a network of state secondary schools for girls. Other measures to promote the secularization of society included the reintroduction of divorce, abolished by the Bourbons in 1816, but re-established in 1884 by a law steered through parliament by the radical republican Alfred Naquet, and an end to the exemption from military service for seminary students. *Le curé sac au dos*—the priest with his knapsack on his back—also had his part to play in the realization of the *état laïc*.

The attack on the Church was not accompanied by any assault on the material interests of the rich. Ferry's ideological warfare allowed the regime to appear more radical than it actually was, providing a useful smokescreen behind which its real business— making the world safe for the bourgeoisie—could be conducted. For this task, Grévy looked less to Ferry than to men like the engineer Freycinet and the conservative financier Léon Say. Their task was rendered all the more difficult by the economic downturn in Europe as a whole from the mid-1870s, which did much to undermine confidence in both economic liberalism and in the liberal state itself. The end of the railway boom and increased agricultural competition from overseas markets had serious effects on both French industry and agriculture and the latter was further blighted by disease in the form of silkworm and phylloxera. Many wine-growers were ruined and, as agricultural prices fell, there were knock-on effects on manufacturing industry and the building trade, leading to unemployment, wage-cuts, and strikes. Though pleased by their achievements in the field of education, republicans were troubled by their inability to create a 'feel-good factor' with regard to the economy.

They did try, however. The Freycinet Plan, devised in 1878, was intended to stimulate economic activity through a massive public works programme aimed at extending the communications network of canals, roads, and, especially, railways (another 23,000 kilometres of track were envisaged). Initially well received by the French financial community, the Plan at first gave the desired boost to the economy but it placed an enormous strain on the public purse and produced huge distortions in the pattern of public spending. The crisis deepened in 1882, when turmoil in the banking sector (which claimed as one of its principal victims a Catholic bank, the Union Générale, set up to challenge the hegemony of Jews and Protestants in the world of finance) was accompanied by a precipitous fall in the prices of agricultural products. Forced to try another tack, the opportunists increasingly turned to protectionism as the remedy for the country's economic ills.

Napoleon III's introduction of free trade after 1860 had never been popular with most French textiles manufacturers, and it was they who took the lead in demanding the reintroduction of tariffs in the late 1870s, seconded by spokesmen from heavy industry. Some of the country's leading landowners (many of them nobles) also began to call for a return to protection and in 1881 a tariff law reintroduced duties on a limited range of mainly industrial goods. Further measures followed in 1882, 1885, and 1887, as support for protection picked up in the countryside, notably among small peasant farmers and southern wine-growers hostile to the importation of cheap Italian wine. The key advocate of the protectionist policy in parliament was Jules Méline, deputy for the Vosges and a close colleague of Ferry, who had strong connections with the textile manufacturers of his region but who at the Ministry of Agriculture increasingly presented himself as the champion of French agricultural interests. Méline, in effect, helped to forge an alliance between industrial capitalists and French agrarians which laid the social foundations for the consolidation of a conservative Republic in the 1890s, particularly in the aftermath of the Méline tariff of 1892, which marked the culmination of the protectionist campaign.

Protection may have been good for captains of industry and large landowners, but it raised the cost of living for workers in the cities.

Inevitably, it also invited retaliation from other countries, with a consequent loss of overseas markets. Aware of this danger, Ferry looked to colonies to provide France with new markets. Equally, for Ferry as for Gambetta, colonies were potentially a vehicle for the promotion of French grandeur, so badly dented by the recent catastrophic defeat at the hands of Prussia in 1870. The Ferry era was therefore notable also for its forward colonial policy, in Africa and Indo-China, as described in Chapter 4, but it was this which precipitated his downfall when news reached Paris in March 1885 that French forces had suffered a humiliating reversal at the hands of the Vietnamese resistance. In the legislative elections of October 1885, radical republicans polled particularly well and now held the balance of power, which is how a protégé of Clemenceau, Georges Boulanger, came to enter the government at the Ministry of War.

The Boulangist crisis, 1885–1889

The Boulangist episode was the first of a succession of affairs which damaged the reputation of the Republic. Boulanger enjoyed the backing of the radical republicans because, mistakenly, they thought that he was the strong man they had been looking for to stand up to Bismarck. Boulanger was less of a traditionalist than most army officers, many of whom continued to harbour monarchist sympathies, but he was not so much a republican general as an ambitious demagogue with a talent for self-publicity. In 1887 his popularity soared to new heights when, in the course of a diplomatic incident involving a border dispute between France and Germany, he appeared to have faced down Bismarck.

What transformed 'Boulangism' from a personality cult into a political movement was the belief, shared on both the extreme left and the extreme right, that Boulanger's popularity could be exploited to rid France of the hated opportunist Republic. On the left, militant republicans such as Paul Déroulède, hoped for reform of the executive power and a war of revenge against Germany. These ambitions were shared by the likes of the renegade aristocrat turned demagogic journalist Henri Rochefort and fellow veterans of the Paris Commune, while other supporters on the left included Georges Laguerre, another protégé of Clemenceau, Alfred Naquet, the author of the divorce law, and a number of 'socialists' of various hues. On the right, royalists, headed by the Pretender, the comte de Paris himself, hoped to make Boulanger into the instrument of a restoration which would set 'Phippe V' on the throne of his ancestors. To that end, and obviously without the knowledge of Boulanger's radical sponsors, they were willing to offer impressive financial backing, no one more so than the eccentric and fabulously wealthy duchesse d'Uzès, who promised three million francs.

Boulanger's own political leanings remain something of a mystery, but the fact was that he willingly played along with both extremes of left and right in order to stay in the political limelight, particularly after 1887, when a change of government cost him his post at the War Office and he found himself packed off to a command in the provinces. Stirred up by Déroulède's League of Patriots and by other elements of the extreme left, a crowd demonstrated at the Gare de Lyon and tried to prevent Boulanger's departure. The atmosphere of political crisis was heightened by a political scandal which broke in October 1887 and compromised the president of the Republic. Daniel Wilson, Grévy's son-in-law, was discovered to have been using his family connections to traffic in the sale of honours, and the president was obliged to resign. His successor, Sadi Carnot, had little to recommend him apart from his name (he was the grandson of Lazare Carnot, the 'organiser of victory' of the Jacobin armies). Such a change at the top was not enough to placate the militant republicans who wanted nothing less than a dissolution of the existing Chamber and fresh elections for a Constituent Assembly mandated to redraw the Constitution.

It was these radicals who formulated the strategy of taking advantage of the 'list' system of voting by departments (*scrutin de liste*), introduced in 1885 supposedly to encourage greater party discipline, by putting Boulanger up for election in a series of by-elections in order to demonstrate overwhelming grass-roots support for change. Through 1888, Boulanger chalked up an impressive series of victories at the polls, in both rural and urban France, obviously benefiting from popular discontent with the economic situation. Amidst great excitement, the campaign culminated in victory in Paris on 27 January 1889, where Boulanger polled particularly well in the industrial suburbs inhabited by the factory proletariat. Expectations of a coup were widespread, both within the Boulangist camp and among the fearful opportunist leadership. Boulanger was no *putschist*, however, and refused to lead an assault on the Elysée. The danger passed and, recovering its nerve, the government moved decisively against him. In a ploy which would become a classic feature of republican political practice, it once again changed the rules of the electoral game to work to the advantage of its own candidates, reintroducing the system of *scrutin d'arrondissement*, whereby candidates stood for a single-member constituency in which local issues and personality factors tended to be crucial. In a further move against demagogy, candidates were debarred from standing in more than one constituency. The government also struck at Boulanger personally, threatening to remove his parliamentary immunity and to prosecute him for conspiring against the Republic. This move was of dubious legality, but Boulanger, fearing for his life, dismayed his supporters by fleeing the country. In his absence, he was tried and sentenced to transportation.

The Boulangist bubble had burst, though there remained the matter of the elections of autumn 1889. Paris continued to vote for Boulanger (who was not allowed to take his seat) and in the country at large the combined Boulangist and right-wing vote almost equalled that of the republicans. Thanks to the gerrymandered electoral system, however, this translated into only 43 seats for the Boulangists and 162 for the right against 350 for the republicans (opportunists and radicals combined). What killed Boulangism off were press revelations of the General's duplicity and his flirtations with royalism. In the Paris municipal elections of 1890, only two Boulangist councillors were returned. Boulanger himself, demoralized by his failure and in despair at the death of his mistress, committed suicide over her grave in Brussels in 1891.

The Republic had survived, and could continue the process of consolidation, profiting from the propaganda opportunities surrounding the celebrations to commemorate the centenary of 1789 and the Universal Exposition of 1889. The Boulangist episode, which had seemed to place the Republic in danger, had ultimately served to reveal its strength. Confronted with a common enemy, republicans of whatever stamp would engage in 'republican concentration' to ensure the survival of the regime. Radicals, however, had had their fingers burned, and in future would be distinctly unenthusiastic about constitutional reform and the search for a charismatic leader. The right, on the other hand, though it had failed in its primary objective of overthrowing the Republic, had learned a great deal about how to mobilize the masses to subvert democracy from within. For its leaders, the Boulangist affair was not an end but a beginning, marking the birth of a new right. The success of Édouard Drumont's *La France juive* (1886), a rant against the allegedly malign influence of Jews on national life, pointed to an enhanced role in future for anti-Semitism in the right's discovery of popular politics and new brand of nationalism. It did not have too long to wait for fresh opportunities to seek to discredit the Republic in the eyes of French public opinion.

The *ralliement*, Panama, and the Franco-Russian alliance

First, however, the Republic enjoyed a new lease of life, even winning support from an unexpected quarter. As explained in Chapter 8, the politics of demagogy held no appeal for Pope Leo XIII, who was convinced that Catholics in France should abandon their attachment to the monarchy and rally to the republican regime. His policy of *ralliement* dumbfounded intransigent royalists, but a number of Catholics heeded the papal call—men like Albert de Mun and Jacques Piou—and set about trying to create a new conservative party which would operate against the real enemy: the revolutionary left, increasingly personified not merely by radicals but by socialists. (The menace of socialism was another of Leo XIII's preoccupations and was one factor—allied to a strong commitment to social justice and revulsion at the inequalities inherent in laissez-faire liberalism—which had prompted him to issue his most famous encyclical, *Rerum novarum*, in May 1891, a call for a new deal for workers and an appeal to Catholics to become actively involved in forms of 'social' Catholicism).

It was against this background of religious détente that another scandal broke in September 1892. As in the Daniel Wilson affair, the issue was sleaze, only this time the circumstances concerned the failure of the Panama Canal Company. The project was the brainchild of France's most celebrated engineer, Ferdinand de Lesseps, builder of the Suez Canal, and his name alone had been sufficient to attract

investors, small and large, to his new venture in the Isthmus of Panama. But the scheme had run into all sorts of difficulties, and as costs
soared, agents of the Company such as the cosmopolitan Jewish
financier Baron de Reinach and the adventurer Cornélius Herz (a
naturalized American citizen) resorted to bribing both the press and
the politicians to maintain public confidence and to secure legislation
permitting further flotations. The Company foundered nevertheless,
going into liquidation in early 1889, just after Boulanger's election
victory in Paris. For a time the full extent of the scandal was hushed
up, as ministers who had taken bribes delayed the judicial investiga-
tions demanded by outraged shareholders. But in 1892 details of the
campaign of corruption began to leak out via *La Libre Parole*, the
newspaper founded by Édouard Drumont. The suicide of Reinach in
November 1892 heightened the drama, while in the Chamber of Deputies the Catholic and Boulangist deputy Jules Delahaye denounced
parliamentary sleaze, claiming that more than 100 deputies—almost
all of them republicans—had been on Herz's payroll.

Reluctantly, the government set up a committee of inquiry and
allowed prosecutions to take place. De Lesseps was convicted as a
scapegoat, but all the politicians (apart from one stupid enough to
confess) were acquitted. The entire episode hardly enhanced the
Republic's reputation for probity, however, and on the Right many
asked why they should be expected to 'rally' to a Republic that was so
manifestly corrupt. Inevitably, some of the mud slung at the regime
by its opponents stuck. Many of the compromised opportunist
politicians realized that their time was up and retired from political
life. The single most notable victim of Panama, however, was the
radical Georges Clemenceau, who, though not directly involved in
the scandal, was discovered to have received subventions from
Herz for his newspaper *La Justice*. The nationalist Paul Déroulède
went further and accused him of being a spy in the pay of the
British—a ludicrous accusation, but one which was taken seriously by
Clemenceau's peasant constituents in the Var, who failed to return
him to parliament in the elections of 1893.

Yet the elections of 1893 were far from the disaster that the
opportunist politicians had feared. The furore over Panama among
the political class had left the peasant electorate unmoved. Propiti-
ated by the Méline tariff, it continued to back a regime which was
apparently committed to its interests. Moreover, if Panama dented

the Republic's image, success in foreign policy enhanced it. The signing of an entente with Russia in 1892, which was developed into a full military alliance in 1894, brought France out of its long diplomatic isolation and revived the feelings of *grandeur* which had been shattered by the defeat of 1870–1. The details of the pact, by which each country pledged to assist the other in the event of aggression on the part of Germany or Germany's allies, were kept a secret of state, but it was clear that France was no longer alone in a hostile world. The conservative Republic began to look capable of delivering not just domestic stability but even prestige in the eyes of foreign powers.

Ironically, therefore, not all Panamists lost their seats in the 1893 elections, while Jules Delahaye, the excoriator of sleaze, was defeated. So, too, were the *ralliés*. Neither Albert de Mun nor Jacques Piou was elected, since much of the Catholic vote abstained, or voted for moderate republicans on the second ballot. The results were a total triumph for the moderate republicans, more than 300 of whom were returned, giving them an absolute majority. Freed from the need to enlist radical support against the right, the new generation of moderates—who included men with a big future like Raymond Poincaré and Louis Barthou—began to call themselves *progressistes*, priding themselves on their non-sectarian outlook and willing to collaborate with all, including Catholics, who supported a conservative Republic. The original opportunist project seemed to have been amply realized. Indeed, if there were a threat to the regime in 1893, it appeared to lie not on the right but on the left.

The rise of socialism

For the other victors in the elections of 1893 were the socialists. Socialism had been making steady converts in various parts of France— notably the industrial Nord—since the late 1870s, but its impact was diluted by the internal divisions which divided the movement into warring factions. A Marxist wing, headed by the doctrinaire and inflexible Jules Guesde, adopted a hardline policy aimed at creating a class-based party which would unite all socialists on a strictly defined Marxist basis. The party (the Parti Ouvrier Français—French Workers' Party) demanded full political control and was dismissive both of the democratic process and measures of social reform. The latter, it was claimed, merely prolonged the death throes of capitalism and bred false hopes in workers.

Reformist socialists, on the other hand, such as the 'possibilists' led by Dr Paul Brousse believed that socialism should help to alleviate the plight of the workers through practical social reforms at the local level. The typographer Jean Allemane agreed, but, disliking the bourgeois leadership of the Broussist faction, split off to form a more solidly proletarian party, which had a strong base among the artisans of Paris who regarded themselves as descendants of the Communards and the sans-culottes. Close in temperament to the Allemanists were the Blanquists, whose moving spirits, Louise Michel and Henri Rochefort, likewise kept alive the Communard tradition, though after the Boulangist adventure their new leader, Édouard Vaillant, reluctantly accepted that a parliamentary regime was preferable to the alternative of 'caesarism'. Anarchists were also a far from negligible presence among the diverse elements that made up the French left. Finally, there were a number of 'independent' socialists who were inspired not by Marxism but by the French revolutionary tradition, and who looked for the completion of the work begun in 1789 to be realized in the creation of a socialist republic. The outstanding figure in the ranks of the independents was Jean Jaurès, a philosophy professor and spellbinding orator who was returned to the Chamber in 1893 as the choice of the miners of Carmaux. The rising barrister, Alexandre Millerand, was another prominent independent, making his mark with a speech at Saint-Mandé in 1896 which formulated a minimum programme for the parliamentary route to socialism.

In all, some fifty socialists were returned to parliament in 1893, including Guesde as deputy for Roubaix in the industrial north. This was enough of a breakthrough to scare the republican bourgeoisie, who became even more frightened when an extremist anarchist faction, invoking the need for 'propaganda by the deed', unleashed a campaign of bomb throwing which resulted in a series of terrorist outrages, including an attack on the Chamber of Deputies and the assassination of President Carnot on 24 June 1894. It was time for the Republic to crack down hard on such opponents and the new president of the Republic, Casimir-Périer, grandson of a minister of Louis-Philippe, gave his full backing to the repressive laws introduced by Prime Minister Charles Dupuy—the so-called *lois scélérates* which were denounced by socialists and radicals for their harshness. Significantly, however, the minister of education, Spuller, once the close ally of Gambetta, sought support on the Catholic right, and spoke of a 'new spirit' which now reigned between Catholics and the Republic. By 1894, the regime had come a long way from the days when Jules Ferry had ordered the removal of crucifixes from school classrooms.

But ideological quarrels could not be made to vanish overnight. The culture war between Catholics and the Republic had still to run its course. Catholics remained resentful when the 'new spirit' did not extend to a revocation of some of the more obnoxious of the 'laic laws' and in intensely Catholic parts of France such as Brittany local populations, headed by their priests, kept up their assault on republican institutions, and notably on republican schools. The Breton *guerre scolaire* ('battle of the schools') was one of the hot spots of the French culture war, and it was a war the republicans lost, since parents continued to show a marked preference for Catholic schools rather than state schools. The *ralliement* never worked on the ground. For their part, republicans of all shades—moderate, radical, socialist—were wary of any compromise with 'clericals'. The parliamentary manoeuvres which forced the resignation of both President Casimir-Périer and Prime Minister Dupuy and allowed the formation of a short-lived radical ministry under Léon Bourgeois in 1896 deepened suspicions on all sides. Nevertheless, the return of a stable moderate government under Jules Méline seemed to augur well for the future of a conservative Republic. No one could have predicted that the greatest of the Republic's moral and political crises was already gestating.

The 'Dreyfus Revolution'

In 1894 the French secret services discovered that military intelligence was being passed to Germany. The alleged traitor was Captain Alfred Dreyfus, a talented officer of Alsatian-Jewish origin on the General Staff who was court-martialled and sentenced to life imprisonment on Devil's Island in December 1894. But Dreyfus had been the victim of a judicial error, as was discovered independently by both his family and the new head of Military Intelligence, Colonel Picquart. The latter became convinced that the real traitor was a disreputable officer called Esterhazy, but to his dismay he found that his superiors were implacably determined not to reopen the case. On the contrary, they set about manufacturing further evidence against Dreyfus and shamelessly fed anti-Dreyfus stories to a grateful right-wing and anti-Semitic press. They also convinced the opportunist politicians in power to reject revision on the grounds that the integrity of the army must not in any way be compromised. But doubts persisted, even among pillars of the republican political establishment like Senator Scheurer-Kestner, and the pressure to investigate Esterhazy grew. The High Command's contemptuous response was to clear Esterhazy and to discharge Picquart.

At this point, however, the Dreyfus case ceased to be the purely judicial matter that the authorities, both political and military, kept making it out to be and turned into a full-blown political scandal. On 13 January 1898, an open letter penned by the novelist Émile Zola and published in Clemenceau's newspaper *L'Aurore*—the famous 'J'accuse'—denounced the acquittal of Esterhazy and accused the military establishment of a crime against Dreyfus that was also tantamount to a conspiracy against the Republic and its values. Zola himself was speedily prosecuted for defamation, and fled to England to avoid imprisonment. But public opinion—at least opinion among the intellectuals and the political class—was now acutely divided between partisans of a retrial and its opponents in the latest manifestation of the Franco-French war which had been plaguing France since the Revolution. Dreyfusard intellectuals such as the poet Charles Péguy argued that the issue was simply one of justice. If the Republic was incapable of righting the wrong done to an innocent man, it would forfeit its own right to exist. Anti-Dreyfusards, headed by the military hierarchy but with strong backing from new right nationalists like Charles Maurras and his Action Française, noisily insisted that the army was a sacrosanct institution which could not be called into question without damaging national security. Reason of state should always prevail over the rights of any individual, as Dreyfus himself, were he a 'good' army officer (and not a Jew), would be the first to recognize.

The debate raged on in the press and in the Latin Quarter of Paris, and it even reached the streets in the ugly form of anti-Semitic demonstrations and riots fomented by the likes of Drumont and other professional anti-Semites. In January–February of 1898 there were riots across the country directed at Jewish property and businesses, the most serious of the disturbances taking place in Algeria. For the nationalist right, anti-Semitism appeared to have huge potential as a myth which could mobilize mass support, principally in the cities but also in rural France. Republican leaders were right to be alarmed, though their own pusillanimity in bowing to pressure from the military not to reopen the case was one reason why the clamour refused to die down.

If the affair excited mainly the politicians and the intellectuals, it also stirred passions in the countryside, though peasants inevitably translated abstract issues about justice into more immediate and tangible local concerns. Nevertheless, the elections of May 1898 returned a Chamber much like that of 1893. Even the resignation of Méline did not at first presage change, since the new government, though headed by a radical, did not favour revision. Indeed, the radical minister of war, Godefroy Cavaignac, went out of his way to proclaim his belief in Dreyfus's guilt, citing the most incriminating evidence against him in a parliamentary speech of 7 July 1898, the text of which was printed and distributed throughout France. What Cavaignac did not know was that the key documents were forgeries, as Jean Jaurès was able to demonstrate in a powerful series of articles which he wrote for the newspaper *La Petite République* under the heading of 'The Proofs'. The forger turned out to be a Lieutenant-Colonel Henry, who, having confessed his guilt, committed suicide on 11 August. The case for a retrial began to seem unanswerable, but still the moderate republicans, headed by President of the Republic Félix Faure, hesitated to expose the army to criticism, particularly at a moment of high international tension between France and Britain over the Fashoda incident.

It was the untimely death of Félix Faure on February 1899—he died in acutely embarrassing circumstances, having overexerted himself while entertaining his mistress at the Elysée palace—which finally opened the way to revision. His successor, Senator Émile Loubet, carried a whiff of the Panama scandal about him, but he was known to be favourable to Dreyfus. On both counts, his election was greeted as a provocation by the right. The nationalist agitator Paul Déroulède was moved to try to mount a *coup d'état* on the occasion of President Faure's funeral, but neither the army nor the Parisian populace heeded his exhortations. Shortly after the Court of Appeal ordered a retrial of Dreyfus on 29 May 1899, President Loubet was heckled and assaulted by rowdy aristocrats at the Auteuil races. Alarmed by the affront to republican dignity, the left retaliated with a massive street demonstration on 11 June which demanded a new and tougher line against enemies of the regime. Loubet's response was to form a government of republican defence under René Waldeck-Rousseau, a successful lawyer and reassuringly bourgeois figure who nevertheless retained from his Gambettist past a strong antipathy to the Church, and especially to the religious orders.

The formation of the Waldeck ministry in June 1899 proved to be a turning point in the political history of the Third Republic. Waldeck himself was a moderate, determined at all costs to uphold the authority of the republican state. His coalition, however, was made up of a broad alliance of the left. It was dominated by radicals and even included a socialist, Millerand, though his presence was balanced at the ministry of war by that of General Gallifet, the butcher of the Communards. It was not Waldeck's intention to close the era of the opportunist Republic inaugurated by Grévy and Ferry, but that in effect was what he did. For the radicals, incarnated by Clemenceau, were now on a roll, having purged their Panamist misdemeanours and recaptured the moral and political high ground through their support for Dreyfus. Inspired by Jaurès, some socialists also rallied to the cause of republican defence, though followers of Jules Guesde remained aloof, claiming that socialists had no business meddling in a 'bourgeois' quarrel, and denouncing the opportunism of Millerand in accepting a ministerial post.

The government's first task was to try to right the wrongs done to an innocent man. Dreyfus was brought back from Devil's Island to stand trial a second time before a military court convened at Rennes. In a highly charged atmosphere, once again the military judges convicted him, though only by a majority verdict of 5 to 2, and 'with extenuating circumstances'. Waldeck had expected an acquittal and quickly offered Dreyfus a presidential pardon signed by Loubet, which, much to the dismay of his most ardent supporters, Dreyfus accepted. Waldeck then decided to strike hard against those whom he deemed to be the authors of the turmoil into which France had been plunged by the affair. Logically, his prime target should have been the arrogant and obdurate army officers who had callously condemned an innocent man to a living hell rather than admit to a miscarriage of justice. To attack the army, however, might jeopardize national unity and the security of the state, especially at a time when anti-militarism was rampant among the more extremist elements of the left. Militarism, however, allegedly had an ally, who presented an altogether easier target: clericalism. Had not the affair revealed a clerical-militarist plot? Retribution should therefore fall on the Church, particularly on anti-Dreyfusard and anti-Semitic religious orders like the Assumptionists, and it came swiftly, as is related in Chapter 8.

The elections of 1902 produced a new and more belligerent left-wing majority. The radicals, formally constituted as a party and not merely as a tendency in 1901, were the big winners at the expense of Waldeck's opportunists, but there were also some forty-three socialist deputies. The radical Republic was now a political reality and under the new prime minister Emile Combes anticlericalism moved to the top of the political agenda. Even so, the separation of Church and state came only in 1905, after Combes's resignation, which was precipitated by the *affaire des fiches*, a scandal which revealed that the minister of war, General André, had carried his zeal to republicanize the army and to deny promotion to 'reactionaries' (that is, practising Catholics) to the point where he had employed the services of the Freemasons to spy on the religious proclivities of officers and their wives. Thanks to the Dreyfus Affair and its aftermath, the radicals were able to implement their main policy objective and to position themselves as the pivotal element in French political life for the remainder of the Third Republic's existence. This may not have amounted to a 'Dreyfus Revolution', as some older histories suggest, but it was certainly a decisive milestone in the evolution of the regime.

A radical Republic? Clemenceau, Briand, and the class struggle, 1906–1910

It was the hope of Pope Pius X, who had been elected in succession to Leo XIII in 1903, that Catholic France would repudiate the Separation Law in the elections of May 1906. Instead, outside traditionally Catholic areas like the west of France, where there were some disturbances when inventories were taken of church property, in conformity with the Separation Law, the voters gave their backing to the anticlerical legislation of the *Bloc des gauches*. Radicals topped the polls with 247 deputies, while socialist representation rose to 74 in apparent vindication of the unification strategy pursued by Jaurès which had led to the formation of a united socialist party, the SFIO (French Section of the Workers' International), in 1905. Catholic and nationalist groups could muster only 175 deputies between them. The ascendancy of the radicals appeared to be complete—all the more so in that they no longer needed the support of the socialists to guarantee their parliamentary majority, relying instead on the backing of the Alliance Démocratique, the pro-Dreyfus and secular wing of the *progressistes* who had formed their own loosely organized party in 1901 to ensure that moderate republicanism was not simply swallowed up by the rampant radical party.

But the 'radical Republic' proved to be something of a disappointment to its most ardent supporters. Radicalism was first and foremost a mentality rather than a political programme. It stood for militant republicanism and a world view shaped by both its identification with the French Revolution and the memory of the epic struggle to establish the Republic in the face of counter-revolution and reaction. It enjoyed grass-roots support above all in the south of France, thanks in no small measure to the influence of the provincial newspaper *La Dépêche de Toulouse*, and it was also a significant regional presence in parts of the centre and in the vicinity of Paris (for example in the departments of Seine-et-Marne and Loiret). A number of organizations—chief among them Freemasonry and the Free Thought movement—did much to nurture the radical outlook, as did the League of the Rights of Man, founded in 1888 to resist the threat posed by General Boulanger and reconstituted in 1898 by concerned intellectuals (who included the novelist Anatole France) when the Dreyfus Affair seemed to herald a still greater danger to the safety of the Republic.

After 1902, however, the radical party was no longer a party in opposition but the natural party of government. Having accomplished its historic mission to separate Church and state, the party began to experience an identity crisis and to manifest signs of political ambivalence. In effect, after 1902 the radical party became mainly a formidable electoral machine operating through local committees to ensure the return of 'sound' candidates to the Chamber of Deputies. In formulating what he called *The Elements of a Radical Doctrine*, the party's principal philosopher, the schoolteacher Émile-Auguste Chartier, better known under his pseudonym Alain, defended this situation. Preoccupied less by a lack of principle and the absence of party discipline on the part of deputies than by the prospect of 'big government' and the expansion of bureaucracy and the tentacles of the state, Alain held that 'that government is best which governs least'. Participation in government was a necessary evil, both to reward one's friends and to exclude one's enemies. But power had to be kept in check in the interests of the 'small man', whom it was the business of the radical party above all to represent. Rather than face up to the challenges of technology and of modern society in the early twentieth century, the radicals preferred to refight the battles of the nineteenth century. Their strong suit was ideology, not economics.

The shortcomings of radicalism in government were soon all too apparent during the premiership of Georges Clemenceau between 1906 and 1909. Already aged 65, Clemenceau was widely viewed as the incarnation of radicalism, yet he was not even a member of the party of which he was nominally the leader when called upon to form a government by Armand Fallières, the suave successor of Loubet as president of the Republic. Clemenceau was a radical by temperament, not by dint of party allegiance. A relentless critic of the opportunist Republic, he was known as 'The Tiger' for his implacable hatreds, expressed in debate and in duels. Cast into the political wilderness after the Panama scandal, he owed his political comeback to the Dreyfus Affair and to a willingness to abandon his long-standing support for unicameralism in order to get himself elected to the Senate in 1902. On becoming premier, he promised to introduce social reforms—an income tax, a ten-hour working day, and old-age pensions—that were espoused in particular by those radicals who adhered to the doctrine of solidarism promoted by the likes of Léon Bourgeois in the 1890s supposedly as a halfway house between liberal individualism and socialist collectivism. In the end, all he could manage was the nationalization of the Western Railway and the establishment of a new ministry of labour, though the deputies showed that they could move with alacrity on the issue of their own salaries, voting themselves a whopping pay rise from 9,000 francs to 15,000 francs in an episode that did little to enhance their popularity with the public.

In office, Clemenceau's main priority was the maintenance of order and upholding the authority of the state rather than social reform. Confronted with a wave of strikes mounted by the trade union movement, whose most militant wing was committed to all-out class warfare in conformity with the doctrines of revolutionary syndicalism enunciated in the Charter of Amiens of 1906, Clemenceau had no hesitation in resorting to repression, sending in troops against the workers as he had already done as minister of the interior earlier in 1906 in order to quell the disturbances in the northern coalfields which had followed in the wake of the appalling pit disaster at Courrières, where over 1,000 miners died. In March 1907 troops were mobilized against the electricity workers of Paris, while in two incidents in 1908 police violence against unarmed workers resulted in a number of deaths and serious injuries. Postal workers who went on strike in 1909 were dismissed from the service. Nor did Clemenceau scruple to order the arrest of workers' leaders on the basis of trumped-up conspiracy charges manufactured by police *provocateurs*. Peasants fared no better. In 1907, when southern wine-growers rioted in protest at plummeting prices brought about by a crisis of over-production, Clemenceau again ordered in the troops, with ensuing violence and the loss of five lives. It was for such actions that Clemenceau was dubbed 'le premier flic de France'—France's first cop—a title in which he revelled. So incensed was the radical party that in May 1909 its executive committee passed a vote of censure against the government which, in the view of one senior radical statesman, Camille Pelletan, had shown itself to be more oppressive than the Second Empire.

The socialists, former allies of the radicals in the heyday of the *Bloc des gauches* between 1902 and 1905, were equally appalled, all the more so when Clemenceau's successor as premier, Aristide Briand—a man who had first come to prominence in the 1890s as an apologist for the general strike—applied Clemenceau's techniques to break a strike of railwaymen in 1910, arresting the strike leaders and placing striking workers under military discipline. Now united under the Marxist banner (Jaurès having bowed to pressure from the German-dominated Second International) the SFIO was officially committed to the class struggle and spurned the notion that it could participate in 'bourgeois' cabinets, radical or otherwise. Many of the original 'independents'—men like Millerand, Briand, and Viviani—disagreed and drifted steadily to the right. But Jaurès kept the faith, and by force of his charismatic personality and with the powerful aid of his newspaper, the socialist daily *L'Humanité*, he succeeded in orienting the party towards reformism while retaining revolution as the ultimate goal. The socialist electorate continued to expand, and by 1914 they had made themselves into the second largest party in the Chamber of Deputies, with 104 seats.

Jaurès had assumed that once the threat from 'clericalism' had been dealt with the combined left would be free to address the socialist agenda. The repressive action of the Clemenceau government came as a bitter blow, but there was little the socialists could do about it. With only 90,000 members in 1914, they were a much less imposing force than the two-million-strong German socialist party, the SPD. Moreover, many of their membership were not workers but pettybourgeois, disenchanted with radicalism, or peasants, like the distressed wine-growers of Provence. True enough, they had a strong base among the textile workers of the north of France, built up by talented activists like the Guesdist Gustave Delory, who became mayor of Lille. But the socialists, who continued to be divided among themselves over the question of revolution or reform (and increasingly over the question of militarism and the threatening international situation), had no monopoly as spokesmen for working-class interests. Other voices also articulated proletarian grievances, none more assertively than the revolutionary syndicalists who had drawn up the Charter of Amiens.

Inspired by anarchism rather than Marxism, the syndicalists rejected any collaboration with political parties, including parliamentary socialism, and preached 'direct action' by the workers themselves, the ultimate form of which was the revolutionary general strike. As theorized later by Georges Sorel in his *Reflections on Violence* (1908), the general strike epitomized the kind of powerful myth which could galvanize the proletariat to rise up and smash the bourgeois state. While there is no evidence to suggest that Sorel's text had any influence whatsoever on the French trade union movement, its glorification of violence was another indication that revulsion from the unheroic and tainted Republic of the radicals characterized the extreme left as well as the extreme right.

Syndicalist intransigence owed more to historical memory than to Marx or Sorel. The workers' movement, headed by intelligent and cultured craftsmen, derived its sense of identity from recollections of repression—in 1871, 1848, and 1831 (when the Lyon silk weavers were crushed at the hands of the July Monarchy)—kept alive in publications such as Benoît Malon's *The Third Defeat of the French Proletariat* (1871). From where these militant workers stood, the state was invariably an instrument of repression, whether in liberal, authoritarian, or democratic guise, and it used its power to deny the aspirations of working people to a better life. When the CGT was formed in 1895, it fiercely proclaimed its independence from any political party. The autonomy of the *syndicats* was further reinforced by the adhesion of the Bourses du Travail, a network of labour organizations which, under the direction of the anarchist Fernand Pelloutier, were envisaged as a proletarian and revolutionary subculture destined ultimately to supplant the existing bourgeois social order. But if trade union militancy in the France of the *belle époque* was explicable largely in terms of a political culture which sought to marginalize organized labour, it was also a product of employer intransigence. For many of the smaller *patrons* in particular, the very notion of a trade union was an affront to their right to be master in their own house. At the same time, however, militancy ultimately testified not to the strength but to the weakness of the trade union movement. In 1911 the CGT numbered fewer than 700,000 members, a mere 7 per cent of the industrial working class (comparable percentages in Britain and Germany were 25 per cent and 28 per cent respectively). Revolutionary syndicalism was the affair of a vociferous minority of activists.

On the other hand, there was no mistaking the steady increase in the incidence of strikes: 890 in 1900, 1,087 in 1904, 1,354 in 1906, and 1,517 in 1910. They also inspired a degree of public sympathy, evident in donations to strike funds, the setting up of soup kitchens, and the enactment of festivities in which women and children often played a significant part as the bearers of banners. The fact that, in the run-up to 1914, strikes frequently gave rise to the expression of anti-militarist and pacifist sentiments added to the sense of crisis which they engendered. Also worrying for the political masters of the Republic was an apparent rapprochement between the SFIO and the CGT, facilitated not only by Jaurès but by a new flexibility on the part of Léon Jouhaux, the new leader of the CGT. Recognizing that the repressive capacity of the French state was such as to preclude any imminent prospect of revolution, he subtly embraced a more flexible approach to reform after 1909, thereby raising hopes on the left that the Third Republic might have something to offer the workers after all.

Feminism and the search for female citizenship

Women, too, had high hopes. Just as CGT militants challenged the inequalities of class, likewise feminists contested the inequalities of sex. France had a long tradition of feminist militancy, stretching back to the Revolution, when the likes of Olympe de Gouges had demanded that a revolution made in the name of the rights of man should also recognize the rights of women. Another generation of feminists, inspired by the ideals of utopian socialism, flourished under the July Monarchy, and made a distinctive contribution to the Revolution of 1848, before succumbing to the repression which followed the June Days. Towards the end of the Second Empire, a new generation of feminists emerged alongside the new republican leadership and believed firmly that the causes of feminism and republicanism would advance hand in hand. Great was their disappointment when they discovered that the political masters of the Third Republic, already nervous about the viability of democracy under an exclusively male electorate, had no intention of making their lives even more difficult by creating female citizens whose political loyalties were more likely to lie with the enemies of the Republic (the 'clericals' and the right generally) than with its friends.

To be fair, in sympathy with the problems faced by the Republic in its early days, liberal feminists like Maria Deraismes and her leading male collaborator, the anticlerical journalist Léon Richer, pursued a strategy of gradualism (the *politique de la brèche*) which prioritized civil rights over political rights and accepted that women's suffrage was too hot a potato for the 1870s. In the 1880s, however, younger militants, of whom the most prominent was Hubertine Auclert, launched a vigorous campaign for votes for women. Political rights, Auclert argued in her newspaper *La Citoyenne*, were 'the keystone (*clef de voûte*) which will give (women) all other rights'. Using the language of the Revolutionary tradition, she insisted that suffrage was a matter of justice: and since the Republic owed justice to all, women should have the vote. Its denial was a violation of the principle of the sovereignty of the people and left the work of the Revolution incomplete. The all-male electorate of the Republic in effect made men 'the feudal noblemen of the nineteenth century', responsible for electing '557 monarchs' as deputies. For Auclert, this created a masculine 'royalty of sex', which, if unremedied, would give rise to a new revolution.

Unfortunately for Auclert, in the France of the 1880s she was not only France's leading suffragette but virtually France's only suffragette. Her refusal to pay taxes—no taxation without representation—and her attempts to run as a candidate in elections aroused more ridicule and abuse than support. According to a police report of 1880 she suffered 'from madness or hysterics which make her think of men as equals'—the kind of misogynous comment all too common among anti-suffragists at that time. Nevertheless, in the 1890s, boosted by the success of an International Congress for Women's Rights organized by Deraismes and Richer in 1889 as part of the centenary celebrations of the Revolution, moderate republican feminists began to win converts, among them the ex-actress Marguerite Durand, who in 1897 founded *La Fronde*, the first feminist daily newspaper and one entirely produced by women. A National Council of French Women (CNFF) was founded in 1900 and, as the suffrage issue moved steadily up the feminist agenda, a French Union for Women's Suffrage (UFSF) was launched in 1909. Additionally, a Catholic feminist movement appeared under the leadership of Marie Maugeret, an intransigent anti-Dreyfusard and anti-Semite but a committed suffragist, while there was also a group of socialist feminists centred on the uncompromising figure of Louise Saumoneau, who always prioritized the class struggle over the issues of political, civic, and moral reform which exercised 'bourgeois' feminists.

The latter, it should be said, wanted no truck with sexual radicalism—'free love' was an anarchist cause—or with the militant activism of the British suffragettes, and therefore repudiated French radical feminists like Madeleine Pelletier who sought to emulate them. French feminists set great store by their respectability and considered militancy both un-feminine and un-French, as well as being an unfortunate reminder of the so-called *pétroleuses*, the women incendiaries of the Paris Commune of 1871. Yet their campaigns were by no means entirely ineffective. French women may not have obtained the vote before 1914, but then, for all their militancy, neither had British women, and at least the French feminists could claim that, as in Britain, the issue of votes for women had been placed on the agenda of parliament (a suffrage bill was introduced in 1906 and was recommended to the Chamber of Deputies by its *rapporteur*, Ferdinand Buisson, in 1909). Additionally, public opinion became less hostile than it had been back in the 1880s. Indeed, in May 1914, to coincide with the parliamentary elections of that year, the mass-circulation Parisian daily newspaper *Le Journal* organized a mock ballot for women, and obtained over half a million 'votes'. On 5 July the same year, feminists combined in a protest rally in Paris to commemorate the Enlightenment thinker Condorcet, one of the earliest advocates of female citizenship. In the summer of 1914 suffragists dared to entertain the hope that women might become electors in time to vote for the next parliamentary elections due to be held in 1916. Little did they imagine that, by then, the year of Verdun, the world would be a very different place, and that they would be obliged to wait for the vote until after not one but two world wars.

Conclusion

When war broke out in August 1914, it came as a bolt from the blue. No one—certainly not the French government—had anticipated that the assassination of an Austrian archduke by a fanatical Serbian nationalist on 28 June 1914 at Sarajevo in Bosnia would unleash a crisis which would culminate in what contemporaries would call the Great War of 1914–18. French public opinion was far more interested in the outcome of the trial of Madame Caillaux, the wife of the radical ex-prime minister Joseph Caillaux and the assassin of the editor of *Le Figaro*, than in obscure Balkan politics and tedious great power diplomacy. Yet at another level, the war was not unexpected, having been widely anticipated in the years before 1914, particularly after 1905, when Germany's policy of *Weltpolitik* and the Kaiser's desire for 'a place in the sun' generated a heightening of international tensions, as explained in Chapter 4.

With the outbreak of the First World War, the Third Republic faced its greatest test—far greater than any of the crises and scandals (the Dreyfus Affair not excluded) which had beset the regime in the years between 1880 and 1914. At stake was a struggle for survival: another defeat at the hands of Germany and the Republic could be expected to go the way of the Second Empire. Despite the intense ideological and social conflicts of the pre-war years, the nation showed remarkable unanimity in the face of what was universally regarded as a war of self-defence against naked German aggression, immediately revealed for all the world to see in the attack on France through neutral Belgium, and the action which guaranteed that the British as well as the Russians would join France in the just fight.

On 4 August, the day of the German attack, President Poincaré spoke of the need for the formation of a 'sacred union' which would allow Frenchmen of all persuasions to rally to the flag. On 26 August a government of 'sacred union' was formed under the former socialist and still left-leaning premier René Viviani. It included, amazingly, two socialists, Marcel Sembat and the hardline Marxist Jules Guesde, and, even more remarkable, would shortly include a Catholic, Denys Cochin, who found himself in the company of none other than the priest-hating Émile Combes. The radical Malvy, who continued to occupy the Ministry of the Interior, had already shown confidence in the innate patriotism of the workers and had decided against rounding up trade union and left-wing agitators who featured on a 'B list' drawn up by the police, thus allowing the mobilization to take place in good order, without any attempt at the kind of general strike envisaged by revolutionary syndicalists and anti-militarist socialists in the pre-war period. All sections of the community rallied to the Republic in 1914. But how long would unity last?

2

The Republic in crisis: politics 1914–1945

Kevin Passmore

The Third Republic withstood four years of murderous combat against invading German armies during the Great War, yet crumbled within six weeks of another incursion in 1940. The triumph of republican France in 1918 contrasts with parliament's abject surrender to Marshal Pétain in 1940. Faced with these paradoxes, some historians have emphasized the weakness of democratic culture, others, its strength.

For pessimists, the political system was undermined by a war between the Catholic right and republican left which had been waged since the 1789 revolution. Each side was dogmatically certain of its rightness, and neither could tolerate the victory of the other. Pessimists argue that the Great War weakened the progressive basis of the left, and permitted the revenge of Catholic Vichy in 1940.

For optimists, the strength of democratic culture preserved France from the extremism evident elsewhere in Europe. The rallying of Catholics and socialists to the war effort in 1914 demonstrated their integration into the Republic; communism prospered only when it accepted the Republic in 1935; fascism made little headway. The 1940 debacle resulted from military blunders, not political weakness. Defeat permitted long-buried traditionalist impulses to re-emerge in the Vichy regime, but this was merely a parenthesis in republican history—Vichy's anachronistic traditionalist project could not have succeeded in modern democratic France.

The interpretation presented here is neither pessimistic nor optimistic. On the negative side, although support for democracy increased as a result of the Republic's victory in the Great War, the political system left the majority of adults without political representation, and there remained fundamental disagreements on what democracy actually meant in class, religious, gender, and ethnic terms. These problems contributed to a crisis of the political system in the 1930s. On the positive side, neither chronic political division nor lack or representativeness was sufficient to bring the regime down. Whilst the Republic had become more authoritarian by 1940, it took military defeat to kill French democracy.

Politics, elites, and society

On the eve of war 1914 the Republic rested politically on an alliance of centres: the centre-left was represented by the radicals and the centre-right was loosely equivalent to the Alliance Démocratique (AD). Both centres were anticlerical, but they differed in other respects. The radicals were liberals who valued private property and the individual highly. But they stressed the need for the individual to further his or her interests through associations, such as trade unions, and were willing to accept state intervention to ensure that the most talented of the underprivileged succeeded in fulfilling their potential. The centre-right was more concerned to reconcile progress with conservative interests, including business. It accepted fewer constraints upon the individual than did the radicals.

To the left, the major party was the socialist SFIO. The SFIO was a revolutionary party which expected capitalism and private property to disappear in the longer term. But the SFIO believed in the parliamentary road to socialism and so from time to time it provided parliamentary support for centrist governments because they were democratic and secular. To the right, the major parties were the republican liberal conservatives of the Fédération Républicaine (FR) and the Catholic Action Libérale Populaire (ALP). Both were systematically excluded from centrist governments because they were regarded as too favourable to Catholics. That the small number of monarchist deputies were regarded as *personae non gratae* in the republican court goes without saying.

Electorally, the Republic depended upon the support of workers, peasant proprietors, artisans, shopkeepers, schoolteachers, small businessmen, and professionals. But the diversity of the electorate in class terms did not compensate for the unrepresentative nature of the Republic in other respects. Not only were Catholics kept out of government, but neither women nor the immigrant workers, on which France relied economically, had the vote. The Great War rendered the Republic even more unrepresentative. Because millions of men were killed or maimed in the conflict, voteless women greatly outnumbered men. And in order to make good the shortfall in the workforce, the number of immigrant workers rose from one to three million in the 1920s. The majority of adults were disenfranchised.

The exclusiveness of French democracy was underlined by the emergence since the 1890s of a republican elite which was culturally distant from the middle classes who provided the regime's agents in the provinces. The typical member of the elite had passed through the Paris Law Faculty and Bar, the École Libre des Sciences Politiques, which had a near monopoly on recruitment to senior positions in the administration, and ministerial cabinets before acceding to parliament and a ministerial portfolio.

The republican elite espoused, under the influence of the neo-Lamarckian, eugenicist, natalist, and quasi-racist pseudo-science dispensed at the École Libre, a restrictive view of who counted politically. The elites believed that a nation's ability to survive in the hostile international atmosphere depended on the unity, quantity, and quality of the population. The republican notion that anyone who accepted the rights and duties of citizenship could belong to the nation remained influential, yet was being displaced by a more exclusive view. Future premier André Tardieu, typically, held that the French people were unified not just legally, but by collective psychology, evident in language, and acquired through long contact with the national soil. This implied suspicion of French people, such as Bretons and Alsatians, who spoke minority languages. And although it was hoped that children of immigrants would be assimilated into the nation through education, adult immigrants were seen as dangerous. Many of the republican elite favoured giving women the vote. But they remained convinced that politics was a man's business and that women's primary duty was to bear children—the nation's future producers, reproducers, and soldiers.

This republican elite advocated democracy, but did not expect the lower classes actually to govern. The elite feared the 'passions' of the masses, and was contemptuous even of the average deputy. For the republican elite the role of the masses was restricted to choosing which of the more enlightened classes would govern. The republican elite espoused various schemes for constitutional reform, all designed to ensure that the 'competent' (themselves) monopolized government. This suspicion of 'parliamentary confusion' gave the republican elite something in common with the conservatives to their right, for the latter had long advocated a stronger state. Particularly at the École Libre, there were contacts between the republican elite and more conservative politicians such as Louis Marin and Louis Duval-Arnould of the Fédération Républicaine. For the moment the religious question remained an insuperable obstacle to sustained collaboration between republican and Catholic elites. The Great War broke down some barriers, but only the fall of the Republic in 1940 made real collaboration between the two elites possible.

By that time developments in the sphere of party politics, related to class, religious, and gender conflicts, had undermined the regime's props. The Great War and interwar crises pulled apart the centre coalition, as the radicals turned to the socialists and the centre-right allied with the Catholic right. Some hoped that, as in Britain, government might alternate between strong left- and right-wing democratic parties. Yet there was no firm basis for government by either side. Socialists were too suspicious of the radicals, and the right was divided by the religious question. The resulting parliamentary instability was grist to the mill of those who wanted a more authoritarian regime. The right had long desired a stronger state, but increasingly the republican elites embraced anti-parliamentarianism too. Under the impact of the depression, moreover, elite politics were threatened by mass political mobilization led by communists and the extreme right. Both appealed to groups hitherto excluded from politics. The elites, in response, became increasingly authoritarian, anti-communist, xenophobic, and anti-feminist.

The Great War and the Union Sacrée

The German invasion of France in August 1914 provoked an unprecedented degree of national unity. Famously, socialist and monarchist deputies shook hands in the Chamber of Deputies. Feminists suspended the campaign for universal suffrage and turned to war work; priests and their traditional enemies, state primary school teachers, worked together too. There had been nothing like this in the 1870 war, and nor would there be in 1939.

Support for the Union Sacrée, as the wartime coalition government came to be known, was logical for all of the main parties. Most predictably, the royalist league, Action Française, supported the war effort—it had, after all, been formed to prepare the nation for armed conflict. The Catholic ALP had little sympathy with papal desire for peace and saw the war as a crusade of the 'eldest daughter of the Church' against German Protestantism. Like the liberal conservatives of the Fédération Républicaine, the ALP saw the war as a chance to integrate Catholics into the Republic. The secular conservatives of the centre-right agreed with the need for reconciliation with Catholics— hence their readiness to ally with the Fédération and the ALP, which before 1914 they had refused to do. On the left, both radical-socialists and the SFIO believed that the Republic, the condition of progress, must be defended against Prussian 'reaction'. Although strongly pacifist, the SFIO had insisted that should war actually break out, it would, as Jaurès put it, be 'the first to the frontier to defend France, whose blood runs through our veins'.

The Union Sacrée was not, however, a national consensus based on mutual concession. Right and left each proclaimed that victory in the war would bring final victory over their domestic enemies. The nationalist Barrès saw 1914 as 'the dawn of our renaissance' and recalled with displeasure the 'filthy cesspool' of pre-war France. The ALP hoped that the triumph of the national idea would bring re-Christianization, and expected their patriotism to be rewarded with repeal of anticlerical legislation. The FR was prepared to make significant concessions in this respect, and the ARD was ready to apply existing legislation more sympathetically. Yet the ARD, like the radicals, also felt that the rallying of Catholics to the nation signified the definitive victory of *secularism*. Socialists, meanwhile, defended the Republic because they regarded it as essential to the victory of social- ism—a view not shared by any of the parties to their right. Feminists expected to be compensated for devotion to *la patrie* by the vote and legal equality, yet soldiers expected women to return to the domestic sphere after the war.

These differences might not have undermined the Union Sacrée had the war been short. The expectation that France, fighting this time with the support of Russia and Britain, would quickly avenge the defeat of 1870, encouraged unity. Yet things did not go as planned. Although a German advance through Belgium was stopped at the Marne in September, the Germans were not driven from French mud for four years. The conflict settled down to a bloody stalemate in the trenches. Hundreds of thousands of lives were sacrificed for the gain of a few metres of shell-churned soil. At Verdun in 1916 the French successfully resisted a German attack; the failure of Nivelle's offensive in 1917 led to mutiny in the army. Philippe Pétain replaced Nivelle as commander-in-chief and settled down to a defensive—some said defeatist—strategy. Meanwhile, a series of tensions arose on the home front.

First, the war posed constitutional challenges. Those who had favoured rule by the 'competent' rather than parliamentary 'chat- terers' saw their chance, for their demands could now be presented as a contribution to the war effort. Reform of the constitution was also embraced by business interests, impressed by the impulse given to large-scale production during the war. Georges Noblemaire, for example, wanted to apply modish ideas of 'scientific labour organisa- tion' to business and parliament. Obsession with 'production' was accompanied by suspicion of 'inefficient' small business and the belief that parliament was excessively favourable to it. The left defended parliament, and the pendulum swung one way then the other. In the first year of the war Joffre and War Minister Millerand established a de facto military dictatorship. In 1916, parlia- ment re-established its authority over the military. Then in 1918 the Clemenceau government established its supremacy over parliament. The legacy of war was ambiguous: was it a victory for the Republic or not?

Secondly, the Union Sacrée was undermined by class struggle. Indeed, class conflict was related to the institutional debate, for proponents of constitutional reform saw it as a means to buttress elite power, while the radicals defended parliament as the representative of the 'people' and the SFIO viewed a parliamentary majority as the precondition of workers' revolution. From 1916 concern for the democratic rights of the European peoples also led the SFIO left—the *minoritaires*—to oppose an annexationist peace. The SFIO was further radicalized by the Russian Revolution, labour discontent, and mutinies of 1917. The socialist Albert Thomas's role as armaments minister became untenable—all the more so as the right accused him of protecting workers from military service. Most socialists did not go so far as Fernand Loriot, who believed that the spread of strikes signified a revolutionary situation. But the party rediscovered its aversion to participation in bourgeois governments. Thomas left the cabinet in August 1917, and in October 1918 the *minoritaires* became the majority at the SFIO congress. Again the legacy of the war was contested. For the right it demonstrated the supremacy of nation over class. For most socialists it had demonstrated the folly of compromise with bourgeois democracy.

Thirdly, cooperation of clericals and anticlericals did not prevent manoeuvring for the resumption of religious conflict. Indeed, the array of state and private associations created to support the war effort provided new areas of activity, from factory social work to orphanages, in which Catholics and *laïques* could compete. Furthermore, many republicans felt that Pope Benedict XV was pro-German, an impression strengthened by his appeal in August 1917 for a negotiated peace. The right's frustration at the refusal of the government to re-establish diplomatic relations with the Vatican finally caused the monarchist Denys Cochin to leave the government in August 1917. Thus the war had raised the expectation of reconciliation of clericals and anticlericals, yet spread conflict to new areas.

Fourthly, the war sharpened concern about ethnic and gender identities. In the short term war seemed to re-establish conventional gender roles, previously threatened by the suffrage campaign—soldiering was a quintessentially male activity, while women kept the home front going. Yet as women moved from jobs in domestic service to arms factories, or took on welfare work, negative views of women reappeared. Spy scares evoked stereotypes of feminine betrayal, while female involvement in the strikes of 1917 underlined the potential disloyalty of women and workers to the nation. Even the SFIO agreed that after the war women should produce babies to compensate for the massacre of men in the trenches. During the war years the population 'problem', often attributed to the modern woman's rejection of maternity, became a political issue. Fear of the 'independent woman' was related to distrust of immigrants, not least because the latter were seen as members of 'feminine peoples'. The centre-right was especially prone to see the war as a struggle of 'peoples', conceived in quasi-ethnic terms. Spy hysteria focused especially on the 'recently naturalized'. Again, the legacy of the war was uncertain. Natalism carried a strongly anti-feminist charge, yet the expansion of welfare organizations opened a field of women's para-political activity, that existing parties would struggle to incorporate. Similarly, the spread of xenophobia was accompanied by increasing dependence on immigrant workers to fill the French population deficit.

These conflicts together pushed the Union Sacrée to the right. The decisive moment came with the military failures of late 1917. In November the parliamentary government of Paul Painlevé was replaced by a semi-dictatorial administration under Georges Clemenceau. Although Clemenceau had been a radical since the 1860s, his government relied almost exclusively on the right and centre-right. Clemenceau arrested 'defeatists' and prosecuted the pacifist president of the radical party, Joseph Caillaux, on trumped-up charges linking him with German agents. Clemenceau's defeat of the partisans of a compromise peace ensured successful resistance to the German 1918 spring offensive. He also persuaded the allies, now including the Americans, to accept Ferdinand Foch as supreme commander of all their armies, and it was under his leadership that they finally prevailed over the Germans in November 1918.

In the short term the elation of victory and the recovery of Alsace-Lorraine undoubtedly strengthened the Republic. Yet the cost was enormous. Over 1.3 million people had been killed, and over a million were permanent invalids. Large parts of north-eastern France had been devastated. The government owed huge sums to Anglo-American bankers; exports had collapsed; inflation was rising and the franc was weak. Class and gender conflict were rife; religious struggle spread to new areas and xenophobia was growing. The narrowly based political system was ill-equipped to cope with these challenges.

The right, 1919–1933

One of the major political consequences of the war was that ARD moved away from its centrist past and fixed itself on the right. Its willingness to join coalitions with the FR and ALP, and even to accept the arms-length support of monarchists, made it possible, for the first time since the 1870s, for the right to win elections and form governments. Indeed, the right dominated the interwar period. Yet the right agreed on very little, and was hardly more capable of governing than the left.

The Bloc National

After the war the ARD attempted to perpetuate the Union Sacrée as the Bloc National, an electoral alliance stretching from the radicals to the ALP, excluding monarchists and socialists. Unity proved difficult to realize. The radicals signed a separate agreement with the ARD which made no mention of the ALP and marginalized the Fédération. The ALP refused to participate unless its banner was visible, and it suspected the ARD of dealing secretly with the radicals alone. Clemenceau offered little leadership, preferring to cultivate his supra-party image. Fear of Bolshevism was immense, but did not necessarily dictate unity, for it often caused Catholics to insist even more strongly that only religion could save France. In industrial Aisne and the Nord, there was no united Bloc list despite the presence of a strong socialist threat. In some conservative western departments, radicals joined the centre-right in an old-fashioned struggle of republicans against monarchists.

Thanks to the even greater division of the left, and a voting system that rewarded the most united camp, the Bloc won a majority in 1919. Yet it achieved little. The Bloc was dominated by old-school liberal republicans of the ARD, who frustrated hopes for reform. Failure encouraged some to prefer extra-parliamentary methods.

In 1919 a plethora of groups, such as the Association Nationale pour l'Organisation de la Démocratie and Quatrième République, called for constitutional reform. Many newly elected right-wing deputies were favourable, especially those organized in the centre-right

Action Républicaine et Sociale (ARS). Yet a timid proposal for modification of parliamentary procedure failed in December 1919. Millerand's campaign for the presidency in 1921 evoked the need for reform, but once elected he sought merely to bolster his authority through personal interventions. Reform failed partly because its partisans had different agendas. The Catholic right saw it as a means to bring the Catholic elites to power. Centre-right reformers wished simply to improve parliamentary efficiency by applying to it the lessons of 'rationalization' learned in the war. Opponents of reform exploited fears of Clemenceau's 'dictatorship'. The failure of reform showed that the older generation remained in control of both ARD and radicals, and opposed attacks on parliament. In subsequent years, some constitutional reformers were therefore inclined to use extra-parliamentary methods.

Economic reform failed too. In 1919 a few technocrats (some, such as Louis Loucheur, educated in the elite business school, the École Polytechnique), entered parliament in order to teach lessons learned in the war economy. They wanted the state to encourage business to form cartels and rationalize production. Some social Catholics added calls for state regulation of industrial relations. The great majority of right-wing deputies and businessmen, however, remained economic liberals. Fearful of Bolshevization and obsessed with the desire to restore the value of the franc to pre-war levels, they demanded reductions in state spending and the break-up of state monopolies. Worse still, in 1923 parliament introduced measures favouring small business. These were bitterly resented by big business in general, and especially by technocrats. Disappointed technocrats did not return to parliament in 1924. Subsequently they tried to influence government policy through think tanks such as Redressement Français, and when that failed some turned to the far right.

The persistence of liberalism also explains the failure of pronatalism. The great majority of Bloc deputies saw the birth rate as a matter of life or death for the nation, and saw reaffirmation of woman's maternal destiny as essential to the re-establishment of proper relations in society at large. But most rightists, whether Catholic or lay, remained convinced that stiff penalties for abortion and pro-contraception propaganda, coupled with pronatalist *education* would convince men and women of the necessity of raising the birth rate. They saw the interventionist solutions proposed by natalist 'experts' as unnecessary. There was, at least, agreement on the need for family allowances, but it was difficult to reconcile the centre-right's acceptance of state involvement with the Church's desire for a share in the administration of allowances. The pronatalist lobby was therefore disappointed, especially as the Bloc's measures (whilst prejudicial to women) had no effect on the birth rate. Subsequently, the pronatalist movement shifted to the right—the pronatalist Duval-Arnould joined the anti-parliamentary Jeunesses Patriotes in 1925.

Another cause of disillusion was failure to satisfy the grievances of Catholics. The programme of the Bloc National included an ambiguous compromise on the religious issue: 'the fact of the *laïcité* of the state must be reconciled with the rights and liberties of all citizens, whatever religion they confess'. For the ARD this meant liberal application of existing laws; for the FR it meant modification or repeal. Some intransigent Catholics were alarmed by the apparent acceptance of *laïcité*, while others announced the imminent victory of religion—thereby stimulating anticlericalism. The Bloc agreed not to apply lay legislation to newly recovered Alsace and Lorraine, re-established diplomatic relations with the Vatican, and settled long-standing disputes on the nature of temporal government within the Church. Yet fundamental questions concerning education remained unresolved. Few Catholics served as ministers in Bloc governments (or thereafter). Although the centre-right was now unequivocally conservative it still preferred to lock the radicals into a right-wing alliance rather than ally too closely with Catholics.

By early 1924 conservatives were candidly talking of the failure of the Bloc. Financial and international problems ensured electoral defeat in June. Successive governments had postponed financial crisis by setting off the deficit against future German reparations payments. But the Germans claimed to be unable to pay. French occupation of the Ruhr in January 1923 achieved little, and in February 1924 the government was forced to introduce an unpopular austerity package. The left returned to power in June.

The reconstitution of conservative parties

In opposition separate right-wing parties, in the background since 1914, reasserted themselves. With some modifications they did so within the pre-war clerical/anticlerical alignment. This evolution was encouraged, paradoxically, by Pius XI's desire to depoliticize Catholicism. His refusal to revive the ALP permitted the Fédération Républicaine, under the nationalist Louis Marin, to become the unofficial representative of the Church, and to take over much of the ALP's leadership, electorate, and parish-based organization. Also, the Pope's condemnation of the royalist Action Française in 1926 caused Catholic royalists like Xavier Vallat to turn to the Fédération. The once liberal republican Fédération became the voice of Catholic nationalism. It attributed pacifism, depopulation, and labour discontent to the influence of irreligious state primary school teachers, freemasons, and sometimes Jews. Restoration of religion and elimination of the enemy within were the solutions to all problems.

Yet the Fédération had no monopoly on the Catholic movement. In the mid-1920s the Church increasingly promoted Catholic Action, a network of professionally and gender segregated groups designed to involve the laity in spreading the gospel. Although Catholic Action was formally apolitical, it was especially concerned to promote the reformist social doctrine of the Church, so it denounced the laissez-faire attitudes of the Catholic right. Women, assumed to be 'innately' religious and caring, were given a primary role in achieving social reconciliation and 're-Christianization'. In 1925 a group of social Catholics and Christian democrats formed the Parti Démocrate Populaire (PDP), which aspired to be a popular party of the moderate right. It formed links with Breton and Alsatian regionalists, Catholic trade unionists, and was the first right-wing party to include women's sections. Inevitably, the PDP came into conflict with the Fédération. The PDP came off second best, and only elected a handful of deputies. In the 1930s some frustrated social Catholics turned to the far right.

The centre-right was notoriously badly organized. Antoine Ratier, president of its most important component, the ARD, was scarcely known. The centre-right was divided on whether to ally with radicals or with the Fédération. Yet it maintained a strong secular identity, reinforced by the clericalization of the Fédération. The centre-right had not abandoned its liberal-conservative conception of politics. Like the FR, the ARD believed in rule by an elite, which would guide the masses through education—republican, not Catholic education. Like the FR, the ARD blamed teachers for social disorder, but would not purge the profession for fear of undermining secularism.

Like the Fédération, the ARD suffered from rank-and-file discontent. The apparent eagerness of the centre-right to collaborate with Catholic politicians caused many of its followers to desert to the radicals. Also, the ARD found it hard to deal with the women's movement. The ARD was largely pro-suffrage, but sought to limit women to the passive exercise of the vote, and had little interest in the social reform advocated by female welfare activists. Some centre-right leaders sought to buttress elite authority through constitutional reform and economic modernization. Some were linked to Redressement Français, founded in 1926 by the Polytechnicien Ernest Mercier, which appealed to 'neo-capitalist' managers and businessmen drawn from sections of the economy that defined themselves as 'modern'. Others joined the so-called 'Jeunes équipes'—a group of journalists, academics, and politicians, whose mouthpiece was Jean Luchaire's journal, *Notre temps*.

The Tardieu governments

When the right returned to power in 1926 modernizers gained influence, especially in the Tardieu governments of 1929–30—Mercier advised on the constitution of Tardieu's second ministry. Tardieu declared parliamentary liberalism to be outdated and advocated a state sufficiently strong to aid the 'vital forces of the nation' (business), and to arbitrate conflicts of interest between them. The centrepiece of his programme was the 'national retooling programme'—a public works project designed to stimulate prosperity and bind peasants and workers to liberal capitalism.

The Tardieu government was among the most dynamic of the Third Republic, and its work was partially continued by succeeding governments under Pierre Laval. Social Insurance and Family Allowance Acts, long advocated by social reformers and natalists, were enacted. Yet the national retooling scheme was scuppered by radical opposition, a sign that Tardieu had not achieved his aim of incorporating that party into a conservative majority. Indeed, Tardieu, a haughty representative of the Parisian republican elite, and a former teacher at the École Libre, was widely disliked by ordinary republicans—an illustration of the chasm between the republican rank and file and elite. Tardieu was also weakened by opposition from the right. As economic depression began to bite, business denounced the expense of welfare reform, while bishops feared that social insurance would harm charity. Tardieu's endorsement of free secondary education also enraged Catholics. Significantly, the small-business Fédération des Contribuables and rural Défense Paysanne formed a common front to oppose social insurance. The right was beginning to lose its grip on its own followers.

For the moment, nevertheless, the right remained in control. The economic situation was good, and the left largely excluded from power. But with the rise of communism and the displacement of the radicals by the SFIO, the situation became harder to master.

The left, 1919–1933

The radicals and SFIO, allied in the Cartel des Gauches, won the elections of 1924, and the former took office under Édouard Herriot. The pursuit of a conciliatory policy towards Germany was popular, but the socialists' demand for a tax on capital frightened the right and precipitated financial crisis. Discovery of the government's use of subterfuge to cover financial difficulties enabled the right to force Herriot out. A series of short-lived left-wing governments came and went before another brief Herriot government gave up the fight in July 1926, permitting the right to return to power. With some justice the left blamed 'the wall of money' for its failure. The Fédération Républicaine deputy François de Wendel had threatened to resign as a regent of the Bank of France unless the government admitted falsifying statistics. But even without right-wing opposition the left was too divided to agree on a programme.

Communism

On 29 December 1920 the majority at the SFIO Tours Congress joined the communist Third International. The failure of the SFIO in the elections of 1919, and the Bolshevik victory in the Civil War in 1920, both increased the prestige of communism, permitting it to mobilize a broad constituency—in 1924 the Parti Communiste Français (PCF) gained 10 per cent of the vote. Bolshevism chimed with certain French traditions. It recalled the Blanquist belief in seizure of power by a revolutionary minority, the dogmatism of Guesdism, and the revolutionary-syndicalists' dream of proletarian self-government. The PCF also attracted peace activists, anti-bourgeois intellectuals, and feminists impressed by the freedoms of women in Russia. Communist support was relatively weak in bastions of working-class socialism like the Nord, but stronger in the newly industrialized suburbs of Paris and amongst the peasantry of the south and centre.

Subsequently the appeal of communism narrowed. 'Bolshevization' of the party began straight away, and was boosted by the July 1924 Comintern Congress, which shifted the emphasis from elections to factory cells. This precipitated the departure of the revolutionary syndicalists, who disliked centralization. The party line was hardened further by adoption of the 'class against class' tactic in 1928, coinciding with Stalin's move against moderates in the USSR. Capitalism was said to be entering its final crisis. All those who were not on the side of communism, including the SFIO, were regarded as fascists.

Yet factory cells proved difficult to organize in the face of employer hostility, while the party's neglect of economic issues in favour of political slogans restricted its appeal in the factories. Although the PCF espoused advanced programmes for women and ethnic minorities, it subordinated them to the proletarian 'interest', and was fearful of alienating indigenous male workers. Some women joined the party, but they were expected to conform to the implicitly masculine image of professional revolutionaries—something most women were not prepared to do. By 1924 most feminists had left the party. The PCF did attract Italian anti-fascist immigrants, for whom internationalism was an article of faith, but the party worried about their preoccupation with Italian issues. The PCF also backed regionalists in Brittany and Alsace. In the latter, denunciation of French 'imperialism' initially won the PCF credit. But the party's insistence that 'the national liberation of Alsace-Lorraine can only be definitively solved by proletarian revolution' (Doriot) alienated Alsatian communists, many of whom were expelled in 1929 for allying with bourgeois autonomists.

PCF militants were not completely inflexible. The party's lack of interest in rural voters permitted local activists to ignore the party line on the expropriation of small property, and to maintain communist support in the south-western countryside. In the Parisian commuter suburb of Bobigny, where there were few factories, communists addressed community issues such as tenant rights. Yet in 1932, the communist vote dropped sharply even in its rural and urban strongholds. It had managed to identify itself in bourgeois eyes with anti-patriotism, women's emancipation, and the supremacy of the working class, whilst alienating regional minorities, immigrants, women, and workers!

The reconstruction of the SFIO

If the PCF had confined itself to the sidelines, the SFIO occupied an awkward position on the margins of the Republic. The SFIO was not a social-democratic party which sought maximization of working-class advantage within capitalism. Neither did it believe that socialism could be achieved gradually through reform. Rather the SFIO was led by revolutionaries like Longuet who rejected Comintern centralization. Revolutionaries, usually Guesdists, dominated the leadership of the party; at first the electorate of the SFIO came largely from the Guesdist bastions of the industrial north-west. Although there was a reformist minority in the SFIO, the main reason for opposition to communism, as Léon Blum said, was that their conceptions of revolution differed.

SFIO activists believed that revolution was inevitable, as Marx had demonstrated. They parted company from the PCF in insisting that socialism would come about through the democratic republic. The SFIO merely had to await the collapse of capitalism, inherit parliamentary power, and complete the socialization of the economy. In the meantime the party would avoid premature action (hence its distrust of PCF hot-headedness) and would avoid participation in radical-dominated cabinets. The socialists might, however, take power if they were able to dominate a cabinet, and would 'prepare the transition to socialism'.

Socialists also shared Jaurès's view that socialism would ultimately benefit all classes. Together with their commitment to democracy, this conviction helped the SFIO to use the republican tradition to broaden its appeal beyond the proletariat. Since republican democracy had to be defended against Catholics, the SFIO could tap into anticlericalism, and compete with the radicals for the allegiance of schoolteachers. The socialists' populist denunciation of the rich struck a chord with many peasants—so long as collectivism was not mentioned. On the negative side, the SFIO took over the nationalist and anti-feminist exclusions of the democratic tradition. It justified France's civilizing mission in the Empire, and agitated for restrictions on immigrant labour. In some areas the SFIO was backed by native workers, while the PCF was supported by immigrants. The proportion of female members in the SFIO was a paltry 3 per cent. Like the PCF, the SFIO held that women's liberation could come only through socialism, and resisted the creation of autonomous women's sections for fear that they might encourage feminism.

The SFIO's contradictions compromised parliamentary government. In 1924, to keep the right from power and to protect itself electorally from the communists, the party joined the Cartel with the radicals. There was no common programme, and the socialists refused to participate in government. Yet SFIO revolutionary rhetoric and demands for a capital levy excited right-wing fear of Bolshevization. The collapse of the Cartel nevertheless confirmed socialists in their conviction that collaboration with socialists was pointless. Jean Zyromski and Marcel Pivert formed the Bataille Socialiste group within the SFIO, which saw collaboration with radicals as undermining the party's revolutionary mission.

This is not to say that reformism was unimportant in the SFIO. Those socialist deputies who had been elected with radical votes were favourable to collaboration with the latter. Often coalition government with the radicals seemed near, only to be rejected by party activists. Frustrated reformists left the party in 1933 to form the neo-socialists. Some neo-socialists, notably Marcel Déat, gravitated towards fascism—an indication of the impossibility of social-democratic politics.

The radicals

The crisis of radicalism in the interwar years is usually attributed to tension between its 'outdated' anticlerical leftist tradition and the economic and social 'realities' of the present. In fact, it was not just sentiment that anchored radicalism on the left, and the 'modernity' of its programme is difficult to assess. The radicals' problem was that they espoused a social-democratic programme for which there was no political base.

Radical anticlericalism was kept alive by the understandable fear that the Catholic right did not accept secularism, and that the centre-right had conceded too much to Catholics. Hence radical sensitivity to symbolic issues like the status of religious education in Alsace-Lorraine and diplomatic relations with the Vatican. Moreover, radical party activists and deputies were recruited largely from the network of lay groups, such as the Jeunesses Laïques et Républicaines, which expanded alongside Catholic associations during the 1920s. Activists drawn from these circles were particularly motivated by the campaign for free secular secondary education—an issue of immense importance in class and religious terms. Radical voters, many of them civil servants and white-collar workers, were also worried by female and Catholic competition for jobs—a consequence of the feminization of white-collar work in the 1920s.

The radicals' social programme also opposed them to the right. Their demand for 'abolition of the proletariat' looked superficially like nostalgia for pre-industrialism. It was really part of a social-democratic agenda involving nationalization of monopolies, state-regulated industrial relations, welfare reform, and profit sharing—a programme indistinguishable from that of the CGT (the moderate wing of the trade union movement). It was endorsed by radicals from the right-winger Lucien Lamouroux, who described it as 'realistic and generous', to the more leftist 'Young Turks', who sought to renovate radicalism after 1926. Rapprochement with the CGT also reinforced radical anticlericalism, for the unions were dominated by state employees, especially railway workers and teachers, who resented Catholic (not to speak of female and foreign) rivals for jobs.

Radicals looked left and right for support for their reformism. Their hopes of attracting the SFIO to a popular, anti-capitalist alliance of peasants, petty-bourgeois, and workers were encouraged by the development of similar ideas by socialists such as Marcel Déat. Yet most SFIO activists had no sympathy for radicalism, for they believed capitalism to be historically doomed. The radicals also had hopes of those conservatives influenced by the Jeunes Équipes (linked to the radical Jeunes Turcs). However, the centre-right was too attentive to big business for radical tastes, remained largely committed to liberal individualism, and did not want to alienate the Catholic right.

Again in 1932, the radicals, under Édouard Herriot, won an election victory thanks to electoral alliances with the SFIO. This time Herriot pursued a much more cautious line in the hope of reassuring the right. But he remained reliant on socialist votes in parliament, and could not disarm right-wing paranoia about socialist manipulation of the government. As in 1924–6 it was impossible to create a viable coalition. In 1934 the radicals were forced to reverse alliances and accept secondary positions in right-wing cabinets. This time the situation was more serious, because economic crisis had spread discontent throughout society.

The Republic in crisis

At first it looked like the world economic crisis might spare France, for Poincaré's stabilization of the franc in 1928 had caused capital to flow into France. Yet industrial production fell from late 1929, and unemployment began to rise. In purely economic terms the depression was less serious in France than elsewhere. Unemployment was notably lower. But the political impact of the depression was serious. First, it hurt the electorate of right and centre parties more than that of the left. Perhaps surprisingly, the labour movement was strengthened. Since laid-off workers were able to return to the countryside, or were returned to their country of origin, there was no large pool of unemployed ready to take the jobs of workers who disputed the boss's line. In contrast, the depression hit business profits very badly, while wheat prices fell by around 75 per cent from 1926 to 1935. This made possible the massive mobilization of the labour movement in 1936 at a time when business, large and small, felt weak. Secondly, the depression caused massive disaffection among the supporters of all parties. Peasants complained of falling prices, civil servants feared wage-cuts, businesses faced bankruptcy, students and professionals resented foreign competition for jobs, white-collar workers demanded the return of women to the home. The list of complainants was endless, and the complexity of demands was worsened by the division of interest groups between Catholic and lay organizations. Herriot endeavoured to institute an orthodox deflationary response to the depression. But public spending cuts were impossible to reconcile with the demands of his own supporters for state subsidies, let alone with the need for SFIO support in parliament, for the latter was keen not to offend the civil servants among its voters.

The result was extreme governmental instability. Schemes for reform of the constitution were dusted off and given a more authoritarian, even anti-democratic, varnish. The discovery that a few radical politicians had been involved in murky dealings with the financier, Sasha Stavisky, led to demands for the cleansing of parliament. On 6 February 1934, a crowd of 30,000 leaguers and veterans demonstrated against the recently formed Daladier government. When the crowd tried to invade the Chamber of Deputies, police opened fire and sixteen people were killed. The riots did not represent a planned 'fascist coup'. Yet their importance should not be minimized. Few conservatives condemned the overthrow of the government by rioters. The Jeunesses Patriotes wanted a 'national revolution'—a term borrowed from Mussolini and Hitler. No one knows what would have happened had the demonstrators broken into the Chamber.

What is certain is that 6 February represented the beginning, not the end, of the crisis. The next day, ex-president Gaston Doumergue formed a government of 'national unity' based on the right and the radicals. He had to face a mobilization of the left against 'fascism', and, crucially, he alienated the right too. His deflationary economic policies hurt the supporters of both right and left. His government was criticized for its alleged inability to protect conservative activists from anti-fascist attacks, and it proved unable to enact constitutional reform. Successive right-wing governments under Flandin and Laval encountered similar difficulties. Behind these failures lay the long-standing divisions of the right. The Fédération Républicaine argued that deflation could be implemented only if parliamentary powers and trade union rights were reduced. Although it included vociferous proponents of constitutional revision such as Tardieu, the ARD largely defended parliament.

Disgusted with their leaders, many conservatives turned to anti-parliamentary leagues, above all Colonel de La Rocque's Croix de Feu, which may have possessed half a million members in May 1936. Like fascist movements elsewhere, the Croix de Feu combined reaction with radical populism. On the one hand it promised repression of the left, which it portrayed as part of an anti-French conspiracy of freemasons and Bolsheviks. On the other hand the league proclaimed that the established right was too feeble to carry out this task, and that the selfishness of big business had alienated the proletariat from the nation. The Croix de Feu would bring to power a new elite of 'real men' drawn (allegedly) from the people, legitimated not by election, but by service to the nation during the Great War. These notions appealed especially to those right-wingers who felt themselves to be excluded from the established right: female welfare workers who felt that the right was insufficiently sensitive to their schemes for class collaboration; natalists exasperated by parliament's failure to address the population 'problem'; Lyonnais industrialists who resented the dominance of the silk industry in that city; German-speaking peasants in Alsace who resented the francophone urban conservative establishment; Norman peasants who saw the big landowners who controlled agricultural unions as insufficiently concerned with the problem of falling prices; factory managers and engineers who believed that businessmen were more interested in profit than efficiency in the factory, and so on.

The Croix de Feu both reaffirmed and undermined the boundaries of the political nation. Immigrants were forbidden to join the movement, or to receive aid from its welfare services. Women would return to the home. At the same time the Croix de Feu shifted politics from parliament to the streets, and mobilized hitherto subordinate components of the conservative constituency, such as workers, women, and Alsatian autonomists. The movement's notorious military-style manoeuvres were designed to demonstrate that it alone could deal with the left—another implicit threat to the established order. In fact, paramilitarism cemented left-wing unity.

The Popular Front

On 12 February 1934 the communists supported a strike called by the CGT in protest against the fascist riots. Anti-fascist committees sprang up. In July 1934 communists and socialists created a Common Front. The great demonstration of 14 July 1935 marked the adhesion of the radical party to the Popular Front. The left's response might suggest a 'reflex' of democratic defence. Actually, anti-fascist unity came about slowly, and its leitmotif was not democracy in a straightforward sense.

The PCF did not initially break with 'class against class'. In February, Vaillant-Couturier wrote in *L'Humanité*, 'Defend the Republic, says Blum? As if fascism was not the Republic and as if the Republic was not fascism.' The PCF was pushed towards unity partly by pressure from militants. The communist mayor of Saint-Denis, Jacques Doriot, called for unity in an open letter to the Comintern. Unbeknownst to the PCF leadership, Stalin, frightened by Nazism, had begun talks for a military alliance with France, and this predisposed him to accept anti-fascist unity in domestic politics too. But much pressure was required to force Thorez, the PCF general secretary, to implement the new line. Eventually the PCF enthusiastically embraced the new line at its Ivry conference in June 1934. At the same moment Doriot was expelled from the party—for being right before the others.

For the first time the PCF defended the Republic. The party attempted to widen its appeal, essentially by seeking to immunize the petty-bourgeoisie against fascism by addressing their particular grievances, and by adopting the nationalist language of the Jacobins. Sometimes this led to a frankly conservative stance: after the signature of the Franco-Soviet Pact (May 1935) national defence was endorsed; depopulation was denounced as a national danger and the virtues of the family were discovered.

Continuities in PCF policy must be emphasized too. The agreement between the SFIO and PCF was initially limited to anti-fascism. Even after the radicals joined, Thorez declared openly that the Popular Front would 'permit preparation for the total seizure of power by the proletariat'. To this end the PCF endeavoured to build a mass movement of Popular Front committees, and demands such as 'make the rich pay' were designed to mobilize the maximum possible number of supporters behind them. Thorez told the Central Committee that when the moment was ripe, the replacement of the police by a workers' militia would be added to the Popular Front programme. The obstacles in the way of this revolutionary policy were enormous. The radicals and SFIO opposed mobilization through committees; Stalin's efforts to woo French diplomatic support often obliged him to force moderation on the PCF. No more than the SFIO had been was the PCF able to reconcile revolutionary convictions with the requirements of immediate action.

In October 1933, shortly before the riots of 6 February, the SFIO expelled 28 reformist deputies and 20,000 members. Blum and party secretary Faure had reasserted the party's revolutionary mission. The rise of fascism initially changed little: Blum feared that participation in government might cause disillusion with the Republic by raising hopes unrealizable within capitalism. This view was partially altered by the direct threat to the Republic on 6 February. Blum declared that 'When the Republic is threatened the word "Republic" changes its meaning'—in other words, democracy must be defended in order to preserve the conditions for revolution. When the radicals joined the Popular Front Blum accepted that given the danger to the Republic, socialists might participate in a radical government, or 'occupy' power themselves.

Yet the impetus for anti-fascist unity came largely from the leftist Seine Federation of the SFIO, which favoured common action with the communists, but not the radicals. It was chiefly leftists who signed the Common Front agreement of 27 July. The SFIO was less keen to endorse national defence than was the PCF, and was reluctant to bow to communist pressure to moderate the Popular Front programme in order to please the radicals. The SFIO hesitated between the view that 'we must proclaim to the masses ... that we wish to lead them towards socialism, which is the only route to salvation' and the desire for structural reforms would alleviate worker and peasant misery. Little attention was paid to those outside the SFIO's traditional constituency. Feminism was still dismissed in the name of revolution. Some socialists were unhappy with *any* concessions to the 'bankrupt' radicals. In 1935 Pivert formed a new faction, the Gauche Révolutionnaire, on this basis.

Radicalism was indeed in crisis. Professionalization of the bar, journalism, and ministerial cabinets were eroding the informal networks on which the party relied. Mass movements and political polarization undermined the culture of reasoned debate in which radicalism flourished. The radicals' social-democratic programme was tailored to the presumed needs of skilled workers and state employees, but addressed the concerns of neither unskilled immigrant nor female workers in the industrial suburbs, nor peasant and lower middle-class voters who provided the party with the bulk of its support. Ad hoc palliatives were insufficient to deal with the depression. Many peasants turned to socialism or even communism, while some small business people were attracted to anti-parliamentary groups such as the Ligue des Contribuables, which had participated in the riots of 6 February.

The radicals responded to events from a position of weakness. They joined the Doumergue coalition because they had no alternative, and counted for little in the cabinet. Yet the pro-left majority of the party reasserted itself. The local elections of October 1934 demonstrated the unprofitability of the right-wing alliance and the anti-fascist enthusiasm of radical activists. Radical participation in the Popular Front was facilitated by the accommodating attitude of the communists. Radical leaders were half-aware of the PCF's ulterior motives, but they expected that radicals would dominate a Popular Front government.

Events did not turn out as expected. In the elections of 28 April and 3 May 1936, the Popular Front won an overall majority. The PCF gained 11 per cent of the vote and 70 seats. The largest party was not the radicals, who lost nearly one-third of their votes, but the SFIO. When Blum took office on 3 May, France was in the grip of an unprecedented wave of factory occupations. Although no strikers considered seizing state power, the implicit revolutionary threat was obvious, and the bourgeoisie was terrified. Not only did occupations threaten property, but the massive participation of women, and the daily descent of workers, including many women, children, and immigrants, upon bourgeois city centres, apparently threatened the whole fabric of society. Blum profited from the panic to implement a series of reforms, including paid holidays, the forty-hour week without loss of pay, collective labour contracts, and a national wheat office. Later, the railways, Bank of France, and arms industries were nationalized.

The Popular Front is generally seen as having squandered its opportunities. In fact it contributed to the failure of the leagues. Anti-fascists had quickly won the initiative in street politics—doubtless helped by the less systematic hostility of the French police to the left compared to their Italian and German counterparts. Anti-fascists were able to portray their violent response to the leagues (frequently underestimated by historians) as defence against the Croix de Feu's threat to the Republic. On 18 June Blum banned the leagues. La Rocque, despite his oft-declared intention to 'act' in the event of grave disorder, did nothing, aware that in current conditions resistance was risky. The Croix de Feu reformed as a political party, the Parti Social Français (PSF), which resolved to win power through elections. Whereas Hitler and Mussolini combined electoralism with

open contempt for democracy, the PSF gradually abandoned paramilitarism, toned down its subversive rhetoric, and focused on welfare work. It never became a genuinely democratic party, but the
defeat of the extreme right was plain. This was confirmed by the
failure of Jacques Doriot's fascistic Parti Populaire Français (PPF) to
break into mass politics. Some frustrated extremists turned to terrorism in the form of the Comité Secret d'Action Révolutionnaire
(CSAR), better known as the Cagoulards.

The Popular Front also disputed the allegiance of the masses with
the extreme right. The PCF, whilst preserving a core of male, French
activists, mobilized immigrants and women. The notion of French
leadership of international anti-fascism struck a chord with workers
of Spanish, Polish, and Italian origin. The PCF organized women in
the Union des Jeunes Filles de France (UJFF), in which political education and leisure were combined—no longer, the party said, did
women need to forget their femininity. Although the party now
accepted pronatalism, with its anti-feminist baggage, the UJFF
provided women with an introduction to activism. The SFIO, meanwhile, was responsible for creation of a National Wheat Office, which
purchased all wheat at a fixed price, and was an undoubted success
with the peasantry. Léo Lagrange, minister of sport and leisure, tried
to show that the left was as capable as fascists of providing recreation
for the masses.

But if the Popular Front helped defeat the leagues, it proved unable
to hold on to power, or to halt the slide into a more unexpected form
of authoritarianism. Like Herriot before him, Blum failed to win
unequivocal support on his left. The PCF refused to participate in
government, preferring to work with 'advanced elements' in the
masses. Blum's effort to reassure the centre by following an orthodox
financial policy backfired. He fatally delayed devaluation of the franc
until September 1936, and had no answer to price inflation. Working-
class discontent revived, and Pivert made himself its spokesman
within the SFIO. The PCF zigzagged between the moderation
imposed by its desire to win conservative backing for a diplomatic
front against Hitler, and the radicalism required to prevent disappointed workers from turning towards Pivert. Moreover, the PCF's
ever more strident nationalism perplexed the internationalist Italians
and Spaniards who provided the shock troops of the Popular Front.
The Popular Front's leisure programme focused on the male skilled

worker, and offered less to women. André Chamson wrote in the left-wing weekly, *Vendredi*, that the face of the Popular Front, was 'that of a young man, bronzed by the sun, muscular, used to walking and to the open air, his soul innocent and yet not naïve, singing "Allons au devant de la vie".' When Blum fell on 21 June 1937, there were no demonstrations in his favour.

The immediate author of Blum's fall was the Senate, a body which reflected radical fears. Historically, the radicals viewed the SFIO as the lost sheep of the republican family, and they were inclined to view the PCF similarly. Yet in 1936, for the first time, radicals began to see the extreme left as a greater danger than the extreme right. They had never favoured attacks on property, and so June 1936 worried them. The white-collar and supervisory personnel among radical electors were alarmed at the threat to hierarchy in the workplace, while wage rises, paid holidays, and the forty-hour week were resented by small business. The socialists would not accept exemptions for small business from labour legislation, and many big businessmen agreed, for fear of giving small business a cost advantage. These issues had been fudged in the Popular Front programme.

As radicals became anti-communist, they abandoned the idea of a people's alliance against capitalism. They spoke instead for the 'middle classes', allegedly threatened by a coalition of big capital and organized labour. The middle classes were defined widely enough to include the 'healthy elements' of the proletariat as well as 'good capitalists'. Clearly, middle-class ideology implied a break with the SFIO and PCF.

By late 1938 Daladier, prime minister since April, was engaged, with the backing of the right, in unrelenting struggle against the left. The Munich Agreement, in September, represented a victory over the war party, headed by the PCF—it was widely felt that the PCF sought war in order to foment revolution. Daladier then confronted the CGT. Arguing that the forty-hour week hindered rearmament, the government effectively abolished it. Government and employers mounted a massive repressive operation against the ensuing general strike (30 November 1938). Foreign and 'recently naturalized' workers were particular targets. Anti-Semitism also resurfaced, stimulated by the arrival of German and Austrian refugees in 1938, and by the perceived association of Jews with communism and warmongering. As always, immigration and depopulation were connected. In

February 1939 the government set up an all-male High Committee for Population, charged with coordinating governmental action in both areas. In July it decreed a 'Family Code', which included various measures for 'protection of the race' and of the traditional family. All these measures were implemented by executive decree. Parliament counted for little. Policy was elaborated by 'experts', drawn from milieux that had long favoured constitutional reform. Technocrats such as the Polytechniciens Alfred Sauvy and Michel Debré joined the finance ministry. Many experts would play leading roles at Vichy.

The Daladier government represented a victory for the republican elite within the centre-right and centre-left over those perceived to threaten the boundaries of the political nation. Yet the Daladier government was not yet Vichy. Administrative persecution of immigrants was counterbalanced by the Marchandeau decree of April 1939 which outlawed press attacks on religious and racial groups. Furthermore, Daladier's rapprochement with the right had provoked a backlash among some radical activists, headed by Herriot. The Catholic right played a subordinate role in government, had not gained all it wanted in the Family Code, and its demand for suppression of the CGT was unanswered. An older generation would have found it hard to recognize Daladier's regime as republican, but there had been no decisive break with democracy. No one can say what would have become of the Republic had not military defeat interrupted its history.

Vichy

When war broke out again in September 1939 the French people were more united than might have been expected. The popular mood was one of resignation rather than defeatism. The right had overcome its anti-war feeling as the extent of Hitler's demands became clear. Also, the conclusion of the Nazi–Soviet Pact permitted the government to suppress the PCF, and thereby reassure the right that war would not lead to revolution. Nevertheless, the struggles of previous years had some impact on military matters. The high command's defensive strategy, symbolized by the Maginot fortifications, owed something to the pessimism of those who believed that the low birth rate signified national decadence. De Gaulle's campaign for mechanized armoured tactics came up against suspicion that he wanted to create an anti-republican professional army. The government's anti-communism led it to be diverted into aiding the Finns in their struggle against the USSR.

As in 1914 the German armies attacked through Belgium. The French and British sent their best troops to meet them, only to find themselves outflanked by a thrust through the Ardennes to the south, hitherto considered impassable by tanks. On 17 June 1940, after six weeks of warfare, the French government gave up fighting. While the conflicts of the 1930s may have affected the army's ability to fight, the high command's fatal decision to send its best troops into the Belgian trap was not socially or politically predetermined.

Pétain's dictatorial regime, with its headquarters in the spa town of Vichy, was, however, a product of French society and its conflicts. Pétain had been brought into the cabinet on 18 May to stiffen national resolve. Ever the defeatist, Pétain immediately set about working for an armistice. On 17 June, now prime minister, he publicly announced that he was seeking one. He already saw defeat as the prelude to national penitence and regeneration. The armistice preserved French sovereignty over most of the country, but the administration had to reckon with an occupying army in the north. The Germans did not, however, dictate the nature of the French government. At Vichy on 9 July the one-time moderate conservative prime minister Pierre Laval persuaded parliament—the Popular Front parliament—to grant full powers to the octogenarian Pétain.

Vichy was not a fascist regime, with a mass party, but a dictatorship based on army, Church, and administration, the only institutions which remained upstanding in the chaos of July 1940. The PCF had been banned when war broke out, and the SFIO was hopelessly divided between pacifists and bellicists. The PSF had been in decline since 1938 and like all the mass parties was disrupted by mobilization and war. Into the breach stepped the administrators and 'experts', who had played such a role under Daladier, joined by the Church, armed forces, big business, and agricultural leaders. Politically, this meant alliance between the Catholic and republican elites. There was also an Action Française fringe presence, especially in Pétain's cabinet. A few dissident socialists also joined the government.

Vichy's 'National Revolution' aimed to restore the authority of the 'natural elites'. This did not mean return to 'pre-industrial' times, but the arrival in power of the 'experts', demanded since the 1890s. Civil servants and military officers took up ministerial positions. The Church gained major concessions in education. Big businessmen dominated Vichy's industrial bodies, the Organization Committees. All had imbibed the amateur general culture, pseudo-science, eugenicism, and social engineering dispensed by the École Libre.

With elitism went exclusion, for the natural elites were defined (it was said) by their roots in French culture and soil. Foreigners and Jews bore the brunt—one of the first acts of Vichy was to suppress the Marchandeau decree. Recent research has rightly highlighted the Republic's role in preparing the way for Vichy's discriminatory policies. Vichy's anti-Semitism also owed much to the Catholic right's obsession with the 'enemy within'. Even where the right's hatred had apparently focused on freemasonry, as in the interwar years, the anti-Semitic subtext was never far below the surface. Vichy's exclusion of freemasons from public employment derived from the same logic as anti-Semitic legislation—both Masons and Jews were 'materialist' forces that undermined the spiritual ties of nation, family, and religion. But whereas freemasons and even communists might be recovered for the nation, Jews were most dangerous since they were unassimilable. In 1942 anti-masonic legislation was relaxed, while anti-Semitic measures escalated. Around 78,000 of the Jewish population of France perished in the Holocaust, of whom 22 per cent were French nationals.

The Catholic right also influenced family policy. The National Revolution was portrayed as a virile reaction against the feminine vices of the Republic. The grandfatherly Pétain was depicted as the epitome of patriarchy. Under Pétain's authority the masses would relearn the feminine virtue of self-sacrifice for the nation. 'Familialism' became one of Vichy's priorities, and shaped natalist policy more than under Daladier. Women were excluded from certain areas of employment, and abortion was made a capital crime—two people were guillotined. Vichy represented the purest expression of conservative attitudes towards women. There was no equivalent of the PSF's efforts to mobilize women politically. Indeed, the latter's growing dependence on female cadres may have added to the regime's suspicion of it.

Although Catholic and republican partisans of the National

Revolution shared common enemies, there was room for conflict, especially concerning the role of the state. Former Republicans accepted interventionism, but Catholics feared the state's secularism. The influence of the Catholic right was greatest in the first months, during which the Church's grievances regarding education were addressed. Under Flandin (December 1940 to February 1941) parliamentarians of the centre-right returned. His successor, Darlan (February 1941 to April 1942) was more anticlerical, and gave a greater role to experts and technocrats. When Laval returned in 1942, his model was the Daladier regime of 1938–9.

All Vichy governments distrusted mass politics, even in the form of extreme-right parties. Attempts to form a single party on the fascist model failed in the first months of the regime. The PSF found itself excluded from power. Instead, the regime relied for its links with society on the Légion des Combattants, the product of a merger of pre-war veterans' associations, which were largely dominated by conservatives. Yet Vichy could not avoid fascism entirely. Competing factions at Vichy used links with the Nazis as weapons in power struggles. Mainstream conservatives had developed ties with the far right during the 1930s, while fascists sought to compensate for their numerical weakness by exploiting contacts with conservatives. Fascist influence was strongest under Darlan, when a number of PPF members held office. Paul Marion at the ministry of propaganda spoke of 'sculpting the masses' like a sculptor remoulds clay. By this time, however, public opinion had turned decisively against the regime.

The resistance

If Vichy soon used up its stock of goodwill, the republican 'reflex' was more sluggish. The first resisters were isolated—not, however, in the sense that they were socially marginal. Rather they were untypically strong-minded. Charles de Gaulle, an army officer who had served in the last civilian government of the Republic, who left France to found the Free French in London, had an extraordinary sense of personal destiny. Resistance drew upon those excluded by the narrowly based political system of the Third Republic, such as aid organizations for Spanish republican refugees and Catholic charitable networks, often run by women. Also, just as the disruption of the mass parties had permitted the elites to take control of the government, so dissident elements within the elites were influential in the early resistance—army officers such as Henri Frenay were especially important.

The early resistance was politically heterogeneous, for it often grew out of chance encounters of the like-minded, who put anti-Germanism before politics, especially in the occupied zone. Nevertheless, the left was relatively weak at the beginning. Neither the SFIO nor the radicals were suited to clandestine activity. The PCF had prepared for subversion, and it violently denounced Vichy, yet the Nazi–Soviet Pact dictated that the PCF attack the Germans only indirectly through the charge that Vichy had compromised 'national independence'. The PCF adopted a parody of Leninist revolutionary defeatism, even-handedly denouncing the imperialism of London and Berlin, and endeavouring to turn war into revolution by encouraging the French to fraternize with German soldiers!

Whereas the PCF attacked Vichy but spared the Germans, many non-communist resisters attacked the Germans but not Vichy. Conservatives within the non-communist resistance shared Vichy's analysis of the defeat. Some resisters possessed contacts with the Vichy government, for not all the regime's functionaries favoured collaboration with Germany. De Gaulle rejected Vichy as illegitimate, but did not at first condemn its policies, and was not interested in mass resistance. In the early days, many of the 'progressive' elements of the resistance were actually drawn from the nonconformist right—Christian democrats such as François de Menthon. They were indulgent towards Vichy, and some of them wished to give the regime a more social Catholic orientation.

By late 1942 conservative apoliticism was declining. Politicization and radicalization had begun in the south, where it became clear that resistance necessitated rejection of Vichy. In the summer of 1941 economic discontent caused strikes with anti-German overtones in occupied Nord-Pas-de-Calais. Radicalization was promoted too by the accentuation of German demands upon France in the winter of 1942–3. Most significantly the introduction of obligatory labour service in Germany (STO) in January 1943 caused young workers to go into hiding, and many joined the resistance, or *maquis*. This provided a constituency for the left. In late 1942 the SFIO, via the clandestine Comité d'Action Socialiste, demanded independent representation in resistance bodies. Although the SFIO did not have its own resistance organization, its members became numerous enough in southern movements to give it leverage. The role of the PCF was also crucial, especially in the north. Following Hitler's invasion of the USSR on 23 June 1941, the party had called for a 'national front' against the invader.

Paradoxically, the victory of the left owed much to the temperamentally conservative de Gaulle. Deterioration of the latter's relations with the allies led him to see the internal resistance as a source of legitimacy, and he wished to prove to American opinion that he was not a fascist. To win Russian approval, he was willing even to accept PCF support. By May 1943 de Gaulle had secured the backing of the internal resistance, communists included, for a Conseil National de la Résistance (CNR). This enabled him to defeat the US-backed neo-Vichyist General Giraud's bid for leadership of the French forces. By July 1943 de Gaulle was sole head of the French Committee of National Liberation (CFLN). Within France the formation of the CNR represented a victory for the SFIO and PCF over the more conservative Frenay, who at the end of 1942 still spoke privately of his dislike of the 'British, Jewish and Masonic' influences around de Gaulle.

Politicization enhanced the role of the left within the resistance, but at the price of narrowing its base. At first, the informal character of resistance had permitted the politically marginal to play a role. The necessity for clandestinity—an allegedly female characteristic—permitted women to become involved as carriers of messages and distributors of pamphlets. Since the resistance did little more than this at first, women such as Lucie Aubrac rose to leadership positions. As in the 1930s, women were most involved in the PCF and Catholic groups (Témoignage Chrétien and Ceux de la Résistance). The former used the pre-war UJFF network to form Women's Resistance Committees. In 1944, thanks mainly to the PCF, the Consultative Assembly in Algiers accepted female suffrage. Since immigrants too had conventionally been conceived in feminine terms, and because many lived a semi-clandestine existence anyway, they too played a significant part in resistance. The PCF's Immigrant Workers' Movement (MOI), established in the 1930s, set up a fighting organization within the communist Francs-Tireurs et Partisans (FTP). It was responsible for most attacks on the Germans in Paris in 1942.

The shift of resistance activity to factories and the *maquis* in 1942–3 reduced opportunities for the marginal. In the *maquis*, working-class men lived in male military camps. To counter Vichy's accusation that camp life was promiscuous, women were usually excluded. Now that resistance was no longer confined to a minority, it was possible to replace the notion of clandestinity with that of the 'outlaw'—the '*man* on the run'. With the complicity of the normally law-abiding, the outlaw expressed the people's opposition to an illegitimate regime. The *maquis* also stressed its roots in the land, and whilst this countered Vichy's idealization of the peasantry, it also connected implicitly with discourses that had legitimated discrimination against immigrants.

De Gaulle played a crucial part in the re-establishment of old hierarchies. Once he had defeated Giroud, he was less interested in the internal resistance. He preferred to establish the CFLN's credentials as the legal continuation of the Republic. Hence also his creation of a Consultative Assembly, and in June 1944 transformation of the CFLN into a Provisional Government. As part of a strategy of 'taming' the resistance, de Gaulle created a women's auxiliary group which confined them to support roles. Meanwhile, as Vichy disintegrated, the resistance created an alternative republican state, with its own shadow administration and army. Preoccupation with continuity of the state permitted many of the administrators and experts, who had served Daladier and Vichy so well, to survive the Liberation. The conservative right was not eliminated from the resistance, for the decay of Vichy led many of its supporters to change sides. The Organisation Civile et Militaire (OCM) and Ceux de la Résistance were both important in this respect. The left-wing resistance newspaper *Franc-Tireur* declared that France no longer wanted to be governed by grands bourgeois, Conseillers d'État, finance inspectors, and pupils of the École Libre. In fact, resistance leaders were largely younger members of the same elite.

Conclusion

The political history of the years from 1914 to 1945 demonstrates the strengths and weaknesses of democratic culture in France. In August 1914 there had been a brief moment of national unanimity, but it was unclear whether it was republican in content. Ultimately the war led to political polarization and undermined the centrist coalition that had sustained the regime in the late 1900s. The revolutionary priorities of the PCF and the SFIO, still in evidence during the Popular Front years, and the existence of mass anti-parliamentarian movements in the 1930s, all contributed to the instability of the regime. Each of these movements endorsed the Republic, but conceived it in radically different ways. The regime continued to exclude women, rejected the demands of regionalists, and discriminated against ethnic minorities.

The instability of parliament was grist to the mill of those who believed parliamentary rule to be 'ineffective'. Proponents of constitutional reform included the Catholic right, some in the centre-right, and a few radicals. Constitutional reformers at first invested hope in the Bloc National, and when that failed they turned to extra-parliamentary lobbying. When elite politics were challenged by mass movements in the 1930s, demands for 'reform of the state' became frankly authoritarian, and were coupled to anti-Marxism, anti-feminism, and racism. The Daladier government realized much of this project, but only under Vichy were Catholics fully included in the government.

How strong was democracy in 1945? Anti-republicans of left and right were weaker than at any time since 1914. The extreme right had been dealt a blow from which it would not recover for forty years. The right had been discredited by association with Vichy. The PCF participated in government and sought to win for the people—not just the proletariat—the maximum degree of freedom possible in a capitalist society. Reformism and humanism, now embraced by Blum, gained ground in the SFIO. For the first time workers won comprehensive welfare reform. Yet by 1948, the PCF had returned to sectarianism, and Gaullism had re-emerged as a movement of the authoritarian right. As in the Third Republic, an unstable centrist alliance struggled to hold the regime together. Women had gained the vote, but failed to win political influence. Indeed, the natalist policy of Daladier and Vichy, minus some of its most repressive features, was reaffirmed by the Provisional Government. Discrimination against freemasons and Jews ended, but de Gaulle's ordinance of November 1945 continued existing policy towards the 'recently naturalized'. This shift in priorities reflected the defeat of the Catholic right, but demonstrated the adaptability of the republican ruling class. Indeed, the tendency of the resistance to portray Vichy as an *exclusively* 'clerico-reactionary' regime, and the acceptance of this idea by many historians and political scientists, helped the republican elite, of which some academics were a part, to escape the taint of Vichy.

3

The Fifth Republic as parenthesis? Politics since 1945

Richard Vinen

Describing the Fifth Republic as a 'parenthesis' may sound gratui-
tously perverse. France has seen five republics, two empires, two
sorts of monarchy, a consulate, and an 'état' since 1789. The Fifth
Republic has already lasted longer than all but one of these, the Third
Republic of 1870–1940. The Fifth Republic did not, as its defenders
would hasten to point out, spring from nowhere. It was established
by a man steeped in the history of France and it incarnates traditions—centralization, *dirigisme*, and the leadership of a ruler who
enjoys direct relation with the electorate—that can be traced back to
Louis XIV, Colbert, and Napoleon.

Furthermore, the Fifth Republic is not, so far as one can tell, about
to disappear. Reform is often discussed but no major figure has suggested a total rethinking of the constitution since the 1960s. In many
ways, however, it is precisely this last point that reveals the transience
of the Fifth Republic. The basis of Gaullist thinking, and of French
politics for the last forty years, was that change came from above and
that, consequently, constitutions mattered. Things looked different by
the end of the century. The French saw their lives governed by market
forces that come from outside France altogether or by the bonds of a
civil society at local level. Perhaps even the constitution itself had
become irrelevant to most French people. The referendum of 1958,
which approved the Fifth Republic constitution, mobilized over

three-quarters of French voters. The referendum of 24 September 2000, which reduced the term of office of the president from seven years to five years, mobilized less than a third of French voters.

All this changes the way in which we look at French history. The Fifth Republic is not the reflection of some timeless platonic absolute (de Gaulle's 'certain idea of France'). Rather it reflected the needs of French society at a particular time. These needs were partly expressed in the constitution (and in the mere fact that the constitution mattered so much) and partly reflected in a variety of other institutions. The aim of this chapter is to look at the social foundations of French politics; how they changed during the 1950s in ways that made the Fifth Republic useful and how they have changed in the 1990s in ways that have made it irrelevant.

Broadly, the political history of post-war France can be divided into three stages. The first is the era of the notable. During this period, French politics operated largely at local level and was dominated by a club of powerful individuals from which much of the population was excluded. The second was the era of the state. During this period, politics operated at a national level and was dominated by a small number of very powerful individuals who derived their legitimacy from direct relations with the electorate, and who governed with the help of a centralized and highly trained civil service. The third era is that of globalization. During this period, the power of the French state was undermined by its inability to control rapid technological change and international economic forces that often seemed to make all national politics irrelevant and which, in terms of party structures, often seemed to recreate the confusion of French politics in the 1950s.

These three eras are not, of course, entirely separate. The transition from one to the other was a slow process which often took place at different speeds in different domains. A single individual may, in different aspects of his or her life, incarnate different aspects of all three eras. Valéry Giscard d'Estaing is a classic product of notable politics, having inherited his constituency from his grandfather, as well as being a supreme example of state politics, since he progressed through the *grandes écoles* and the *grands corps* to become president of the Republic, but he is also a prophet of globalization who spoke English to German Chancellor Helmut Schmidt. To put it crudely, however, the era of the notable coincided with the Fourth Republic

(1946–58). The era of the state was born with the Fifth Republic in 1958 and then reborn with the constitutional changes that brought about direct election of the president in 1962. The era of globalization began in the 1990s.

The Fourth Republic, 1946–1958: notable politics

As France was liberated, de Gaulle finally acquired recognition as leader of a provisional government from the allies but he had not, so far, been endorsed by any electorate of more than a few hundred people. The first legislative elections in post-war France, and the first in French history in which women voted, were held on 21 October 1945. The elections had been accompanied by a referendum on the drawing up a constitution. The new assembly was granted the right to draw up a constitution but was also obliged to submit its constitutional proposal to a new referendum within seven months. The assembly was dominated by communists (who had obtained 26 per cent of the vote), socialists (23 per cent of the vote), and members of the newly formed Christian-democratic Mouvement Républicain Populaire (MRP) (24 per cent of the vote).

De Gaulle formed a coalition government after the elections (in which the communists held 5 of 20 seats) but on 20 January 1946—bored with party politics and probably, though wrongly, convinced that public opinion would call for his return—de Gaulle resigned. France was now governed by a coalition of communists, socialists, and Christian democrats. The communists and socialists attempted to impose a constitution that would have granted considerable power to a single chamber assembly, but this constitution was rejected by a referendum of 5 May 1946 (by roughly 11 million to 9 million). A second constitutional draft was finally accepted by a narrow majority of the electorate (9 million against 8 million) on 13 October 1946.

The new constitution differed from the rejected draft of May 1946 in that it granted greater powers to the upper house (the Council of the Republic) and also provided a more important role for the president of the Republic. These differences became important for two reasons. First, in January 1947, Vincent Auriol was elected as president, by a joint meeting of both houses of the Assembly. Auriol, a tough socialist who had lost an eye in the Great War, undertook his duties, particularly with regard to government formation, with great vigour during his period of office (1947–54). Secondly, the means of electing the Council of the Republic was changed in 1948 in a way that made it less like the lower house and more like the conservative Senates of the Third Republic.

The parties of the Fourth Republic

The largest party in post-war France was the one that broke all the rules of notable politics. The Parti Communiste Français (PCF) was disciplined, centralized, and strikingly indifferent to the material interests of its supporters. The PCF was supported by more than a quarter of the electorate in the late 1940s. There were over 900,000 party members in 1947 (three times the pre-war figure). In part, the PCF's success came from the prestige that it derived from its per-ceived role in the resistance and its success in this domain earned it some support outside the working class. However, most of its sup-port, especially after the few heady years that followed the Liberation, came from workers (half of its electorate was working class in 1956), and the party's fortunes were therefore improved by the fact that the working class was both larger and more homogeneous than ever before in the years that followed the Liberation. The war economy and the reconstruction envisaged by the Monnet Plan encouraged the concentration of industrial production into ever larger plants and particularly the development of the coal and metallurgy industries, which were centres of communist strength. French industry had trad-itionally drawn on large numbers of women and foreigners. Divisions of sex and nationality had made working-class unity, or at least the kind of working-class unity that the communist party wanted, dif-ficult to achieve. This problem had been exacerbated by the frequency with which workers changed jobs. From the early 1930s onwards, this changed. Women and immigrants were driven out of the labour force by economic depression while employment for men stabilized. The result was a large, native, stable, highly skilled and male workforce—precisely the kind of working class that fitted in with PCF preconcep-tions and one that greatly facilitated the party's electoral success and hold over institutions such as the Confédération Générale du Travail (the main trade union confederation).

Some on the right believed that the way to counteract the power of the communists was to create an equal and opposite force: a strong and well-disciplined party of the right. The earliest and most explicit attempt to do this was seen in the foundation of the Parti Républicain de la Liberté (PRL), founded in 1945, which aimed to imitate the British Conservative Party. The role of the Christian democrat MRP was more complicated. The party had similar ambitions to the PRL in that it aimed to create a centralized and disciplined national movement and it attracted many conservative voters (indeed it attracted precisely the voters that the PRL had hoped to win over): its opponents jibed that it was the 'machine à ramasser les pétainistes' (a vehicle for picking up the ex-supporters of Marshal Pétain). The MRP might well have played the role that the Christian democratic parties played in Germany and Italy—that is, that of a party of mass conservatism. Yet curiously, the only party leader who seems to have appreciated this possibility was Georges Bidault, the only one with a left-wing past, which discredited him as a leader of the right.

More generally, like the PRL, the MRP fell victim to the continued power of notables. Notables were men who drew their power from control of patronage, local newspapers, and ability to broker electoral deals in particular constituencies. Notables claimed to draw power from their own personal prestige and contacts rather than from their contact with a party or any other institution. Membership of a family that was established in an area could confer such power. Exercise of certain professions was also useful. The radical party was dismissed in 1945 as 'good for the vets' but in fact vets had great influence in agricultural regions and it is no accident that Roger Duchet, éminence grise of conservative politics after 1951, was a vet. Sometimes men—such as André Baud in the Jura—exercised enormous power at local level while remaining almost unknown at national level.

The circumstances of the few years after the Liberation increased the gulf between local and national level and between formal and informal power. Many Third Republic politicians were declared ineligible for all public office because they had voted full powers to Marshal Pétain or held office under Vichy. Such men, of course, preserved their contacts, and often their prestige, in their home areas even when they were prevented from entering parliament. Notables resented centralized, disciplined, Paris-based parties of the kind that many who emerged from the resistance tried to create in 1945.

The preferred parties of the notables were small ones assembled in loose alliances. The radical party, and its associates in the Rassemblement des Gauches Républicaines (the constituent parts of which were, in fact, mainly on the right of the spectrum) was very much a notable party. The radical party's central discipline was so weak that its leaders did not even have a clear idea about the number of members of their party, but its use of alliances and electoral manipulation was so adept that it managed to increase the number of seats that it held in parliament even when its vote declined. Many candidates stood as 'independents' and indeed the Fourth Republic gave birth to the apparent paradox of political parties that grouped 'independents'. The Centre National des Indépendants (formed in 1949), which later became the Centre National des Indépendants et Paysans, was the most important such grouping but it coexisted with bodies such as Union des Nationaux et des Indépendants Républicains and the Rassemblement des Groupements Républicains et Indépendants Français. Roger Kir, mayor of Dijon, even fought the 1951 legislative elections as an 'independent Independent'.

How did a political system based on small, loosely structured parties hold together? The answer to this lies largely on the left of the political spectrum. From January 1946 until April 1947, the communist party governed in coalition with the Christian democrat MRP and the socialist SFIO. However, the French communist party was ferociously loyal to Moscow and, as the division of Europe was frozen by Soviet installation of puppet governments in central Europe and by communist rejection of Marshall aid, communist ministers left the French government. From then until the death of Stalin, in March 1953, French politics were divided in the most bitter way imaginable between communists and their opponents. Fear of communism was associated with a fear of the proletariat, which was an isolated but powerful minority in a nation of peasants and artisans. Fear of communism also sprang from fear of the Red Army which was, as de Gaulle memorably remarked, separated from the French frontier by a distance that was barely equivalent to two stages of the Tour de France.

Finally, anti-communism sprang from genuine moral disgust: a disgust that was felt especially strongly on the left. The party's claims to be the party of the resistance sounded hollow to those who remembered the inactivity of its leadership during the Hitler–Stalin pact era or who knew that the very PCF members most associated with resistance were being purged from the party on the grounds of suspected 'Titoism'. France's historic associations with eastern Europe made the purges there especially traumatic. French communists professed to believe ludicrously improbable stories about the guilt of 'conspirators' in the east. Some of those condemned had spent years of exile in France. The Czech Arthur London was a hero of the French resistance who was denounced by his own French wife and brother-in-law, both loyal members of the PCF. Yet, among the non-communist left, anyone who could be bothered to listen to the exiled Hungarian François Fejto knew that innocent men were being hung.

The threat that the communist party was seen to pose in the late 1940s ensured a certain degree of unity among the opponents of communism. Numerous differences (over religion, Vichy, or industrial concentration) were subordinated to the one great difference (between communists and their enemies). The very looseness of political groupings allowed them to bring together a wide spectrum of opinion. Thus the Rassemblement des Gauches Républicaines brought the Union Démocratique et Socialiste de la Résistance into an alliance with several groups that were primarily composed of Pétainists. Jacques Isorni, Pétain's defence council, was refused admission to the Independent grouping in parliament after his election in 1951 but soon became 'attached' to the peasant party which was, in turn, part of an alliance with the independents. At local level, cross-party alliances were expressed through *apparentements* (agreements which allowed parties to pool their votes under certain circumstances). In government, they were expressed through coalitions. Cross-party cooperation was assisted by bodies that operated outside conventional party politics to distribute funds, provided by business or the Americans, and to coordinate anti-communist activity. Often such bodies were run by men such as André Boutemy (prefect of Lyon during the occupation) or Georges Albertini (a leader of Marcel Déat's collaborationist movement) whose support for the Vichy government had made it impossible for them to occupy an open position in political life.

The resilience of the Fourth Republic political system was revealed by the Rassemblement du Peuple Français, founded by Charles de

Gaulle in April 1947. The RPF was a child of the Cold War. Its leaders juxtaposed their own dynamism with the alleged weakness of the established parties of the Fourth Republic and argued that France needed a broad supra-party alliance that would take vigorous action against the communist party. The problem for them was that the political system of the Fourth Republic was already, in effect, a supra-party alliance designed to exclude the communists from power. The president (Vincent Auriol) and the prime minister (Henri Queuille) proved adept at constructing broad alliances that stretched from the socialist left to the Pétainist right. The minister of the interior, Jules Moch, was ruthless in his suppression of agitation by both communists and Gaullists. The CRS (a militarized police force) kept control of the streets.

The high point of notable politics came with the legislative elections of 1951. Conservative parties (mainly grouped in the Centre National des Indépendants et Paysans (CNIP)) won 87 seats (a gain of eleven); the Rassemblement des Gauches Républicaines (RGR) won 77 seats (a gain of 23). The parties that had attempted to impose discipline on the right of the spectrum did badly. The PRL had effectively ceased to exist; the MRP won 84 seats (a loss of 83). The communists and the Gaullists were the biggest parties in parliament (with 95 and 106 seats respectively) but this did not translate into real power. Both parties were bidding for something much more dramatic than mere representation in government. The Gaullists wanted to overturn the Fourth Republic and the communists wanted to overturn capitalism. Having failed to fulfil these monumental ambitions the two parties were then entirely excluded from the bargaining of Fourth Republic government formation. The communists, hardened by years in the political wilderness, endured this fate with stoicism. The Gaullists did not. Twenty-seven Gaullists deserted the party to support the investiture of the Independent Antoine Pinay in 1952 and de Gaulle, disgusted by the *politique à la petite semaine* of his supporters, announced his own withdrawal from political life in 1953.

The fall of the Fourth Republic

Why then did the political system of the Fourth Republic disintegrate and why did France, which had rejected Gaullism in 1951, turn to Gaullism in 1958? Part of the answer to this question lies in three developments during the 1950s. First Pétainists made an increasingly open return to political life after the amnesty laws of 1951 and 1953. This upset the tacit deals on which bourgeois alliances of resistance and Pétainist forces had been based. Men who had been agents of unity when they stayed in the corridors of political life became agents of division when they tried to re-enter the National Assembly. This was notably the case with André Boutemy who functioned effectively as a distributor of business funding to anti-communist parties in the late 1940s but whose arrival in the Senate evoked vociferous complaints.

Secondly, Poujadism, which began as an anti-tax protest in south-western France, transformed itself into a political party which won 52 seats in the legislative elections of 1956. Poujadism was particularly dangerous for the notables of provincial France because it attacked the very institutions— chambers of commerce, small business associations—from which they derived their power. Thirdly, the war to defend French Algeria against a nationalist revolt, which began in 1954, destabilized the Fourth Republic as increasing numbers of European settlers, army officers, and right-wingers in metropolitan France argued that the regime was too weak to take effective measures in north Africa.

Most of all, the Fourth Republic collapsed because the political cement that had held it together (i.e. anti-communism) became less effective. The communist threat diminished in the 1950s. Stalin's death in 1953 made Cold War divisions less intense and the French communist party's purge of its own independent-minded leaders in 1950 (often leaders who had risen through the Resistance) removed the very men who were most likely to contemplate revolutionary action. Increasingly, the communist party became what Georges Lavau termed a 'tribune party'—that is to say a party dedicated to representing the working class within the existing system rather than a party dedicated to overthrowing the system. The changing atmosphere of French politics was reflected in reactions to strikes. Large-scale strikes in 1947 and 1948 had engendered real fear among the bourgeoisie because they were seen as part of a broader revolutionary project. A large-scale public sector strike in 1953, by contrast, was seen simply as a reflection of specific grievances. In short, the Fourth Republic collapsed because it had been designed mainly to counter a communist threat that no longer existed. Just as its predecessor had been well fortified against an attack on the German frontier but badly prepared against an attack through Belgium, the Fourth Republic had built all its fortifications to survive an attack from the extreme left and these fortifications were irrelevant when assault was mounted from the right and centre of the political spectrum.

De Gaulle's Republic

Algeria was the immediate issue that brought the Fourth Republic down. In May 1958, soldiers and settlers' leaders (enraged by the execution of three French soldiers captured by the FLN) seized the government headquarters in Algiers. Some of them called for de Gaulle to return to power. In mainland France, many feared a military coup. Left-wing parties demonstrated and even called for arms to be issued to the people. The government had no stomach for such measures. The president (the conservative Coty) and the prime minister (Pflimlin of the MRP) were less robust than Auriol and Queuille, who had fought off Gaullism seven years previously.

De Gaulle had been absent from French public life for five years and had made no public statement on Algeria. This gave him an enormous advantage. Those in favour of French Algeria attributed support for their view to de Gaulle without de Gaulle himself being obliged to say much that might imply a commitment on his part. Even after he came to power, de Gaulle maintained a studied ambiguity: he told an enthusiastic crowd of *pieds noirs*, 'I have understood you,' a remark that might have meant a lot of things. The truth is that de Gaulle probably believed that France should keep Algeria (albeit with a different kind of status) but that he did not consider Algeria to be the most important issue that he confronted. Most of all, he wanted to return to power with free hands. He was not willing to lead a putsch, which would have left him with debts to the generals, but he was also unwilling to accept office as an ordinary Fourth Republic prime minister, which would have left him with debts to the parties. After much negotiation, it was agreed that de Gaulle should be granted full powers for six months by a vote of the National Assembly on 1 June 1958. The following September a new constitution, drawn up by a small group of men close to de Gaulle, was accepted by the

French people in a referendum. The president was given new rights, notably that of choosing ministers, while parliament was transformed by the institution of simple majority voting in single member constituencies, which deprived small centre parties of the particular advantages that they had enjoyed in the Fourth Republic. The constitutional changes of 1958 did not, in themselves, bring about a political revolution. For the first four years of the Fourth Republic, the president was still chosen by 80,000 notables rather than by direct elections. De Gaulle's first prime minister, Michel Debré, was an established politician with roots in the radical party and he dominated internal policy for the first few years of the new regime.

Politics in the first four years of the Fifth Republic were overshadowed by Algeria. Charles de Gaulle took direct responsibility for Algerian policy and it became slowly obvious to everyone, perhaps more slowly obvious to de Gaulle himself than to most of his compatriots, that only complete withdrawal from Algeria would fit in with his desire to modernize the French army and preserve French influence in the world. De Gaulle's drift towards granting Algeria independence provoked settlers to protest during 'barricades week' of 1960 and, much more seriously, provoked part of the French army to attempt a *coup d'état* (the 'generals' putsch') in April 1961. These attempts at resistance failed, and after long negotiations, France accepted Algeria's right to independence in the Evian Accords of March 1962.

Algeria split several political formations: it put loyal Gaullists, such as Michel Debré, in an awkward position and it drove a number of important politicians, notably the Christian democrat Georges Bidault and the Gaullist Jacques Soustelle, into illegal action. The Fifth Republic survived such traumas partly because the very structures that the pro-Algérie Française campaigners had helped to destroy were also the ones that had made Algeria into a central issue for French politics. Algeria mattered to a large part of the French political class and, in particular, it mattered to the cadres of the radical party, which drew a substantial electoral advantage from its position in Algeria, but it did not matter much to most of the French people. The increasingly direct democracy of the Fifth Republic cut out the notables and created direct links between ruler and ruled. The link between direct democracy and de Gaulle's Algerian policy was reflected in the use of referenda to legitimize decisions taken over

Algeria and in the institutions of direct election of the president of the Republic in 1962 (at the very moment when French withdrawal was finalized).

The stabilization of French politics after 1962 was not, however, simply a product of constitutions or even new political parties. It was also the result of broader political, economic, social, and technological changes. In purely political terms, the shift was seen in the foundation of a new party, the Union pour la Nouvelle République (UNR). This was a party that supported de Gaulle without necessarily being supported by him. The general was never a member of the party and often chose his ministers from outside its ranks. The UNR had a comparatively small membership and one that did not necessarily exercise much power over policy. This was a 'voter-oriented' party, one designed to mobilize the largest possible section of the electorate rather than to provide a home for militants or notables. De Gaulle's own support, especially in presidential elections and referenda, always reached beyond the supporters of the UNR but broadly France seemed to be moving from the multi-party politics of the Fourth Republic towards something that resembled the two-party politics of the Anglo-Saxon countries. In the 1965 presidential election, de Gaulle obtained most of the right-wing vote: about 5 per cent of the population (mostly made up of those who had been most hurt by the loss of Algeria) voted for the extreme right candidate Jean-Louis Tixier-Vignancour, but most of the mainstream right voted for de Gaulle. Most of the left rallied behind François Mitterrand in the second round of the election and thereafter Mitterrand sometimes talked of himself as 'leader of the opposition'.

In economic terms, France became more prosperous in the 1960s. This was the age of consumerism: the age of Georges Perec's novel *Things* and of Barthes's essay on the Citroën DS. Consumerism blunted political discontent. The production of consumer goods also began to undermine the foundations of the working class culture that had been created after the war. Consumer goods were often produced outside traditional working-class areas. They were manufactured on production lines that used an unskilled, often female, workforce that was relatively untouched by the culture that had built around the skilled male workers in metallurgy and heavy industry.

The transition from Fourth to Fifth Republic was associated with a transition of the economy from one that revolved around comparatively small enterprises operating in a local framework to one that revolved around companies that operated at national level. The transition was associated with the formation of a new kind of economic/political and administrative elite. Under the Third and Fourth Republics, there had been a sharp division between the political elite (made up mainly of lawyers and journalists) and the administrative elite (made up of graduates of the *grandes écoles*). The latter intersected with a section of industrial management which ran a small number of large companies based in northern France. In the 1960s, two things changed. First, large companies became more important in the economy. Secondly, a new elite was created that encompassed industrial management, administration, and politics. The single institution that had most to do with the creation of this elite was the École Nationale d'Administration (ENA). ENA had been founded in 1945 but its graduates first began to reach senior positions in the 1960s. The school had been designed to train high-ranking civil servants but many of its graduates indulged in 'pantouflage', that is to say they transferred into lucrative jobs in private sector companies where they were able to trade on their prestige and political contacts. An increasingly interventionist state made it more important for companies to draw on the contacts that former civil servants could provide and the increasing scale of private sector industry meant that its decisions became more and more governed by formal planning, which resembled that carried out by the civil service. Large private sector companies, nationalized companies, and the departments of the civil service charged with administration converged. The administrative/managerial elite began, in turn, to intertwine with the political elite. De Gaulle, contemptuous of those who had made their careers in Fourth Republic political parties, drew on men from the civil service who would provide an 'apolitical', technocratic solution to France's problems. Valéry Giscard d'Estaing (de Gaulle's finance minister) and Maurice Couve de Murville (foreign minister and then prime minister) had both begun their careers as *inspecteurs des finances*.

De Gaulle, more than any other politician in history, made his reputation through broadcasting. He had been brought to the attention of the French people through the BBC during the Second World War. After 1958 his reputation was increasingly spread by television, which communicated his speeches to the French people. They played an especially large role in his facing down of the rebellious generals in Algeria in 1961—de Gaulle's speech on this occasion was broadcast to the conscript soldiers in Algeria via the transistor radios with which many of them were equipped. In the 1960s, the number of television sets in France increased rapidly. De Gaulle drew special benefit from this partly because he was such an effective television performer and partly because all broadcasting was controlled by a state agency (ORTF) that was subject to political manipulation.

Another piece of technology was crucial to the success of the Fifth Republic. France exploded her first nuclear bomb in the Algerian desert in 1959. The possession of nuclear weapons underwrote a new kind of foreign policy that allowed France to achieve a certain kind of grandeur even after she had lost her overseas empire. Being a nuclear power made France into a member of an exclusive club. It allowed her to lay claim to an independent foreign policy that was eventually incarnated in her withdrawal from the North Atlantic Treaty Organization (NATO) in 1966. Nuclear weapons did not give France the kind of power that was exercised by America or the Soviet Union. What they did do was to provide her with the prestige of independence. This tied in with a broader policy that emphasized the diffusion of French culture (particularly expressed through the use of the French language) and France's privileged relations with certain countries (Romania, China, Syria). Curiously, the very division of the world between American and Soviet spheres of influence worked to France's advantage. It allowed her to cast herself as leader of the 'non-aligned world' and gave her gestures of independence a resonance that they would not otherwise have had. It also ensured that France became the spoilt child of the Western alliance. The Americans did not exercise direct influence over her policy, but they could not afford to remain indifferent to her fate either. In private, French generals admitted that French nuclear weapons were merely 'trip wires' and that their deterrent value came from their capacity to provoke a general conflict rather than from their intrinsic destructive capability.

1968

The very success of France in the 1960s began to sow seeds of opposition. The increase in the birth rate, which had begun in the 1940s,
and the increase in prosperity, which began in the 1950s and accelerated in the 1960s, meant that an ever larger proportion of young
people went to university. The number of people in higher education
rose by a factor of ten in the post-war years. However, neither university facilities nor graduate opportunities expanded fast enough to
absorb this increase. Students' discontent about their own material
circumstances combined with a more utopian rebellion against
materialism itself and with a range of, often contradictory, critiques
of capitalism. Students herded into the new campus of Paris University in the grim suburb of Nanterre went on strike at the beginning of May, the strikes spread to the centre of Paris and then, most
unexpectedly, to parts of the working class. Nine million workers
went on strike, student demonstrations closed universities, rioters
confronted the CRS on the boulevard St Michel, and, in a move that
seemed to challenge everything that the Fifth Republic stood for,
énarques refused to accept the places in the *grands corps* to which their
ranking would normally have entitled them.

Uncharacteristically, Charles de Gaulle seems to have lost his nerve.
His only response to the students was repression. On 29 May he
himself flew to Baden-Baden where he met general Massu (a loyal
Gaullist but one who had disagreed with de Gaulle over Algeria). The
precise nature of their discussions is not clear. Some believe that de
Gaulle had panicked and sought a refuge from revolution in France;
others that a deal was done in return for maintaining the army's
loyalty (a number of officers imprisoned after the Algerian war were
released soon afterwards); Massu himself claimed that he simply
strengthened de Gaulle's resolve. Whatever the truth the meeting
with Massu compromised the lofty independence that de Gaulle had
so assiduously cultivated.

In some ways, 1968 did represent a challenge to the Fifth Republic.
Rigid rules and strict hierarchies were all called into question. The
consumer prosperity, which had appeared to be the Republic's most
concrete achievement, was dismissed. The student demonstrations, in

particular, laid the foundations of movements—such as a revived regionalism in the west of the country—that posed a long-term challenge to a centralized state. Perhaps the most dangerous legacies of 1968 for the Republic were paradoxical ones. The students professed a hostility to both capitalism and American 'imperialism', yet they were attacking a state that affirmed itself in international terms against simple deference to America and in national terms against the unbridled operations of the free market. The students were often fascinated by American popular culture and by the informality of American life that contrasted so much with the world of the French education system. Sometimes such people, once they had abandoned their youthful ideological baggage, fitted rather well into the American-owned advertising agencies and software houses that were to transform France at the end of the century.

In the short term, the events of 1968 had an odd effect. They strengthened the political right. The parliamentary elections of 1968 produced the biggest right-wing majority in French history and the right was to remain in charge of the Élysée and Matignon palaces for another thirteen years. However, they weakened the nominal leader of the French right—Charles de Gaulle. Everything about de Gaulle's background—his family, his profession, his Catholicism, and his manner—made him seem like a man of the right, but he had always been most successful when he had operated in alliance with the left. This was most obviously the case during the Second World War, especially his period of association with the communists after 1943, and during the Algerian war, particularly as he became committed to granting independence. The strongest single theme of de Gaulle's career, a theme expressed in his first book and illustrated by his distaste for both Vichy and the Algérie Française lobby, was the need to subordinate the army to civilian power. His appeal was greatest when he promoted movement and change rather than order, and when his charisma reached out to touch working-class voters, who would ordinarily have been immune to the appeal of a conservative. The events of 1968 put de Gaulle in an uncomfortable position. A politician who had spent his whole life ensuring that the strongest emotions of the electorate were focused on him as an individual suddenly found that he was seen as an irrelevance. The partisans of Algérie Française had made numerous attempts to kill de Gaulle but they had never, unlike the students of 1968, ignored him. A man who had always tried to rise above his natural constituency found that he was its prisoner. He had been sustained by a demonstration of *Figaro* readers and by a pep talk from a general. For the first time in his life, de Gaulle looked like what he was—an old, retired, army officer.

De Gaulle attempted to regain the initiative with a referendum on participation (a vaguely defined concept designed to re-establish a specifically Gaullist approach to politics). When he lost, in April 1969, he immediately resigned, retired to his country house, and refused to make any public statements. His sudden death in November 1970 (not preceded by the indignities of illness or attempts to return to political life) seemed almost calculated to preserve the Gaullist myth. Alfred Fabre-Luce, who understood de Gaulle with the intimacy that came from hatred, compared his death to the ritual suicide of the Japanese poet Mishima.

Politics after de Gaulle

Curiously, the defeat of de Gaulle marked the triumph of de Gaulle's republic. The political hatreds that followed the Algerian war had been so focused on de Gaulle as an individual that his mere departure eased the tension—especially since his replacement, Georges Pompidou, had advocated reconciliation after both Vichy and Algeria. The Fifth Republic was shown to be a system that functioned on its own and not simply an incarnation of charismatic leadership that was dependent on the intervention of a single man. The regime was dominated by de Gaulle as an individual for its first eleven years but in the eleven years that followed his death it had three presidents drawn from three different political parties.

In 1974, Pompidou died and the subsequent presidential election was won by Valéry Giscard d'Estaing of the centrist Union pour la Démocratie Française (UDF). Giscard's appeal was based on a mix of technocracy and sentimentality. Though he had been a minister under de Gaulle, Giscard's enthusiasm for Gaullism had always been very lukewarm—an attitude summed up in his phrase 'yes but'. Giscard broke up some of the rigidities of the Gaullist state. The ORTF was divided into its component parts and, in a move that was to have important consequences, Paris was given its own elected mayor in 1975.

Giscard's first prime minister was Jacques Chirac. Though leader of the Gaullist Union des Démocrates pour la République (UDR), Chirac's political style was, in many ways, more removed from de Gaulle than that of any other major politician in post-1970 France. Chirac was jovial and emollient where de Gaulle had been haughty and regal. De Gaulle regarded political parties and electoral politics as, at best, necessary evils. Chirac lived for them. De Gaulle refused to speak English in public; Chirac loved to show off the American accent that he had acquired in Cambridge, Massachusetts. De Gaulle's politics functioned at national level, Chirac's greatest skill was in cultivating support at local level. Revealingly, Chirac's political base was the Corrèze, a region that had once been dominated by the quintessential Third and Fourth Republic radical Henri Queuille, and that had previously been impervious to Gaullism.

In August 1976 Chirac resigned as prime minister. He subsequently transformed his political party into a new formation—the Rassemblement pour la République (RPR) and in March 1977 established a new power base as mayor of Paris. Chirac ran against Giscard in the presidential election of 1981, and the refusal of his supporters to rally behind a united candidate of the right in the second round contributed much to Giscard's defeat.

Mitterrand and the Parti Socialiste

The victor in the 1981 presidential elections was François Mitterrand of the Parti Socialiste. Mitterrand was not a lifelong socialist. For much of his career he had been associated with anti-communist centrism (indeed before 1940 he was a supporter of the extreme right). Although a resistance hero, he had been associated with the Vichy government and maintained cordial relations with former Pétainists (notably the lawyer Jacques Isorni) after the Liberation. Mitterrand had been a violent opponent of the Fifth Republic constitution, which he denounced as the 'permanent *coup d'état*'. In 1965, working without any real base in a political party, he had succeeded in imposing himself as the main challenger to de Gaulle in the presidential elections. His chance to consolidate his position came in 1970 when the SFIO (the socialist party that had existed since 1905) was transformed into the Parti Socialiste (PS). Mitterrand was not a founder member of the new party but he effectively took it over at the Épinay Congress of June 1971.

Novelty was an advantage for the PS. Previously left-wing parties had looked back to the French Revolution (1789) or the Russian Revolution (1917), or to the Congress of Tours (1920). The right, free from such ideological baggage, had been more flexible and innovative. Furthermore, though its founders probably did not realize this, social trends in France in the early 1970s were propitious for a new party. French levels of industrialization had peaked, the extreme class consciousness of a large, male, French-born, and relatively skilled workforce in heavy industry was being undermined by deskilling, feminization, and immigration. In short, the circumstances that had made the communist party the natural party of the left in France had come to an end. The actual membership of the PS was not, initially, very different from that of the SFIO (both were dominated by teachers). What was new was the absence of guilt about social origins. The PS reached out to a middle-class electorate much more openly than the SFIO could ever have done.

The most important political relationship of the 1970s was that between the PS and the communist party. It was a relationship defined by an initial alliance (the common programme of 1972), then by a falling out (before the legislative elections of 1978) and finally by the presence of communist ministers in Mitterrand's government between 1981 and 1984. Mitterrand was always an anti-communist. He had never, however, shared the visceral and hysterical anti-communism that affected so many bourgeois Frenchmen. His experiences in the resistance had shown him how ruthless communists could be but also taught him that alliances with democratic forces could be used to trap the party. Mitterrand embraced to destroy.

Mitterrand won his struggle with the communists for several reasons. First, the party was weakened by the social changes described above. Secondly, the party suffered from the behaviour of its masters in Moscow. The loyalty of French communist leaders to the Kremlin had not always been a disadvantage. The party's support in France had peaked at the time of Stalin's most grotesque atrocities in the late 1940s. The sense of being at war with the world may actually have contributed to the intensity of feeling among communist militants during this period. By the early 1970s the Soviet leadership was less barbaric and the PCF was less slavish in following Moscow's line but, curiously, these two developments damaged the party. French communist leaders had raised the possibility of criticizing the USSR, particularly after the Warsaw pact invasion of Czechoslovakia, while never, unlike their Italian comrades, taking such criticism far enough to develop a genuinely independent line. This left dissidents inside the party and ordinary communist voters dissatisfied and prone to seek alternatives elsewhere. Furthermore, the old, corrupt, authoritarian members of the Brezhnev politburo epitomized everything that the French left disliked, especially after 1968. The crimes of the Soviet Union were smaller than they had been under Stalin but they were more discussed on the French left. The central European émigrés in Paris who had been denounced and ostracized in the early 1950s exercised a great influence in the 1970s.

Worst of all for French communists was the impact of détente. The whole basis of PCF identity hinged around the idea that the USSR was not just like any other country. Yet the more that the USSR had relations with Western countries, the more it became obvious that her leaders were driven by the same sense of national self-interest as any other government. Particularly galling for French communists was the warmth of relations between the USSR and the government of Giscard d'Estaing. Giscard laid a wreath on Lenin's tomb when he visited Moscow and Moscow made it discreetly known that it would not be sorry to see him re-elected as president in 1981.

The triumph of the PS over the PCF during the 1970s was, in some respects, the return match for 1905. At the formation of the SFIO, Guesde's views (with an emphasis on class interest) triumphed over those of Jaurès, which laid a Dreyfusard emphasis on individual human rights. As class politics receded, individual human rights came to the fore again. One of Mitterrand's first campaign pledges to be redeemed was that his government would abolish the death penalty. Race was another issue where the PS felt more comfortable than the PCF. Traditionally, large numbers of French workers, including communist workers, had been immigrants. However, most of these immigrants came from European countries. Their language, culture, and religion fitted in relatively easily with that of their host country. The immigrants of the 1960s, by contrast, came mainly from north Africa. The cultural gaps between them and native workers were much greater and these gaps were exacerbated by economic downturn, which meant that immigrants were seen to be competing for scarce resources. The communist party was swept along on a tide of anti-foreigner demagoguery that produced ugly incidents in working-class suburbs of Paris.

The triumph of the PS was marked in elections. From 1978 onwards the PS polled more votes than the PCF. In the legislative elections of 1981 it won 283 seats when the communists gained 44. Mitterrand's government was formed in an atmosphere of euphoric hope that was shared by everyone on the left except, probably, Mitterrand himself. His first prime minister was Pierre Mauroy, mayor of Lille, and his government contained several communist ministers.

Mitterrand's first few years in office were dominated by two international crises. The first was the world economic slowdown triggered by oil price rises in 1980 (rises that came on top of those that had happened in the mid-1970s). France was particularly vulnerable to the oil price because she had few natural energy reserves. It was too late to deal with such economic problems by applying Keynesian remedies inside national frontiers (the franc plummeted when such remedies were tried) and it was too early to coordinate measures at a European level (though Mitterrand and Jacques Delors, his finance minister, considered such a possibility). In the end, the French government accepted the need to live in a world of international capitalism and this recognition was marked by the appointment of Laurent Fabius (a 37-year-old *énarque*) as prime minister in 1984. The second international crisis was the intensification of the Cold War which was produced by Soviet action in Afghanistan, the declaration of martial law in Poland, and the election of Ronald Reagan as president of the United States. Mitterrand took a strongly anti-Soviet line during this period. It was a line that fitted in with a socialist commitment to human rights but also one that had the useful effect of making life difficult for the communist ministers who were forced to associate themselves with government condemnations of Soviet action. In 1984, communist ministers, dissatisfied with economic policy and embarrassed by foreign policy, left the government.

The Front National

The other party whose fortunes were transformed in the 1980s was the Front National (FN). The FN had been forged out of a variety of extreme-right *groupuscules* in 1972. Its prospects did not look good. De Gaulle had split the leaders of the extreme right from their potential rank-and-file support. The leaders were a small group gathered around publications such as *Rivarol* and *Écrits de Paris*. They were obsessively concerned with the wrongs that had been done to them and their cause at the Liberation and, especially, after the Algerian war. Their hatred for de Gaulle was so intense that it blotted out almost all other considerations. Rank-and-file right-wingers, by contrast, found de Gaulle's nationalism and conservatism appealing—especially in the aftermath of 1968. The extreme right's absence of popular support had been covered in the 1965 presidential election by the fact that the *pieds noirs* (European settlers) who had returned from Algeria could be relied on to vote for the most anti-Gaullist candidate available. However, after de Gaulle's death, most *pieds noirs*, who were not naturally right-wing, drifted back to supporting mainstream parties. The extreme right seemed bereft of mass appeal.

This situation was changed by three things. First, Le Pen's vulgarity qualified him to take the extreme right's appeal to levels of society that would not have been touched by the intricate debates on Maurrassianism or the cult of the martyred Robert Brasillach that had formerly dominated the 'opposition nationale'. Indeed the Front National deliberately abandoned much of the traditional stance of the extreme right during the 1980s. It was economically liberal, pro-American, and pro-Israeli (though its leaders were often anti-Semitic). Le Pen's success in breaking out of the political ghetto was illustrated by the fact that over half of FN voters described Gaullism as a 'positive experience'—a statistic that would have been unthinkable two decades earlier. Secondly, the economic crisis of the 1980s created resentments linked to unemployment and the general quality of urban life that the FN was able to exploit. Thirdly, elections fought under proportional representation gave a relatively small party an advantage. This was useful to the FN in the European elections of 1984 and even more so in the legislative elections of 1988 (in which the FN polled 14.4 per cent of the vote).

The main impact of the FN was to weaken the right. It took votes from the Gaullists and the UDF. It also put them in embarrassing positions at local level when their power seemed dependent on FN support (this was precisely why Mitterrand had instituted proportional representation). However, the political frontiers of the Fifth

Republic were not as permeable as those of the Fourth. The Pétainist right after 1951 had been able to slip back into loosely structured alliances such as the RGR and the CNIP. There was no chance of alliance between the RPR or the UDF and the FN. Transmission remained at the level of individuals—who sometimes moved from one formation to another—and, perhaps more significantly of ideas—after 1988 some talked of a parallelism between Charles Pasqua (Gaullist minister of the interior) and the FN.

Mitterrand: the *fin de régime* and after

Mitterrand remained in the Élysée palace for fourteen years—which makes him the longest serving president of any French republic— indeed no head of state or prime minister proved more durable in any democracy in the late twentieth century. A man who had spent a decade denouncing de Gaulle became curiously Gaullist in his methods after 1981. His reserve and aloofness contrasted sharply with the manners of either Giscard or Chirac. His cavalier attitude to his own party and ruthlessness towards his own subordinates was also a very Gaullist trait. Perhaps the high point of presidentialism in the Fifth Republic came after the socialists were defeated in the legislative elections of 1986. For the next two years, Mitterrand ruled with a Gaullist prime minister (Chirac) and ministers taken from the political right. Far from weakening the presidency, this 'cohabitation' seemed to strengthen it. Mitterrand insisted on punctilious respect for the dignity of his office. He left the management of economic and social affairs to the ministers (while making no efforts to help them in their task) but kept a tight grip on the *domaine réservé* of defence, foreign, and, especially, European affairs.

The socialist campaign in the presidential elections of 1988 was largely based on Mitterrand's personality and the subsequent socialist victory in the legislative elections seemed to strengthen his power in both the party and the country. As it turned out, Mitterrand's second *septennat* disappointed many of his supporters. The president was, though this was not revealed until later, dying. The smell of corruption lingered around his government and Mitterrand's own Pétainist past became a matter for wide public discussion. The socialists lost the legislative elections of 1993, thus bringing a second period of cohabitation (this time the prime minister was Édouard Balladur).

The lowest moment of the Mitterrand presidency came when Pierre Bérégovoy, the recently ejected socialist prime minister, faced with charges of corruption and apparently abandoned by the president, shot himself.

Mitterrand ended his career with a very Gaullist flourish by dying soon after he left office (in 1995). At one time it seemed likely that he would take the socialist party with him like an Egyptian pharaoh being buried with his slaves. It was widely assumed that the party was both discredited by the squalor of Mitterrand's *fin de régime* and incapable of finding any other rallying point once he was gone. This assumption turned out to be wrong. Lionel Jospin, until recently a comparatively junior member of the party, imposed himself as Mitterrand's successor (never having been seen as an obvious Dauphin, he had avoided both the resentment of rivals and the jealousy of Mitterrand himself). He scored unexpectedly well in the presidential elections that pitted him against Chirac in the second round.

In some respects, the right looked weaker than the left at the end of the century. Chirac, unlike Jospin, had to contend with other politicians from his own side who considered themselves to be serious candidates for the presidency as well as with the relentless personal animosity of Valéry Giscard d'Estaing. European integration exposed divisions on the right with particular harshness and it was largely this issue that provoked Philippe Séguin to split away from the RPR and establish a new Gaullist Rassemblement pour la France (RPF) with the Eurosceptic Philippe de Villiers. Worst of all Chirac's personal position was weakened by public interest in the misuse of state funds to support political parties. This was an issue that affected all political parties but the left was somewhat protected because its recent renewal of leadership had removed the people most concerned with past abuses. Chirac, by contrast, was particularly exposed because he had been mayor of Paris for much of the period between 1977 and 1995 and allegations of electoral fraud and misuse of public money were particularly rife in Paris. Chirac was humiliated. His party tried, and failed, to impose a discreet disappearance from the public scene on Jean Tibéri, Chirac's former associate and successor as mayor, who was said to know where many bodies had been buried. By the end of 2000, Chirac was under pressure to appear as a witness before judges investigating corruption charges. Earlier, in 1997, he had blundered badly by his decision to dissolve the National Assembly and call legislative elections. The left won the elections and formed a government under Lionel Jospin, thus imposing all the frustrations and humiliations of cohabitation on Chirac, who was blamed by many on the right for having provoked an unnecessary trial of strength.

Chirac was saved, or at least reprieved, by the astonishing presidential elections of 2002. It was assumed that his main opponent would be Lionel Jospin but fourteen other candidates were declared (a fact that reflected the fragmentation and complexity of French politics— see Box 3.1).

On the evening of 22 April 2002 it was announced to general astonishment that Lionel Jospin had been eliminated from the second round of the presidential election. He had obtained 16.18 per cent of the vote, Chirac 19.88 per cent, and Jean-Marie Le Pen (who had only narrowly secured the signatures from elected representatives that he needed to validate his candidacy) 16.86 per cent. The consequences of this were dramatic. Jospin immediately announced his retirement from public life. The great majority of other candidates called on their supporters to vote for Chirac in the second round in order to exclude the extreme right (only Arlette Laguillier flatly refused to play the games of bourgeois politics). Chirac duly won the second round with more than 80 per cent of the vote, appointed a new prime minister —Jean-Pierre Raffarin—and mobilized a new political formation (the Union pour une Majorité Presidentielle) which won 309 seats in the subsequent legislative elections (all its opponents put together were only able to win 210 seats).

Chirac's victory in the presidential election came mainly from the weakness of his opponents. The left-wing vote was divided, abstention was high, and many people seem to have used their first-round vote as a means of registering protest rather than a means of supporting a candidate whose programme they believed in. Voters sometimes seemed almost indifferent to the actual policies of those that they supported—a large number of the unemployed voted for Jean-Marie Le Pen, who was committed to sharp cuts in public spending. Some *soixante-huitard* left-wingers voted for an authoritarian Trotskyite candidate. More generally, the left seemed to suffer from the collapse of class-based loyalty to the socialist and communist parties. In recent years, left-wing parties had almost begun to take it for granted that the route to power lay in avoiding the ghettos of class politics and

Box 3.1   Candidates in the First Round of the 2002 Presidential Election

Olivier Besancenot. Ligue Communiste Révolutionaire. Obtained 4.25% of the vote. Born 1974. A postman (a slightly artificial professional situation which was acquired after university studies in history). The successor of Alain Krivine, Besancenot represented a 'soft' Trotskyism and urged his supporters to vote for Chirac in the second round.

Christine Boutin. Forum des Républicains Sociaux. Obtained 1.19% of the vote. Born 1944. Journalist. A former associate of the UDF, Boutin represented Christian conservatives especially on the matter of abortion.

Jean-Pierre Chevènement. Mouvement des Citoyens. Obtained 5.33% of the vote. Born 1939. *Énarque.* A former socialist, Chevènement was increasingly preoccupied with the defence of national sovereignty and republican unity (in some ways the most 'Gaullist' of the candidates).

Jacques Chirac. Rassemblement pour la République. Obtained 19.88% of the vote. Born 1932. *Énarque.*

Daniel Gluckstein. Parti des Travailleurs. Obtained 0.47% of the vote. Born 1954. History teacher. The least successful of the Trotskyite candidates.

Robert Hue. Parti Communiste Français. Obtained 3.37% of vote. Born 1946.

Lionel Jospin. Parti Socialiste. Obtained 16.18% of the vote. Born 1937. *Énarque.*

Arlette Laguillier. Lutte Ouvrière. Obtained 5.72% of vote. A prominent and attractive figure who seems to have been a mere front for those who really ran her highly secretive and authoritarian party. Only candidate to give her supporters no advice about the second round.

Box 3.1 continued

Corinne Lepage. Citoyenneté d'Action Participation pour le 21ème Siècle. Obtained 1.88% of vote. Born 1951. Lawyer specializing in environment. Minister of the Environment under Chirac in 1995.

Jean-Marie Le Pen. Front National. Obtained 16.86% of vote. Born 1928.

Alain Madelin. Démocratie Libérale. Obtained 3.91% of vote. Born 1946. Like Boutin had been associated with the UDF though his politics were founded on extreme economic liberalism.

Noël Mamère. Les Verts. Obtained 5.25% of vote. Born 1948.

Bruno Mégret. Mouvement National Républicain. Obtained 2.34% of the vote. Born 1949. *Polytechnicien,* he left the RPR to join the Front National in 1985 and then left the FN in 1998. Only candidate to urge his supporters to vote for Le Pen in second round.

Jean Saint-Josse. Chasse, Pêche, Nature, Traditions. Obtained 4.23% of the vote. Born 1945. Ostensibly apolitical though had been associated with the RPR. Said that he would give no advice to supporters in second round but did, in fact, urge them to vote against Le Pen.

Christine Taubira. Parti Guyanais de Centre Gauche. Obtained 2.32% of vote. Born 1952. Former campaigner for independence converted to cause of multiculturalism.

in cultivating a more modern image that was based on technical competence or the willingness to embrace new issues. The elections of 2002 seem, amongst other things, to have been a protest by working-class voters whose support had been taken for granted.

The weakness of the left did not, however, mean that Chirac's position was strong. Behind the spectacular statistics of the second round of the presidential and legislative elections lay the hard fact that less than a fifth of French voters had supported him as president in the first round and that many of those who voted for him in the second round justified their support with the slogan 'rather the thief than the fascist'. Most of all, Chirac's victory was in many respects the defeat of the political tradition that he had once purported to represent. Chirac's whole stance in 2002 was strikingly un-Gaullist. While the general had affected to disdain electoral politics and the mechanics of party organization, Chirac appeared to devote all his energies to these matters. De Gaulle played at being Cinncinatus— always keen to return to his plough and Colombey-les-Deux-Églises if the French proved not to be up to fulfilling his visions of grandeur. Chirac, by contrast, was more or less condemned to stay in power because of the difficulties to which he would be exposed if he were to lose his immunity from prosecution.

There was a whiff of the Fourth Republic about the 2002 elections with their multiplicity of apparently hopeless candidacies and electoral manoeuvres. The person whose standing seemed to have increased most in the course of the events was Chirac's prime minister Jean-Pierre Raffarin and several commentators drew attention to the fact that his carefully cultivated image as a modest provincial businessman bore striking resemblances to that of Antoine Pinay.

Conclusion: a Sixth Republic?

Chirac seems to epitomize a slide of the Fifth Republic presidency— once seen as the incarnation of aloof authority—into short-term political calculations. This slide takes place at a time when other quintessentially Fifth Republic institutions are also in crisis. The ORTF has been undermined by satellite broadcasting. The École Nationale d'Administration has been undermined by the propensity of bright young French people to seek a more international education that will fit them for the lucrative world of the private sector rather than the prestigious positions of the French state. France's possession of a nuclear bomb no longer confers any special prestige at a time when Pakistan and Israel possess similar capabilities and, more generally, France's pretensions to an independent foreign policy have been damaged as the unpredictable threats that followed the end of the Cold War have increasingly forced her back into association with the United States and NATO, as in intervention in Kosovo. The sense of French *rayonnement* (cultural diffusion) which mattered so much in the early years of the Fifth Republic has been called into question by the spread of a culture that expresses itself in English. National sovereignty often seems meaningless in an age of economic and cultural globalization.

All the certainties of the Fifth Republic—including the certainty that it actually makes a difference who occupies the Élysée, Matignon, or the Palais Bourbon—have been shaken. As early as 1993 Jacques Attali looked back on the early Mitterrand presidency as part of a vanished age, when the president of the Republic disposed of huge, 'potentially dictatorial' powers, which have been eroded by the new international scene that emerged in the wake of the collapse of communism and the shift towards greater European unity:

In France the State has lost its prerogatives, to the regions, to Brussels, to business. And the magic of nuclear weapons, which made France one of the five miracle-workers of the planet, wore off simultaneously with the disappearance of the Soviet menace.

Social, economic, and technological change in the 1950s helped produce a new Republic. Will there be an equally explicit change in the early part of the twenty-first century? Almost certainly, the answer to this question is no. The social changes of the 1950s intersected with violent struggles rooted in Vichy and, especially, Algeria. No division of comparable violence affects France now. If France is to undergo significant constitutional change that will come from Brussels and Strasbourg, but, more probably, the changes that will most affect French people in the next few years will come from economic and social changes that are so pervasive that they are independent of any particular political configuration.

4

France, Europe, and the world: international politics since 1880

David Watson

Introduction

This topic is treated here primarily in the form of an account of policies followed by French governments over this period. Whatever the future may hold, in the year 2002, as in the year 1880, France is a nation state, a community which has a sense of identity, and which is represented by a government with the task of defending the national interest. The primary element of this task is defence of the national territory, and of its inhabitants: second is safeguarding the economic basis of their existence. Beyond these objectives is the feeling that the French language and French culture are elements of importance in the human heritage, and that France ought to play an important role on the world stage. Relations between France, Europe, and the world clearly have non-governmental aspects, such as demography and immigration, which are dealt with in Chapter 5. The fact that the French population from long before 1880 had been growing more slowly than that of other European states had major consequences: it not only meant that France received large groups of immigrants long before other European states but it led also to fear of a national decline. But this chapter will be mainly concerned with the government policies devised to deal with the political and economic problems facing the nation over this period.

Relations with the outside world have been of vital importance to the evolution of French history throughout the period. There are three reasons for this: geography, historical tradition, and demography. Its geographical position meant that France had a double preoccupation. First, it needed to protect its vulnerable north-eastern frontier, especially against Germany. Secondly, its long coastlines on the Atlantic and the Mediterranean tempted France to become a maritime power with concerns across the Mediterranean in north Africa, and, potentially, throughout the overseas world. Historical tradition meant that memories of the period 1648–1815 when France had claimed, and temporarily achieved in the revolutionary and Napoleonic period, a position of European hegemony were always a factor in political calculations, however impossible it might be to recover that hegemony. Alain Peyrefitte reports de Gaulle as saying on 22 August 1962, 'if France manages to be the first among the six (members of the European Community) she can use this Archimedean lever to become again what she has ceased to be since Waterloo, the leader of the world'. Although such ambitions proved unrealizable, they have certainly been a factor in French relations with the outside world throughout these 120 years and more. Finally the impact of demography must be remembered. One reason for the decline of France from her dominant position after 1815, besides the counterbalancing territorial settlement provoked by Napoleon's overweening ambition, was that France ceased to be the most populous European power. In addition, France entered the demographic transition far earlier than other parts of Europe; her population increased only marginally between 1850 and 1950, when that of other nations increased dramatically.

Thus, after her defeat in the Franco-Prussian war of 1870–1, France remained a great power, but weaker than the German Empire. This disparity grew steadily greater down to the division of Germany in 1945. However, the balance of power system of international relations meant that, in a world of five great European powers, France would be able to contain Germany when Bismarck's policy of moderation was subsequently abandoned. Moreover, France came to accept the 1871 treaty, including the loss of Alsace-Lorraine, but refused to accept further German bullying: as Clemenceau said in the Senate in 1912,'the difficulty between Germany and us is this: Germany believes that domination is the logical result of her victory, but we do not believe that the logical result of our defeat is serfdom'.

Towards war: 1880–1914

The thirty-four years of peace between 1880 and 1914 saw the evolution of these factors. France sought to learn the lessons of 1870–1 by embarking on far-reaching reforms, such as the gradual extension of conscription until it became genuinely universal, but of a much wider range of institutions that were seen as having been inadequate in the face of the German challenge. Nevertheless, the idea of *revanche*, a war of revenge that would overturn the Prussian victory, became steadily more unrealistic, especially as at this stage France remained without allies. Every passing year saw an increasing German population and the development of German heavy industry based on coal reserves lacking in France. In addition, Bismarck created an alliance system including Austria-Hungary, Italy, and Russia that prevented France from finding allies. Finally Bismarck encouraged France to extend her colonial empire because it would lead France into rivalry, possibly conflict, with other powers such as Britain, Italy, and perhaps even Russia, thus making her more dependent on Germany. Some in France, notably the republican left, rejected colonial expansion because, as was said, it would distract attention from the blue line of the Vosges: Déroulède declared that 'we have lost two daughters (the provinces of Alsace and Lorraine) and we are offered twenty negro maidservants'.

However, the Opportunist Republicans, who constituted the majority in Parliament throughout this period, accepted the exchange. A war against Germany was impossible, but France could maintain her status in the world by extending her small overseas territories into a major empire that would rival that of Britain. Léon Gambetta and his successor Jules Ferry both advocated this policy. It began with the occupation of Tunis in 1881–2, which was turned into a French protectorate to the anger of Italy. Conquest of Indo-China followed in 1884–5, involving a war with China itself. In the next ten

years Madagascar was taken, together with a huge expanse of territory in west and central Africa. Other European states similarly
expanded their colonial possessions, most notably in Africa: the
'scramble for Africa' was in part the result of French action as a
catalyst.

The new French Empire looked enormous on global maps, and
was second only to Britain's in population and territorial extent.
Although advocates of territorial expansion from Ferry onwards
stressed the potential economic advantages, these turned out to be
minimal. There was only limited emigration to the colonies, and
although France was a major exporter of capital, only a tiny proportion went to her colonies. Another negative factor was that, as well as
the alienation of Italy, these developments produced a twenty-year
estrangement of France from Britain. This resulted in large part from
French resentment about British control of Egypt. In 1882, the two
powers had planned a joint debt-collecting expedition to enforce
their joint claims to interest payments resulting from the construction of the Suez Canal. But the French withdrew at the last minute, an
example of weak government making coherent policy difficult to
achieve. Britain went on to establish her unofficial control of Egypt
that lasted until 1954, while France sought vainly to limit this control.

However, other colonial acquisitions served to bolster French self-
confidence after the Boulangist crisis of 1886–7 had demonstrated
that *revanche* had to be abandoned. Gradually France's international
position improved as Bismarck's system of alliances began to unravel.
In the long run it proved impossible for Germany to be the ally of
both Austria-Hungary and Russia. Even before Bismarck's fall,
French capital began to flow into the Russian Empire, which it continued to do on an enormous scale in the years down to 1914 when
nearly a quarter of all French foreign investment was there. From an
economic point of view this proved a disaster as it was lost with the
repudiation of the debt by the Soviet Russian regime, but it was of
considerable importance politically in the pre-war period, paving the
way for the military alliance between Russia and France achieved in
1893.

At this stage, France's increased self-confidence was expressed
mainly in a desire to recover a stake in Egypt. Both Hanotaux (foreign
minister for most of the period 1894–8 and Delcassé (foreign minister
1898–1905) were determined to overthrow British predominance in

Egypt, an ambition which had the support of much of the republican political elite. The French navy was being developed in these years in ways which it was hoped would make it a thorn in the flesh for the British fleet. Events came to a head with the Fashoda crisis of 1898 when the Marchand expedition, intended as a token of French claims to the upper Nile, met a British army that had reconquered the Sudan. Faced with two unpleasant realities, the absence of diplomatic support even from her Russian ally and the superiority of the British fleet, France was forced into a humiliating retreat. It was left to Delcassé to draw the conclusion that France had to abandon her ambitions in Egypt, but that Britain might be prepared to compensate her. Thus the essential bargain of the 1904 Franco-British entente was that France gave Britain a free hand in Egypt, while Britain gave France support to round out her north African territory in Morocco.

Although the Entente Cordiale was not intended to be an alliance, the German reaction virtually turned it into one. The place of Morocco in the diplomacy of 1905–14 is not due to its intrinsic importance, but as a symbol of the relations between the European powers. Germany hoped to persuade France that the price she would have to pay for Morocco was breaking off the entente with Britain, while Britain and France were determined not to give way to what they increasingly saw as aggressive German bullying. Thus the Moroccan crises of 1905 and 1911, with the interlude of the Franco-German agreement on Morocco of 1909, led to the creation of a French protectorate, which like that over Tunisia, was seen until after the Second World War as tantamount to absorption within the French Empire.

More important than this small addition to French colonial territory was the complete reversal of the mental climate after Fashoda. Britain was now the friend, if not formally the ally of France, while Germany was the enemy. As Russia recovered from defeat at the hands of Japan in 1905 and concentrated attention on European instead of Far Eastern affairs, the stage was set for the First World War. The second Moroccan crisis in 1911 was resolved by a compromise which greatly favoured France. Yet, in the changed atmosphere, this was seen almost as a French defeat, and led to the fall of Caillaux, who had negotiated the deal, and to his replacement by Poincaré, who dominated French foreign policy as prime minister and then as president from 1912 until after the outbreak of war.

Poincaré used to be attacked by his left-wing opponents ('Poincaré la guerre') as being responsible for the First World War by encouraging Russian ambitions in the Balkans, and as a man from Lorraine deliberately engineering war for the recovery of the lost provinces. A more balanced view is that Poincaré was convinced that France had to support her Russian ally in the face of German attempts to weaken the Franco-Russian alliance. In the event, the crisis erupted in the Balkans with the German-backed Austro-Hungarian ultimatum to Russia's protégé, Serbia. German military strategy ensured that the conflict became a general war, involving all the great powers. Germany's Schlieffen Plan dictated an immediate onslaught on France through Belgium. From the German point of view, this produced the unfortunate result that they inadvertently made it much easier for the British government to convince doubters at home that Britain must join the Franco-Russian alliance.

From the Great War to defeat: 1914–1940

Domestic political conflict in the years before 1914 had made some fear that France would not have the strength and unity to survive a major war. In the event, although the 'sacred union' of all French people proclaimed in 1914 was challenged before the end of the terrible struggle, the political system proved resilient enough to take France through the war to allied victory. It was the authoritarian empires which eventually collapsed in revolution and defeat. Nevertheless, however noble the effort and however great the achievement of keeping the French army fighting to the end, the First World War was in a very real sense a pyrrhic victory. The effort proved to be too great for the resources of the country in men and in economic and financial terms. Moreover, the western front of the war was largely fought on French soil. France's low birth rate before 1914 meant that her military effort was greater proportionate to that of any other belligerent. The terrible losses of French troops before April 1917 could never be overcome. Thus, by the end of the war, although the French army was still a major force, it had been outclassed by the British and American armies. Even more serious was the exhaustion of French financial assets, exacerbated by the loss of the major portion of her foreign investments in the Russian and Ottoman empires and the crippling demographic impact of the war, all the more serious because it came after half a century in which the low French birth rate meant that the population had been growing more slowly than that of other European states.

Clemenceau, prime minister of France from November 1917 to January 1920, now known as 'Père la Victoire', with the prestige given him by victory had full authority to negotiate with the other allies about the peace terms to be imposed on Germany in the Treaty of Versailles. The terms, decided by the Council of Four—Clemenceau, Lloyd George for Britain, Wilson for the United States, and Orlando for Italy (who played no important part)—were submitted to the German delegation and were only modified to a small extent in the face of its indignant protests. Clemenceau's advisers were minor figures who had no independent political base. Thus Clemenceau has been held responsible in France for the entire 1919–20 settlement, and when war came twenty years later, contemporary criticism that he had botched the negotiation was renewed. This ignored the fact that he had to negotiate with his two allies, both of whom had greater military and economic power than France. France had defeated Germany only as the weakest member of a coalition, and the removal of Russia from the diplomatic scene made the maintenance of alliance with the Anglo-Saxon powers all the more imperative.

The peace settlement was criticized by some, mainly in Britain and America, as too harsh, and by others, mainly in France, as too lenient. The reply to the first line of argument is to ask what terms would not have been seen by Germany as too harsh. It is clear that only a settlement which ignored the fact that Germany had attempted to win total domination of Europe, and had been defeated, would have been acceptable to Germany. Any settlement that was tolerable to the victors would have been resented in Germany. So the problem was how to make a settlement which could provide a basis for future peace against inevitable German attempts to amend it. Conversely, those who criticized Clemenceau on the grounds that the treaty was not harsh enough argued that a safeguard should have been provided by the breaking up of Germany into smaller states, or, at least, by the creation of a buffer state in the Rhineland. This had been argued for by General Foch, commander-in-chief of allied armies at the end of the war, and by President Poincaré.

However, such harsh terms were not acceptable to Wilson or Lloyd George, and France did not have the power to impose them unilaterally. Clemenceau negotiated a compromise by which the Rhineland would remain part of a unified German state but would be occupied by allied forces for fifteen years, longer if Germany failed to fulfil the terms of the treaty, and would be demilitarized indefinitely. In addition, France was promised treaties with Britain and the USA guaranteeing her against a German attack. Clemenceau could tell his critics that France had the best deal possible, terms which did provide the basic security she required, and also the continuation of the triple alliance which had won the war. However, when the United States Senate refused to ratify the treaty in 1919, these guarantees evaporated, as Britain took the line that they were joint guarantees, and that if the United States backed down Britain would do so too.

The problem with the 1919 settlement was not that it was too harsh, or too lenient, but that it was not enforced. That failure of enforcement was a factor from the very beginning in that the continuation of the wartime alliance on which France had counted never occurred. The United States withdrew into isolation, while Britain attempted to maintain a position of balance between France and Germany. There was also the linked problem of reparations and war debts. Germany had almost no external debts, while France and Britain had incurred enormous ones towards the United States, and France also towards Britain. Although the United States withdrew from European politics, it nevertheless insisted on its allies repaying their debts. Such an outcome placed Britain and France in a very weak financial position compared to Germany. Hence the need for reparations, which had been part of the armistice terms. Germany had agreed to pay the cost of repairing the damage caused by her invasion of France and Belgium. But, in a strained interpretation of this provision to allow Britain to share in the reparations, the cost of war pensions was also included and as a result the total reparations bill handed to Germany was of astronomical proportions. France was soon to feel as cheated in this respect as over the treaty of guarantee, when Britain, after insisting on her own right to a sizeable share of German reparations, refused to help France apply pressure on the Germans to force them to pay.

This led to the Ruhr crisis of 1923. After two years of failed attempts to get any appreciable payment from Germany, France decided to use her military supremacy to enforce German payment even without British support. French and Belgian troops occupied the Ruhr, the major centre of German heavy industry. German passive resistance lasted throughout 1923, transforming already serious inflation into hyperinflation that completely destroyed the German currency. The Ruhr occupation was the decision of President Millerand, a former socialist who had moved far to the right, and the prime minister, Poincaré.

By the end of 1923 they seemed to have won as Germany was forced into negotiation. Some on the right in France thought that having taken unilateral action, France should have continued to go it alone and implement the policy of detaching the Rhineland from Germany. But Poincaré decided, as Clemenceau had done in 1919, that it was more important to remain in step with Britain and the United States. So the Ruhr crisis ended not with a bilateral settlement between France and Germany, but with negotiations involving France, Britain, Germany, and the United States. The United States was involved, in spite of its political isolationism, because of the link between reparations and war debts. By the time the negotiations took place in the summer of 1924, France's position had been greatly weakened. Stabilization of the German currency led to speculation against the French franc, which now fell temporarily to one-tenth of its 1914 value, at a time when the pound was restored to its 1914 parity with gold and the dollar.

The franc was stabilized in 1926 at one-fifth of its former value, an undervaluation which brought France a brief period of prosperity and external financial strength. At the same time the 1924 elections replaced the right-wing chamber that had supported Poincaré's firm policy with a centre-left coalition led by the radical, Édouard Herriot. It was Herriot who went to Britain to negotiate with Ramsay Mac-Donald's Labour government. In the eyes of the French right, Herriot threw away the strong cards won by Poincaré's firmness in 1923. The French occupation of the Ruhr was to end, and provision was made for the possible ending of the allied occupation of the Rhineland before 1935, the date set by the Treaty of Versailles. The financial settlement, known as the Dawes Plan, was that private American loans would finance German payment of greatly reduced reparations, while Britain and France would begin repayment of their war debts towards the United States. This transatlantic circular movement of money provided a brief four years of prosperity, the background to an equally brief political détente.

The political settlement in 1925 took the form of the Locarno treaties guaranteeing the Franco-Belgian-German frontiers, and paving the way for German entry to the League of Nations. While Locarno merely repeated what had already been promised at Versailles, it was supposed to be different in the sense that Germany now willingly accepted what had then been resented as a *Diktat*: it was also significant that no mention was made of the eastern frontier of Germany. Britain declared that it could not possibly guarantee that frontier, ironical indeed in view of the guarantee to Poland that brought war in 1939.

The leading figure in French foreign policy in the years after Locarno was Aristide Briand, later remembered as 'the pilgrim of peace'. He sought to build on Locarno to ensure permanent peace through the League of Nations, and other mechanisms, notably the Kellogg–Briand agreement by which every major state in the world renounced war, and an abortive scheme of European union. At the same time, French military planning turned to the construction of the Maginot line, a system of fortifications to defend the frontier with Germany to prevent another invasion. It was hoped that by that means, if war did come, it would be fought outside French territory.

Ominous signs soon indicated that war had not been banished by any of the diplomatic developments of 1925–9. The financial stability given to Germany by the Dawes Plan proved short-lived, as it depended on private American loans that dried up as early as 1928. By the next year, Germany was again plunged into a financial crisis, this time a deflationary one which had far more serious effects than the earlier inflation. The year 1930 saw the democratic system in Germany facing pressure to which it succumbed in 1933. Meanwhile illusions of peace continued with a momentum of their own. Reparations demands were scaled down even more in the Young Plan, and the allied troops occupying the Rhineland were withdrawn, both in 1930. A year later, Germany, with the encouragement of the American President Hoover, stopped paying reparations. A farcical disarmament conference began in Geneva, at which France faced heavy British pressure to disarm while Germany sought the right to rearm. Even the Nazi takeover in Germany in 1933 did not end the British idea that it was the French army that threatened world peace. Eventually the disarmament conference disbanded, but the intellectual climate had been created under which, over the next two years, Germany began to rearm and to denounce the provisions of the Versailles treaty without resistance.

Economic developments in this period seriously weakened France internationally. The reserves accumulated as a result of the franc's undervaluation between 1926 and 1930 allowed France to remain on the gold standard when Britain and the United States abandoned it. This meant that the franc became the overvalued currency until the Popular Front government was forced to go off gold and devalue in 1936. So, perversely, the earlier financial strength which had led the French to believe that they would escape the Depression meant that she suffered from it more, and for longer, than other major countries. Among them, France alone had lower output in 1939 than in 1929.

A crucial turning point came in March 1936, when the German army marched into the demilitarized Rhineland. This meant the end of the guarantee system established by the treaty to prevent a renewed German challenge. Subsequently the question has often been posed: why did France not react to this blatant move? The answer is both practical and psychological. In practical terms, the problem was that French military organization was based on a short-service conscript army, which meant that the army in being was only a body of troops under training: any military response required recalling the reserves. The psychological atmosphere, dominated by hatred of war, made such a move virtually impossible, coupled with the fact that any such French reaction would have produced intense criticism in Britain. Instead, from 1936 onwards, France took the line of subordinating her foreign policy to the need to remain in step with Britain, in spite of the fact that Britain was not prepared until very late in the day either to form a proper alliance or to organize for serious military intervention on the continent.

Thus France was dragged under British leadership into the policy of appeasement, which seemed logical enough as policy makers believed that Hitler was as horrified by the prospect of another world war as everyone in Britain and France. The policy had two strands. First, 'legitimate' German complaints about the 1919 settlement were to be rectified: reparations, the demilitarized Rhineland and Saar (returned to Germany in 1935) had already gone. The two further German nationalist demands—incorporation of Austria and the

Sudetenland—followed in 1938. They were not resisted in spite of the fact that this made the German Reich by far the most populous and powerful state in Europe, and strategically weakened any opposing coalition. The second strand of British and French policy from 1936 onwards was rearmament. Again, this had its logic, and was more effective than early critics of appeasement admitted. The idea was that Germany's 'legitimate' demands had been met, but further demands would be deterred by the military strength of Britain, France, and their allies, among whom it was hoped the Soviet Union could be counted. One basic element in the calculation was that the Maginot line and the strength of the French army ensured that, as in 1914–18, a continuous front would hold for years in the west: the difference would be, it was hoped, that the front would be beyond French territory. The strategy was thus for a long war, in which an economic blockade of Germany and the mobilization of the superior resources of the anti-German coalition would eventually bring victory as in the First World War.

Appeasement turned to resistance in March 1939 when Hitler took over the rest of Czechoslovakia, going beyond the incorporation of Germans into the Reich, and ignoring the diplomatic fig leaves that he had allowed to be pinned on him at Munich in 1938. Britain now joined France in issuing guarantees to small states in eastern Europe and in seeking a military alliance with the USSR. French policy was now completely dominated by that of Britain, in spite of the fact that the land forces which the allies could deploy in Europe were overwhelmingly French.

Two developments destroyed the basis of these Anglo-French plans for resisting the new German bid for domination of Europe. The Nazi–Soviet Pact of 1939 removed the eastern prop of the intended anti-German coalition. The importance of this was not the strength of the Soviet military forces, largely discounted with good reason, but that Germany could not now be denied the economic resources needed for a major war, undermining the whole strategic scheme of the allies. The second, fatal blow was the collapse of the French army in May–June 1940 when Hitler launched his attack.

Nothing like this collapse was foreseen, as the French army was in theory a formidable force, and belief in the advantages of defence over offence was the deeply ingrained lesson of 1914–18. After the defeat, the French military leadership sought to divert the blame, claiming that they had been denied the resources to rearm on the same scale as the Germans, and that pacifist and 'decadent' sentiments among the troops had destroyed morale. The consensus of many years of historical research refutes these claims. In spite of the delayed British rearmament, the military equipment of the two sides was roughly equal. Nor is there evidence that the morale of the French rank and file was the cause of the collapse. Morale collapsed *after* the German army had made its decisive breakthrough, and the French proved to have no plan to deal with the situation. The simple lesson of 1940 was that the French military leaders—above all generals Gamelin and Weygand—had proved to be inadequate both in their pre-war planning and even more in their ability to react when the German army achieved the unexpected.

The year 1940 is the halfway point in the 120 years under consideration, and the military collapse in that year bringing about the fall of the Third Republic marks the nadir of France as one of the players on the stage of international politics. The efforts that had brought her back from the less complete collapse of 1870 seemed to have been in vain, and the Franco-German duel seemed to have ended in total German victory. However, the very depth of this collapse was a vital element in the subsequent reassertion of France's place on the international scene.

From defeat to recovery: 1940–1969

The shock of the 1940 defeat and the subsequent subordination of France to Germany during the collaborationist Vichy regime ensured that the reassertion of France's national independence was of first importance to all ruling elites of the post-war period. General de Gaulle certainly played a crucial role in this scenario both between 1940 and 1946 and between 1958 and 1969, but he was far from alone in this endeavour. The weak Fourth Republic took crucial decisions that were necessary foundations for de Gaulle's achievements after his return to power in 1958. This applies in the area of nuclear development and in the formation of the European Community. In both cases, the years after de Gaulle's departure demonstrated continuity of policy even after the arrival of the left in power in 1981.

The Vichy regime that replaced the Third Republic in 1940 suffered from the illusion that, despite draconian armistice terms, there could be a reasonable degree of autonomy for an independent France in Hitler's Europe. Pétain and his advisers envisaged an early end to the war, and thought that when peace came there would be scope for their National Revolution, a conservative system that was very different from Nazism. But actual developments, especially after the German attack on Russia and the allied landings in north Africa leading to German occupation of the whole of French territory, led on to collaboration with a foreign regime of unimaginable horror. The question, which has recently been much examined after being ignored for thirty years, of what happened to the Jewish population of France is relevant here. On the one hand, about half of that population survived, which may be regarded as remarkably high for territory under German control: on the other hand, half did not, and they were in most cases handed over for deportation by the Vichy authorities whose earlier establishment of Jewishness was the basis on which deportations could be conducted. The main distinction was between Jews who had been established in France for generations, as opposed to recent refugees. In that last category, which also included non-Jewish political opponents of Nazism, Vichy's earlier cancelling of naturalizations under the liberal law of 1927 facilitated deportation.

Vichy's foreign policy, based on the idea that 1939–40 was a European war that Hitler had won, was rendered obsolete when the events of 1941–2 made the Second World War a truly global struggle. From 1880 to 1941, France had been a participant in the game of power politics that was essentially conducted among the traditional great powers of Europe. This game had culminated in the 'European Civil War' begun in 1914 and was to end with the relative eclipse of all the purely European states, now overshadowed by the two global superpowers. This helped France to regain her own status instead of appearing, as a result of her ignominious defeat in 1940, far weaker than Britain or Germany. The position ten years or so after 1945 was that France could claim at least parity with her two ancient rivals. Neither Britain, nor France, nor Germany were in the premier league, occupied by the two superpowers, but France could claim to have recovered her place in the second division. In fact, de Gaulle was obsessed with the idea of outclassing the other two, an ambition apparently within his grasp because of the various handicaps placed on Germany resulting from Nazism and defeat, and because of the failure of nerve and confusion of purpose that came to envelop Britain. But France had first to be removed from the status of a German dependency, and restored to the rank of an ally of Britain, the USA, and the USSR.

The 1940 defeat and the collaboration between the Vichy-based government and Germany meant that at first France was hardly seen as one of the victorious allies at all. It was a major achievement of de Gaulle to impose his own version of the war years, namely that the Vichy regime had never had legitimacy and that he himself and the resistance and the 'Free French' forces represented the true France. In spite of the difference between the small French military forces and the huge armies of her three major allies, de Gaulle was able to achieve formal recognition of France as one of the great powers. This was largely because of British support against the indifference or hostility of the USA and the USSR, in spite of moments of intense antagonism between de Gaulle and Churchill during the war, and in spite of a treaty of alliance between France and the USSR of December 1944. During the negotiation of this treaty, de Gaulle told his Russian hosts that there were no matters in dispute between their countries, while Britain and France were traditional enemies. France was given permanent membership of the Security Council of the United Nations, and an occupation zone in Germany. To some extent the old disputes of 1919 were revived, with France seeking to impose her control over German coal and to achieve military security through occupation of the Rhineland area, while the Anglo-Saxons resisted. France was again allowed to establish a special status for the Saar coal-mining region, which she hoped might eventually lead to its incorporation into France.

These matters were soon overshadowed by the developing Cold War between the capitalist West and the Soviet Union. The Cold War ensured the achievement of the two major French aspirations that had been frustrated in the aftermath of the First World War: the ending of German national unity, and a long-term alliance with Britain and the United States. The steps towards this last were the Treaty of Dunkirk of March 1947 between Britain and France, explicitly directed against Germany, followed by the Treaty of Brussels of March 1948 extending its cover to the Benelux countries, and finally the establishment of NATO on 4 April 1949, bringing in the United States and Canada. By this time it was clear that the enemy for France and her allies was no longer Germany, but the USSR. There is no room here for analysis of the origins of the Cold War, but the brutal takeover of Czechoslovakia, the Berlin blockade, and the Marshall Plan for the economic recovery of Europe were the salient events that underlined the complete change of diplomatic alignment that had occurred by 1948. Notably, France's participation in the Western alliance was never threatened by the fact that, at this time, a quarter of its electorate voted for the communist party: this simply ensured that there was a firm line between the communists and everyone else.

Although the East–West conflict laid down the basis for France's international position, fear of German revival remained acute. The intensification of the Cold War, after the outbreak of war in Korea in 1951, brought demands for the rearmament of West Germany. France advocated the creation of the EDC (European Defence Community) so that German units would be incorporated into this joint European army instead of forming an independent German force. However, after more than two years of delay, the French parliament refused to ratify the EDC treaty, in August 1954. This was followed rapidly by the entry of Germany into NATO and the creation of a German army under NATO command in July 1955. In any case, by this time Stalin's death had greatly reduced international tension.

At this point, it is necessary to discuss the international aspects of French economic evolution since 1880. In 1880 France had taken only a few steps away from the free trade policies of the Second Empire, but very soon she moved decisively towards a system of protective tariffs, culminating in the Méline tariff of 1892, as explained in Chapter 1. For the next century France adhered to economic protectionism, which was only partly dismantled by the creation of the European Economic Community. In consequence, the economy was distorted, and small-scale peasant farming survived, at some considerable cost in terms of national economic production. The First World War brought an enormous reinforcement of protectionism; economic blockade of Germany and her allies was seen to be a vital weapon and it was indeed a major factor in their defeat. For a time it seemed that the policy might be continued into the international economic relations of the post-war world. At the Paris economic conference of 1916 France got Britain and Russia to agree to continue economic cooperation against Germany into the indefinite future after the end of the war.

However, the collapse of Russia and the entry into the war of the United States where President Wilson's views about the principles that should govern economic relations in the post-war world were diametrically opposed to this brought an end to this scheme. A French plan to build on German defeat and the concomitant return of the Lorraine iron ore field to France so as to replace the German coal-iron complex with a French one, proved impossible to achieve. When commercial relations returned to peacetime normality in 1925 the situation was not very different to that of 1914. France, like most other major states, followed a moderately protectionist policy. It was not free trade, but it was very different from the policy of continuous economic warfare envisaged in 1916. It was also very different from the autarchic systems that developed as a result of the Great Depression. From 1929 to the Second World War international trade collapsed as one country after another erected vastly higher tariff barriers, or retreated into state-controlled systems, aimed at economic autarchy. Although not a leader in this retreat from economic liberalism, France followed suit, and turned to a system of tariffs and quotas to protect domestic economic activity. One aspect of this retreat from the pre-1914 world was the greatly increased importance of trade between France and her colonies.

The defeat of 1940 meant that the French economy was exploited to the hilt in the service of the German war effort, and consumption was reduced to a very low level. If France had been free to follow her own instincts, the post-war years would have seen a resumption of the highly protectionist policies of the 1930s. This did happen to some extent but it was tempered by the acceptance of American ideas in return for the economic aid of the Marshall Plan. Beginning with the European coal and steel agreement of 1951 France began the process of reconciling protectionism with economic liberalism which governed the world of the second half of the twentieth century. The European Economic Community (EEC), initiated in 1959, envisaged the opening of France to industrial competition from Germany; in return the protection of French agriculture was enshrined for all future time in the form of the Common Agricultural Policy. Thus the main lines governing French economic relations with the rest of the world have been fixed by the EEC. In broad terms it can be agreed that they have served her well, by allowing her to move away from the straitjacket of protectionism, fixed on her between 1892 and 1939. The return to free trade in everything except agriculture played a vital role in the transformation of the French economy in the last half century.

The twelve years from the failure of the EDC in 1954 to France's withdrawal from the integrated command system of NATO in 1966 are the crucial ones for the evolution of France's position in the world in the second half of the twentieth century. They see the change from the high point of the East–West Cold War confrontation (marked by the Berlin crisis and the Cuban missile crisis of 1960–2) to what could be called a stable Cold War when, in spite of vast expenditure on weapons of mass destruction, the psychological atmosphere became very different. Nor did the sideshow wars in South-East Asia and Africa, in the end, seriously threaten the balance that had been achieved between the United States and the USSR. This balance allowed de Gaulle to create an international role for France far greater than her small military weight could justify in a world where there really was a serious threat of war between the two sides of the Cold War.

EDC would have made French military strength a subordinate and minor part of an armed coalition. Twelve years later France had withdrawn from NATO's military system. An important step in this evolution was French participation with Britain in the 1956 Suez expedition in reaction to Egyptian nationalization of the Suez Canal. France and Britain drew opposite conclusions from the American pressure that forced them to abandon the Suez affair: Britain, that in future, policy should be more closely coordinated with that of the United States, and France, that it should strive more vigorously to develop the capacity to follow an independent policy. The last governments of the weak Fourth Republic took two other vital decisions: the Treaty of Rome was signed in 1957 to set up the EEC with effect from 1 January 1959, and the decision in April 1958 that the existing nuclear programme should be extended from civilian to military purposes. De Gaulle's Fifth Republic was to benefit from these initiatives, and to make them vital pillars of its policies.

Meanwhile an even more basic turning point was passed with the working out of the Algerian crisis: Egypt's role in support of the Algerian rebellion had impelled France into Suez rather than the nationalization of the Canal. The impulse to reassert France's imperial presence had seemed vital at the end of the Second World War: it was asserted that only the Empire would allow her to retain the rank of a great power. From the interwar period, the economic links between France and her colonies had grown far more important than they had been in the pre-1914 world of relatively free trade. The experience of the Second World War, when to some extent Free French armies had been deployed in the colonies, and the autarchist economic ideas that were very widely held between 1929 and the end of the 1950s, meant that the Empire seemed to be of vital importance. The Brazzaville conference of 1944, which represented not the native populations but French elites, had provided a blueprint for the Union Française that was legislated into existence in 1946. It did not even envisage autonomy for the colonies, let alone independence. It was, in theory, the high point of assimilationist theory: in practice, not much real assimilation took place. But the idea that the colonies would accept this reimposition of French rule was shattered by revolt in Madagascar and the developing war in Indo-China. In 1954, Indo-China was abandoned; soon afterwards Morocco and Tunisia were allowed to claim their independence. A negotiated withdrawal was made easy in their case because in legal terms they had been simply protectorates, with native political institutions remaining in place, although in reality for much of the period down to 1955 they had been treated as if they were colonial possessions.

But Algeria was very different. It had been French since 1830, and was home to a population of European origin more than a million strong, the majority relatively poor, though in a much better position than the native Arabs and Berbers. Its legal status was that it was simply an extension of French territory across the Mediterranean, although the distinction between the rights of natives and Europeans was one of several facts that contradicted that claim. However, these factors, together with the determination of the military elite not to accept another humiliating defeat after that in Indo-China, ensured that the Algerian rebellion would turn into the worst political crisis of post-1945 France. This crisis ended the Fourth Republic, restored de Gaulle to power, and allowed him to reshape French political institutions after his own design, providing for a strong executive power. The first fruits of this change allowed de Gaulle to impose a settlement with the Algerian nationalists that in 1962 saw the exodus of the European settlers, although that had not been the intention of the

Evian agreements, and almost certainly had not been de Gaulle's plan from the beginning.

The Algerian crisis and de Gaulle's solution are central to discussion of France's role in the world over the period from 1880 to the present day. Withdrawal from Indo-China and then from Algeria opened the way to an amazingly rapid withdrawal from the rest of the colonial empire, with minor exceptions, mainly tiny Caribbean and Pacific islands. Elaborate constitutional recasting of the Union Française of 1946 into the Communauté proved to be ephemeral indeed. The colonial dream of the 1880s proved in the long run to have been a mirage, as did the empires acquired by other European states around the same time. The African colonies taken so easily by France in the late nineteenth century were given independence with remarkable ease and rapidity. However, economic and cultural links remained close; before long there were more French citizens working in the former colonies in various forms of aid and training than there had ever been in the colonial period. Continuation of the French presence was helped by the fact that a large part of the cost shifted to the European Community.

This revolution could come about because de Gaulle reversed his earlier advocacy of the idea that France needed her Empire to continue to play a leading role in the world. He now accepted that the burden assumed in Indo-China and in Algeria had weakened France in every way; without it, France had much greater scope to assert her place on the world stage where it really mattered. Simultaneously with the end of the Algerian crisis came the greatest Soviet–American confrontation of the Cold War, the Cuban affair in 1962. Successful resolution of this confrontation meant the end of the period of high tension following Korea, years marked by misguided fears of Soviet technological superiority, the Berlin, and then the Cuban crises. The Cold War settled down to almost thirty years of stable confrontation in which, in spite of a massive build-up of nuclear armaments by both sides, peace did not seem to be threatened in the acute ways that it had been in the first phase of the Cold War. This stability allowed France to assert her independence from American tutelage by leaving the NATO command system, expelling American forces from French territory, and concentrating her military expenditure on creating an independent nuclear force. Other elements in de Gaulle's programme for the reassertion of France's independent place in the world were the exclusion of Britain from the European Economic Community in 1963 and 1967, the Élysée treaty of 1963 between France and Germany, and the challenge to the American-dominated international financial system when France changed her currency reserves from dollars into gold. There were also more rhetorical challenges to American hegemony, such as criticism of American policy in Vietnam and the Middle East.

Although a good deal of this programme was achieved, de Gaulle's furthest ambitions proved to be out of reach. The events of 1968 dictated this outcome. First the Soviet invasion of Czechoslovakia destroyed hopes of a real détente between East and West; de Gaulle had seen such a détente as the way in which Europe could really be freed from American hegemony. Although France continued to be less critical of Soviet policy than other NATO states, any real diplomatic revolution was postponed until the collapse of the Soviet Union changed all the terms of the question. Secondly, domestic events in France in 1968 weakened her claim to be the dominant force in the European Community.

Although France retained the position of being a nuclear power while Germany was not, the French economy was less successful than the German. Furthermore, de Gaulle's hope that France could have a stable currency backed by gold proved to be an illusion. Inflation returned and when the dust settled from the currency upheavals of the 1970s, the franc proved not to have posed a lasting challenge to the dollar or the mark, although it remained for some years stronger than a collapsing pound. The economic miracle which had transformed the French economy in the thirty glorious years after 1945 was brought to an end by the oil shocks of 1973 and 1979, and reaction to these economic difficulties had important effects on foreign policy. De Gaulle's fall from power in 1969 opened the way to the long delayed admission of Britain and other states to the European Community in 1972. It became something quite different from the tight community of six which had been the ideal instrument for de Gaulle's ambitions.

Gaullism by other means: French policy since 1969

Nevertheless the fundamental elements of the French elite's view of France's role in the world have continued throughout the years that have elapsed since his fall. The upheaval of 1981, bringing the left to power under Mitterrand as president, did not produce a major change in foreign policy; his policy has been described as 'Gaullism by any other name'. The collapse of the Soviet bloc in 1989 brought more fundamental change. It removed one of the poles of the bipolar world which had allowed scope for France's balancing act, protected by NATO but not part of it as a coordinated military alliance. It also led to the reunification of Germany in 1990, transforming even more the relative weight of France and Germany in the European Community. This seismic shift in the world of international politics opened up transformations of NATO and of the European Community which are still ongoing. It is impossible to come to firm judgements about the evolution of French policy since 1990. What can be said is that up to the end of the millennium and beyond, the French elite, whether power was held by left or right, or shared between them in cohabitation, was still governed in its aspirations by a vision of France's role in the world most clearly articulated by de Gaulle.

The basis of this vision was nationalistic, in spite of protestations to the contrary in French support for supra-national elements in the European Community. The common currency and the European Central Bank were seen as ways of ensuring that France could exercise influence on economic matters that would otherwise have been more exclusively controlled by the German Central Bank. Having secured this economic basis, France would continue to see herself as the dominant political force in Europe. France claims to be the third strongest military power in the world, behind the USA and Russia, but ahead of Britain because of her independent nuclear force. It is impossible to decide on the degree of reality in this claim as long as the world is spared a major nuclear war, or even a nuclear confrontation involving the superpowers. What is important for this analysis is not the answer to an unanswerable question, but the fact that there is such wide support within France for such a claim, and for the financial burden involved. Over the last thirty years, a salient fact has been the virtual absence of any anti-nuclear movement in France, in notable contrast to Britain and Germany.

How can this be explained? It is to be hoped that an answer emerges from this historical account. French opinion is governed by the idea that their nation needs to defend itself in an alien and dangerous world. Even if the German threat, so nearly mortal in 1940, has been removed forever by German defeat in 1945 and the subsequent evolution of NATO and the European Community, in a wider sense power politics is still seen as the basis of international relations. An understanding of the French attitude is helped by considering why it should be absent in the other two contenders for leadership in Europe, Britain and Germany. The explanation lies in their contrasting experiences in the fifty years beginning in 1914. German nationalism burnt itself out by its enormous excesses, which do not need to be detailed here, leaving a society without any such ambitions even if it were not controlled by post-1945 restrictions. On the other hand, Britain was never brought to realize, as was France between 1940 and 1944, what military defeat could mean for the survival of the nation. In addition to the largely illusory idea that Britain had successfully defeated her enemies in the Second World War, there is the importance of the linguistic and cultural links summed up in the terminology of 'les Anglo-Saxons', so much used in France. However often we are told that the United States does not see itself as having a special relationship with Britain, Britain acts as if it has a special relationship with the USA. The contrasting reactions of Britain and France to their betrayal by the USA over Suez in 1956 has set the pattern ever since, with Britain seeking always to retain US support, and France determined, whenever she could, to take an independent role, even if that has often meant simply verbal and rhetorical stances. The feeling of being alone in a dangerous world has long since faded in Britain, while in France it has remained, governing both military-political decisions and also the desire to defend *francophonie* and French cultural aspirations against the rising tide of Anglo-Saxon language and culture. The French stance in regard to the outbreak of the Second Gulf War in March 2003 is the most recent, and notable, case in point.

In short, France's basic stance in the world of the new millennium is the product of her history. The two dominant elements are first the legacy of Louis XIV, the Revolution and the Napoleonic Empire, with France claiming political-cultural hegemony over Europe, and secondly the acute feeling of vulnerability resulting from the shattering defeats of 1870 and 1940, and from the more diffuse unease produced by the demographic and cultural decline of the century before 1945, which took France from being the most populous European state to being behind several others. From 1945 to the present, a major strand in French history has been the impulse to turn around what could be seen as more than a century of decline. This impulse was most clearly articulated by de Gaulle, but it began under the Fourth Republic and has continued for more than thirty years after his rule.

5

The transformation of society

John Horne

If there is a 'peculiarity' of French social history since 1880, it is the opposite of that sometimes attributed to Germany. The industrial revolution transformed German society, eventually producing a cataclysm in a political system still rooted in the *ancien régime*. France possessed a democracy inspired by the Revolution, yet society and the economy changed more slowly than in Germany, with periods of stagnation. The contrast should not be overdrawn. French society like German politics had advanced elements and moments of transformation. There is also no highroad to political or social modernity; each country takes its own route. It remains the case that modern republican politics were elaborated in a society that changed gradually and only partly developed the class structure of an industrial revolution.

Peculiarities of the French economy

Nineteenth-century society internalized some key consequences of the French Revolution. Market liberalism and the ideal of an elite open to talent replaced *ancien régime* privilege and corporatism with an economy apparently based on change. At the same time, the abolition of the seigneurial system without the compensation imposed elsewhere confirmed the peasantry as a major social group, possessing half the land in some regions. Railways helped develop the internal market and open up the countryside. Although peasants farmed for self-sufficiency, many produced a surplus for cash and also engaged in artisan and 'proto-industrial' manufacture. Artisan production was highly developed in the towns and cities, with Lyon silk weaving and Paris luxury goods enjoying international renown. Yet the revolutionary vocation of urban artisans and labourers from 1789 to the Paris Commune of 1871 inflected the pattern of French industrialization, which also faced competition from British mass production. Manufacturers sought to locate heavy industry in rural or mono-industrial settings, avoiding large industrial conurbations (a goal encouraged by scattered raw materials), and they favoured the 'putting-out' system among peasant-artisans for the same reason.

France by the 1880s had islands of heavy industry and mass production but was characterized by small-scale, family businesses, whether rural or urban. The major cities (apart from Lille and Rouen) were not centres of factory labour, and the reputation of Paris as a symbol of modernity owed more to consumption than production—to its quality goods, department stores, and fashionable boulevards. The vibrancy of the French economy should not be underestimated. Re-evaluations have pointed to the relatively strong per capita growth of GNP in the nineteenth century even by comparison with Britain and Germany. Labour-intensive agriculture proved able to feed the urban population until the 1880s. Handicraft manufacture adjusted to a more intensive division of labour. Yet the economy was constrained. Ideals of broad property-ownership and economic balance suggested a desire to avoid the social upheaval entailed by the industrial revolution in Britain. Since the family was the central productive unit, limiting its size in order to preserve its inherited patrimony preoccupied many groups, including peasants. Population increase slowed and France, formerly a demographic giant, was outstripped by Germany and rivalled by Britain. There was less internal migration and no French diaspora, weaker domestic demand, and labour shortages in industry.

The depression of the 1880s starkly illuminated these limitations. Agricultural competitivity was threatened by cheap food imports from the 'new world' and labourers and artisans (though not peasants) left the countryside. Bankruptcies soared while unemployment and strikes signalled the stirrings of labour. Recovery came in the 1890s, but was driven by new technologies of cheap steel, electricity, chemicals, and the internal combustion engine—a second industrial revolution that transformed the terms of economic development. At the same time, anxieties deepened about French demographic as well as economic performance, both of which seemed vital to France's world role and even security. Social evolution over the subsequent century involved all these issues and more. While it became clear that the scale and pace of change had altered irrevocably, the desire to find a path compatible with the essential post-Revolutionary values of balance, family enterprise, quality, and inventiveness, remained strong.

What that path turned out to be is broadly indicated by three sets of data—on population, economic production, and the social structure. With a low birth rate, French population growth (Table 5.1) was weak from 1871 to 1910 (36.1 to 39.6 million) compared to her major neighbours, and stagnated between the wars, when births dropped below replacement rate. Yet France was now less exceptional as other western European countries moved to low birth rates and smaller families. By a remarkable reversal, birth and population growth rates rose sharply during and after the Second World War, when a more sustained baby-boom than elsewhere pushed the population from 41.4 million in 1949 to 50.3 million in 1969—an unprecedented increase.

Taking average annual rates of increase in Real National Product as a measure of economic growth (Table 5.2), France performed relatively strongly compared to Britain and Germany from 1890 to 1930. It fared worse during the 1930s slump, during which negative growth

Table 5.1 Comparative population growth (millions) in France, Britain, and Germany

	France	Great Britain[a]	Germany[b]
1870/1	36.1	26.1	40.8
1910	39.6	40.8	64.9
1929	40.8	45.7	64.7
1949	41.4	50.3	68.1
1969	50.3	55.5	77.9

[a] Includes Northern Ireland from 1929.
[b] East and West Germany from 1949.

Source: Carlo Cipolla (ed.), *The Fontana Economic History of Europe*, vol. v, part 2 (London, 1973), 747, and vol. vi, part 2 (London, 1976), 642–3.

Table 5.2 Average annual rates of growth of Real National Product, 1920–1981, for France, the United Kingdom, and Germany (%)

	1920–9	1929–38	1950–60	1962–73	1974–81
France	4.9	−0.5	4.6	5.6	2.5
United Kingdom	1.9	1.9	2.7	3.1	0.6
Germany[a]	4.5	3.9	7.8	4.4	2.1

[a] West Germany from 1950–60.

Source: Gerold Ambrosius and William H. Hubbard, *A Social and Economic History of Twentieth-Century Europe* (Munich, 1986; trans., Cambridge, Mass., 1989), 144.

was registered, and the economy was devastated by the Second World War. But it surged ahead of West German growth rates in the middle of the post-war boom to become the fourth-largest economy in the West (after the USA, Japan, and West Germany) by the recession of the 1980s.

Comparison of employment in the different sectors of the economy (Table 5.3) reveals that agriculture (principally peasant farmers) accounted for 44 per cent of the active population in 1906 and over a quarter in the 1950s, but was merely a shadow of its former self with 7.5 per cent by the 1980s. Conversely, industry and building became an important minority with around a third of the active population, reaching nearly 40 per cent in 1968 before falling back to the 1906 level in the 1980s. The tertiary sector (sales, services, professions, administration) employed a quarter of the active population at the

Table 5.3. Employment in different sectors of the economy (%)

	Primary	Secondary	Tertiary
1906	44.0	30.5	25.5
1946	36.0	32.0	32.0
1954	27.3	35.4	37.3
1962	19.9	38.0	42.1
1968	15.7	39.6	44.7
1975	10.1	38.5	51.4
1982	8.2	34.2	57.6
1987	7.5	30.6	61.9

Source: J. Dupâquier (ed.), *Histoire de la population française*, vol. iv, *De 1914 à nos jours* (Paris, 1988), 363.

start of the century and increased steadily until it occupied just over 60 per cent by the late 1980s.

In outline, therefore, French society embarked on a demographic roller-coaster in the century after 1880, sliding below, then rising above, the norm of comparable societies. It sustained the challenge of economic growth and industrialization, tentatively before 1930, triumphantly between the Second World War and the 1980s. Yet it remained significantly rural until the 1950s, and industrial workers— by contrast with Britain (and the predictions of the French communists)—never approached a majority. The expansion of the tertiary sector was clearly a major source of change. In terms of periodization, growth and adaptation from 1890 to 1930 were followed by stagnation during the depression and Second World War, when the active population in the primary sector actually went up. The *trente glorieuses*, or 'thirty glorious years' of economic boom after 1945, transformed France more than had the previous century according to Jean Fourastié, the economist who coined the term. We shall return to the 'peculiarity' of this path after examining in greater depth the main processes of social change.

Weakening population growth made the state, industrialists, and social statisticians in France aware earlier than in other countries that human reproduction was a fundamental variable in the evolution of society, and a target of action. The influential Alliance Nationale pour l'Accroissement de la Population, founded in 1896, and a series of governmental bodies established during the interwar and Vichy years, turned the study of demography into a French speciality. Spurred by the catastrophe of the First World War, in which the birth rate plummeted and France lost 1.45 million actual or potential fathers, propaganda was intense and backed by legislation in 1920 that banned birth-control publicity and stiffened penalties for abortion. The conservative family movement deplored the 'moral decay' that resulted in small families or worse, childless couples, and it was joined by the more technically minded pronatalist movement in agitating for financial inducements to encourage procreation. The state responded with a small grant to large needy families in 1913, and followed this in 1932 by obliging industrialists to contribute to the family benefits that many had instituted voluntarily in a paternalist spirit. But the lobbyists' case only began to be met in 1939 when, in response to a tumbling birth rate following the sharp decline of twenty years earlier and the renewed threat of war, the government introduced a 'Family Code'. This instituted a grant for the first child and allowances for second and subsequent children. It was amplified by Vichy, which blamed the debacle on too few babies (amongst other things) and saw paternalism and pregnancy as sources of national renewal. Family social allowances became, and remained, central to the French welfare system.

Women were the ultimate target of the pronatalist effort. Yet their general reluctance to oblige was embedded in the logic of the family-based economy. Despite the increase in single women and widows due to the Great War, French women generally married and had children, but typically not more than one or two—though a significant minority with over six kept pronatalist hopes alive. The preamble to the 'Family Code' tellingly blamed the low French birth rate on the modest comfort of a society that placed the preservation of the family patrimony above the search for 'new sources of wealth'. The surging birth rate from 1943 was partly a response to the new family-aid regime, and the more impressive since a million POWs and a quarter of a million male workers were in Germany in 1942 (the latter rising to nearly three-quarters of a million by spring 1944). Family benefits (almost 40 per cent of welfare spending by 1949) helped sustain the baby-boom of the post-war years. Yet this was due to much else, including reduced infant mortality. Above all, the decline of family businesses (including the peasant farm) in favour of salaried labour, urbanization, and a major effort to redress the chronic housing shortage, combined to produce a new and buoyant attitude to family size. The *trente glorieuses*, by transforming the social structure of post-Revolutionary France, removed the malthusian restraint that had come to characterize it.

The reverse face of that Malthusianism was immigration. France had a long tradition of foreign minorities and political exiles. But industrial growth from the 1890s at a time when the peasant farm remained largely intact forced industrialists and big farmers, backed by the state, to use immigrants on an unprecedented scale. To the Belgians of the north were added Italians in southern docks and vineyards and the new iron-field of French Lorraine. The state brought half a million foreign workers to France during the First World War, from Spain, Greece, and for the first time from the north African and Indo-Chinese colonies. There was still stronger immigration in the 1920s under the impetus of economic growth, reconstruction, and the demographic deficit of the war. To the dominant Italians were added Poles (e.g. in the coal mines of the north), Spanish, and others, including a new influx from the colonies. By 1931, with 7 per cent of the population foreign-born, France was the leading immigrant country in the world.

Many immigrants came under bilateral treaties (Italy, Poland), and were kept under tight control. Concentrated in heavy industry, building, mining, and agriculture, they provided a pliable labour force that spared French workers some of the heaviest tasks of accelerated industrialization and cushioned indigenous proletarianization. Some returned home or were repatriated, especially in the 1930s. Many stayed, however, posing the question of their relationship with French society. The relative rigidity of national identities and political forms in France excluded an American-style 'melting-pot', even as an ideal. The abstract values of republican citizenship provided an alternative, but it was one that found it hard to acknowledge the cultural difference displayed by immigrant communities. Laws in 1889 on nationality and in 1927 on naturalization sought to define and regulate the transition from foreigner to French, but this was a lengthy process. Xenophobia surfaced in depressions (the far right exploiting it in the 1930s as it had in the 1880s–1890s), and Vichy institutionalized it by official discrimination, cancelling naturalizations, and turning over foreigners (Jewish and non-Jewish) demanded by the Germans.

Despite the natural population increase after 1945, immigration rose above pre-war levels driven by the sheer intensity of economic growth plus the ingrained recourse of industrialists to foreign labour. In addition to an influx of southern Europeans, there was a sizeable flow from current and former colonies (plus nearly a million settlers from Algeria), making colour and religious difference major factors. Foreigners built 50 per cent of the housing, 90 per cent of the motorways, and one machine in seven during the post-war boom. They dominated the non-skilled grades of the automobile industry. When a young intellectual, Robert Linhart, joined the Citroën assembly-line in 1968, he found his comrades were from villages in Yugoslavia, Turkey, and north Africa. The foundations of the *trente glorieuses* were in no small measure laid by immigrants. Both the arrival of their families and intermarriage made it clear (as did renewed xenophobia in the 1980s, exploited by the Front National) that France had become multicultural. This was confirmed by the influence of earlier and second-generation immigrants—with Polish sociability marking the northern working-class, eastern European Jews embracing republicanism and communism, and various groups making their mark in show business (e.g. the singers Serge Reggiani and Charles Aznavour), politics, the media, and more.

Almost as much was at stake with industrial production as with human reproduction in a period when productivity, and therefore increased profits and living standards (not to mention military capacity), turned on a nation's ability to engage in industrial innovation and related social reorganization. France stood to benefit by the second industrial revolution, with abundant supplies of iron ore available for large-scale steel production, hydroelectricity to supplement poor coal supplies (despite productive fields in the north), capital, and a wealth of inventiveness in big firms and the family-based economy. Louis Lumière devised a combined movie camera and projector, and he and his brother organized the first commercial cinema in Paris in 1895 before selling their rights to Charles Pathé. Louis Renault used the capital of the family drapery business to set up a car factory in 1898 at the Renault's holiday property on the Seine, west of Paris. By 1914, France was a major producer of movie films and automobiles and was well represented in several leading sectors—steel-making and armaments (de Wendel in Lorraine, Schneider at Le Creusot), engineering, and chemicals (Péchiney).

The First World War galvanized the industrial economy. Despite the loss of 16 per cent of industrial firms and 41 per cent of total steam power in the invasion of 1914, a major industrial effort was improvised with over 1.6 million workers in munitions who, by the end of the war, supplied the American army in France with much of its military equipment. The conflict revealed to the French how crucial industrialization had become. The latest machine-tools and industrial ideas were imported from the USA and French experts toured American factories. New links were forged between state and industry, and at least some in business, politics, and the labour movement dreamed of a concerted effort to modernize the industrial economy after the war. Such ideas remained a dream, but renewed growth, the rebuilding of industry in the liberated regions, and a competitive franc that buoyed exports from 1926, confirmed the positive response of industrialists to the new phase of industrialization, even if some sectors remained backward.

The rise of the worker

These developments created an industrial working class. Perhaps more than elsewhere, the artisan was a vital link, testifying to the continued vibrancy of small workshops and supplying the substantial skilled grades which mechanized production required. Artisans also transmitted labour organization and political radicalism to factory workers. But by 1921, when 57 per cent of the industrial labour force worked in enterprises with over 100 workers, the factory had triumphed, even if large factories remained less common than in Britain or Germany. American 'scientific management' theories associated with F. W. Taylor were adopted and spawned French variants. These ideas 'rationalized' production into simpler, repetitive tasks performed by 'semi-skilled' labour on piece-rate payment and under strict discipline, with an elite of skilled workers and a host of experts and technicians to plan and regulate the process. Heavy industry and mining were often still isolated, and rural outworking continued, but the workforce in burgeoning engineering and other factories was less easily contained by strategies of industrial paternalism. Rural migrants, foreigners, and artisans crowded into industrial districts, creating suburban working-class communities around Paris, Lyon, and elsewhere.

The depression of the 1930s and the Second World War marked a long hiatus. Economic historians argue over whether this is best understood as the dislocation of a conservative industrialization, which shied away from an economic transformation that would disrupt the 'balance' of society favoured by the peasantry and middle classes, or as an interruption to basically strong French growth from the 1890s. The former view finds it hard to account for the scale and speed of the economic transformation after the Second World War, since it underplays the earlier dynamism of the French economy. The latter fails to address the real difficulties faced by backward sectors (including much artisan production) in modernizing to meet the harsh climate of the 1930s, and the brake placed on recovery by restricted domestic demand. Forty-nine per cent of the population still lived in the countryside in 1931, and urban workers' living standards remained low.

In social terms, however, the depression and Occupation marked the point at which a collective working-class identity—symbolized by the resolutely masculine trio of the miner, railway worker, and metal-worker—became a central feature of French society. Jean Gabin, as the heart-throb in a series of brooding films, dramatized the figure of the Paris worker to mass cinema audiences which now included much of the working class. Collective identity found expression in a level of industrial and political militancy that had been anticipated, but not matched, just after the First World War. The mass strikes and factory occupations of May–June 1936 following the Popular Front's electoral victory, and the resulting wage increases and social reforms which turned on labour rights and greater leisure (with the forty-hour week and paid vacations), helped consolidate the working class and served notice of future claims. Although worker militancy bore no single ideological label, the political beneficiary was undoubtedly the Parti Communiste Français (PCF) and the communist-dominated trade union movement, the Confédération Générale du Travail (CGT). French communism won its legitimacy from purporting to speak for this working class, and in turn its political culture became a central, though never exclusive, feature of the latter—a symbiotic relationship confirmed by the role of both workers and communists in the resistance.

Anti-communism explains the vehement reaction by industrialists and much of the middle classes to the Popular Front. But equally, the way in which the government's fairly modest reforms were portrayed as a Moscow conspiracy suggests that what was really at stake was a shift in the balance of forces in French society. Arising partly from this and partly from the prolonged experience of the depression, the issues of how and whether France should become a fully industrialized society were debated more intensely and divisively than ever, with numerous groups (political, business, labour, intellectual) proposing divergent solutions. These culminated in the opposed (yet oddly parallel) projects drawn up by Vichy and the resistance. The nadir of French economic and military fortunes was accompanied by a crisis of orientation in much of society.

The post-war boom

Liberation, reconstruction, and the prolonged post-war boom resolved the question of French economic development, though in ways that brought their own ambiguities and conflicts. The goals of social justice and economic modernization that informed much resistance and Free-French thought shaped the post-war order. Despite a number of nationalizations, communists and many socialists were rapidly disabused of their dream that France might advance towards a collectivist economy. Yet social reforms were introduced that reinstated and extended the achievements of the Popular Front and seemed to acknowledge working-class claims to a more central place in society. Among these were the renewal of the forty-hour week (1946), the creation of a social security system for illness and old age incorporating the pre-war system of voluntary insurance (1945–6), the institution of a minimum wage (1947), and the extension of family allowances. The redistributive effect of these measures was considerable; by 1950 social payments represented 12 per cent of the resources of the average French household. Additionally, worker representation on factory committees and an official system of collective bargaining entrenched the re-established authority of trade unionism.

Economic modernization, however, came from a different source. This was the agreement by a knot of experts, civil servants, industrialists, and politicians, that the state must break with the past and lead the way to a revitalized capitalism. The ferment of the 1930s and first-hand observation of the American economic mobilization during the war furnished crucial ideas. The need to prioritize the rebuilding of a shattered infrastructure supplied the stimulus. Flexible state planning in consultation with business, labour, and other groups was the instrument, and control of scarce investment capital, especially American dollars, gave the state its leverage. As conceived by Jean Monnet and his associates, who operated on the margins of the state bureaucracy and formal politics, the recipe proved a brilliant success. It infused the economic and political elites and the civil service with a heady belief that economic transformation was the basis of national renewal.

Industrialists recovered rapidly from their over-involvement with Vichy, apart from those, like Louis Renault, whose firms were nationalized as punishment for collaboration. They reorganized the defence of their interests and pushed for economic liberalism. But earlier tendencies to temper growth by social balance disappeared in the face of euphoric expansion and the drive to win markets, at home and abroad. Plant was modernized, business methods were imported from America (with technical missions visiting the USA and American companies investing in France), and as firms grew larger, they were increasingly managed by salaried professionals. Graduates of the exclusive *grandes écoles* (such as the venerable École Polytechnique or the new École Nationale d'Administration, created in 1945) circulated between politics, the civil service, and business (a tendency known as *pantoufflage*), producing an administrative elite wedded to economic modernization.

Some features of the interwar working class were reinforced by post-war growth. The technologies of the 'second industrial revolution' lay at the heart of the extended boom. 'Rationalized' factory production became more prominent, yet workers were also better protected, benefiting from the 'heroic' victories of 1936–45 and from a PCF that coexisted with, and made claims on, the status quo which it theoretically rejected from 1947. In other respects, however, the post-war boom changed workers. The industrial labour force grew by over two million. While the skilled tended to be children of the interwar generation, the new semi-skilled were peasants and immigrants. Light industries and automobile production (where the semi-skilled predominated) diversified from the industrial suburbs to green-field sites, especially in the west of France, partly to avoid the fortresses of organized labour. French industrial geography was redrawn as cities like Caen (Citroën) and Rennes (Renault) became centres of manufacturing. Workers benefited from the increased living standards brought by higher growth and productivity. By 1975, nearly three-quarters of working-class families had cars (compared to 8 per cent in 1953), and 88 per cent possessed a television. Many lived in the subsidized apartments or HLMs (dwellings at a moderate rent), built by the state since the early 1950s. Persistent inequalities and the alienation felt by the post-war influx, however, bred dissatisfaction, which the PCF and CGT were less able to harness. This was demonstrated by the emergence of a rival trade union body, the Confédération

Française Démocratique du Travail (CFDT, 1964) and the explosion of May 1968, with the largest strike movement in French history. By the 1980s, communism was shrinking as it sought to defend its heartlands (Lorraine steel, industrial Paris) against recession and the shift to post-industrial technologies. As the post-war cycle of growth came to an end, it was clear that while manufacturing continued to occupy an important minority of the workforce, the working-class identity of the middle decades of the century was dissolving.

Revolution in rural France

The proportion of the workforce engaged in agriculture since the 1880s has been quite close to that of neighbouring countries—27 per cent in 1950, compared to 42 per cent in Italy and 23 per cent in West Germany, with Britain the exception at 5 per cent. Yet perhaps no other western European society has celebrated its rural roots as much as France. This doubtless stems from the creation of a landowning peasantry by the French Revolution, on which male suffrage was conferred in 1848. The Third Republic was consolidated by peasant votes in the 1870s and politicians under successive Republics paid tribute to the rural backbone of society. Jules Méline, the moderate republican who introduced the major tariff protecting French agriculture in 1892, set the tone with a book entitled *Return to the Land* (1906), which painted a prosperous peasantry as the antidote to the frenetic battle of industrialization between Britain, Germany, and the USA, and to the false glamour of city life. The most reactionary variant of the refrain came with Vichy, whose Corporation Paysanne unsuccessfully sought to recolonize the countryside, but even the reforming governments of the 1960s believed that preserving a smaller number of family farms was vital for society.

There was some substance to the official rhetoric, for all its exaggeration. Although labourers and independent artisans left the countryside during and after the depression of the 1880s, the family farm was consolidated. The number of peasant exploitations reached its peak in 1906, secured by the absorption of the smallest holdings but also by the capacity of peasant farmers to adapt to the market (e.g. converting from tillage to pasture). At the same time, rural society, even on the remote perimeters, was drawn not only into national politics but also into an urban-based culture. Small-town markets became meeting-places for rural society, as well as points of economic exchange. The café replaced the traditional *veillée*, or home-spun entertainment, as the place of (male) conviviality, and the bicycle freed rural youth to socialize (and court) at a greater distance. Significantly, the quintessential French sporting event, the Tour de France (1903), constructed a mass audience from a population dispersed in the countryside. Confirmation of the peasantry's integration came when it unhesitatingly accepted mobilization in 1914–18 and supplied the majority of the infantry who defended the nation in the trenches.

Yet the survival of the peasantry was ultimately at odds with its place as the largest group in society—as it still was after the Second World War (see Table 5.3). For economic growth was premised on intensified specialization and on a rising standard of living in which food took a declining share. True, recent research has stressed not only the market specialization achieved by small farms in parts of France (e.g. market gardening in western Brittany) but also the extent to which the peasant family remained a basis for other activities— from artisan production to work (with increased transport) in local factories. Flexibility emerges here as the key to a social and economic unit that was pivotal to the adaptability of French society across the twentieth century. Against this, however, must be set the core strategy of the peasant family which was the preservation, and if possible expansion, of its own patrimony and in many cases the continued practice of polyculture for the family's own consumption. Such features put a brake on growth and hence on demand for manufactures and services. The price, for the peasantry, was the growing gap with urban (including working-class) living standards, of which military service, newspapers, and the radio made them increasingly aware.

The First World War was ambiguous in this regard. Intense demand and inflation increased rural incomes, allowing family farms to be expanded. Yet losses were highest among the peasantry and the war accelerated the rural exodus. A brief period of post-war prosperity was followed by a slump in agricultural prices, which plummeted in the 1930s depression. Although industrial production fared even worse, the real wages of workers who remained fully employed rose in the 1930s as prices fell. The perception spread that rural lifestyles could not match those of the cities. In some ways, the peasant farm showed its resilience. Ephraïm Grenadou, a smallholder on the edge of the rich grain region of the Beauce, near Chartres, took to baking his bread and doing his own blacksmithing. But by the same token, there was a further decimation of rural commerce, and some peasant farmers in the west and Massif Central protested by supporting the minority self-styled 'fascism' of Henri Dorgères's Front Paysan.

The Occupation reversed the terms of urban–rural relations as city-dwellers scavenged the countryside for scarce food while peasant farmers were able to feed themselves and supply the black, as well as official, market: 'With all the cows and calves we killed during the war', remarked Grenadou, 'enough skins were buried in the garden to shoe a battalion' (*Grenadou, paysan français* (1966), 205). With the post-war boom, however, the terms were reversed again, and this time decisively. Smallness of scale, technical backwardness, and limited specialization became major handicaps, and if rural living standards rose they trailed those of urban workers.

Peasants became acutely conscious of their grievances. A bloc of peasant deputies in the Fourth Republic sought to protect farmers with price subsidies and food-surplus stockpiles, though these flew in the face of economic modernization. From 1953, increasingly frustrated farmers adopted direct-action tactics. Starting from the region of mass wine production in the Midi, which was suffering a glut, tractor blockades and demonstrations spread through the small-farming districts of the Massif Central, Poitou, and Charentes. Although temporarily placated by parliamentary measures, revolt broke out anew in Brittany in 1961 as surplus artichokes were dumped on the roads and a subprefecture was occupied, with road-blocks spreading to the Massif Central and Midi. Yet out of this crisis, and a revolution in the farmers' own professional associations, a solution emerged.

A group of young farmers saw the central point that the peasantry could only survive if it modernized and specialized, which in turn meant reducing its size. They argued that less efficient farms should gradually have their land redistributed to the progressive minority. In one sense, they were pushing at an open door. The agricultural labour force declined by nearly a million between 1954 and 1962, with 400,000 farms lost. The technocrats of the Plan urged land reform and modernization. De Gaulle saw agriculture as a brake on France.

But farming was a powerful lobby, and it was only when Michel Debatisse (from a 35-acre farm in the Auvergne) and a Catholic young farmers' organization, the Jeunesse Agricole Chrétienne, took over the youth section of the Fédération Nationale des Syndicats des Exploitants Agricoles (FNSEA)—the principal farmers' body—that government and technocrats had the allies they needed.

Edgar Pisani, de Gaulle's unorthodox minister of agriculture (1961–6), carried out the central reforms which turned on the amalgamation of holdings to provide fewer, larger, family farms, credit for mechanization (the 'tractor revolution'), and a restructuring of price supports. The reforms had the full backing of the young farmers, who finally captured the FNSEA. By 1985, the number of farmers had halved, from 3 million to 1.6 million, while average farm size had nearly doubled, and living standards were much closer to those of the city. Modernization had dissolved the mass peasantry but conserved a small-farming component in doing so. Together with an influx of non-farmers into the countryside (commuters, retirees, second homeowners) and a widespread sense of connection with the land at one or two generations' remove, the imprint of the peasantry remained strong.

The evolution of the bourgeoisie

Even more important than peasants for the self-image of French society were the bourgeois. The end of noble privilege and the diverse sources of wealth in the nineteenth century (with land, finance, and commerce as important as industry) resulted in a heterogeneous but self-confident bourgeoisie that stamped society with its values of work and independence and its own sense of status. Although family dynasties structured access to the upper echelons of society and fostered economic privilege, a certain fluidity and upward mobility into the bourgeoisie were preserved. Moreover, the importance of small-scale family businesses in commerce and manufacturing meant that France had a broad category of *classes moyennes* (or lower middle classes), whose values and aspirations were modelled on those of the bourgeoisie. To these was added a growing number of white-collar employees in public and private-sector bureaucracies. Language is more than usually subjective in this area, since there were no uniform official categories, and *bourgeoisie* or *classes moyennes* fluctuated as terms of self-identity, or even abuse. Yet a 1956 survey calculated that 20 per cent of households belonged to the middle and upper classes by their income and activity, while the growth of the tertiary sector in the twentieth century (Table 5.3) indicates expansion in areas (services, commerce, management, the professions) that were especially important to these groups.

The self-confidence of the bourgeois before 1914 was shaken in the interwar period, though less severely than in Italy and Germany. War deaths affected the elites (whose sons served as junior officers) as much as they did the peasantry. The basis of bourgeois wealth changed as inflation eroded income from fixed-interest investments and from urban property, which was subject to ongoing rent controls introduced in the war. The dynamic industrial economy in the 1920s offset the sense of menace, with boom-sector industrialists such as Ernest Mercier (in electricity) embracing an early form of technocracy under American influence, and launching a movement (Redressement Français, or French Recovery) calling for unapologetic expansion through high domestic wages. Yet this remained a minority view. Bourgeois opinion favoured balanced growth and the continued dissemination of property and family businesses as an antidote to social breakdown and Bolshevism. Significantly, the two main currents of French sociology—one descended from the conservative Catholic values of Frédéric Le Play, the other from the high Republicanism of Émile Durkheim—were preoccupied by what Durkheim termed *anomie*, or the breakdown of community in industrial society and the need to counteract it. Durkheim's successor, Maurice Halbwachs, wrote several books with this concern uppermost.

The prolonged depression with its toll of bankruptcies and declining investment revenue brought bourgeois self-belief to its nadir. This contributed to the crisis of orientation in French society already referred to. Determination to defend what one study termed the 'barrier' against access to the elites (Edmond Goblot, *La Barrière et le niveau*, 1925) was demonstrated by the successful resistance against the *école unique*, or integrated education system, which sought to open the elite *lycées* at the secondary level to popular access (though hostility between the different teachers' associations also played a role). Universal primary education, instituted by the Republic in the

1880s, remained a largely self-contained system and the *école unique* only began to be applied with the Fouchet law of 1963.

The interwar years had a parallel impact on the *classes moyennes*. The collective term *artisanat* ('artisanry') was first formulated in the early 1920s, as part of the move towards a class-based public terminology for French society. In 1925, a law gave the *artisanat* formal status and by 1933 the leading artisanal organizations claimed 340,000 members. The claim was perhaps more significant than the substance. Artisans remained eclectic in their political allegiance, with many if not most continuing to support a Republic they were confident would reflect their interests. Likewise organizations purporting to represent the *classes moyennes*, which had emerged before 1914, proliferated in the 1930s under the depression, and if a politicized hostility to both organized labour and big business was sharper than before, it continued to be invested mainly in the republican centre—at the price of the social division accompanying the Popular Front.

After 1945, however, economic and social modernization redefined and transformed both *classes moyennes* and *bourgeoisie*. The most traditional sectors of retailing and artisan production vehemently opposed this process. In the early 1950s, small shopkeepers in western Brittany boycotted Édouard Leclerc, the son of an army officer and a former Jesuit, who tried to break the hold of price fixing and low turnover by selling in volume on small profit margins—the supermarket principle. Modernizers in government supported him and Centres E. Leclerc spread across France, sparking price wars with the older chain-stores (Monoprix, Prisunic) and stimulating a retail revolution that forced the smaller shops to specialize or decline. Refusal to modernize reached its zenith with the populist campaign of Pierre Poujade, a bookseller in the Massif Central who in 1953 founded a Union de Défense des Commerçants et Artisans and led a tax revolt which turned into a broader rejection of modern industry and retailing. 'Around the so-called rich regions, they'll concentrate industry', wrote Poujade, 'which progressively, will be run by a minimum of people [. . .] The shopkeepers and artisans will have to give way to supermarket branches' (*J'ai choisi le combat* (1957), 114–15). 'Poujadisme' peaked with 11.6 per cent of the vote in the 1956 election, though its influence lingered into the 1970s. Ultimately more significant were the small producers and retailers who accepted the pace and opportunities of accelerated growth. The Confédération

Générale des Petites et Moyennes Entreprises (CGPME), founded in 1944 in the wake of Vichy corporatism by Léon Gingembre, a needle manufacturer from Normandy, initially allied itself with Poujade's anti-tax stance. But from 1958, Gingembre embraced competition, modernization, and the Common Market, and the CGPME helped its members to adapt and specialize.

Even more far-reaching in its consequences was the growth and professionalization of the white-collar labour force, a development that straddled the bourgeoisie and *classes moyennes*. The untranslatable word *cadre* ('manager' is a rough equivalent) provides a way of tracing this process. It was first used during the Popular Front by engineers who, fearful of being excluded from collective bargaining, formed their own professional bodies distinct from the conflict between industrialists and workers. Influenced by Catholic Action ideals of hierarchy and self-organization, they saw themselves as an elite defending the *classes moyennes* and fitted perfectly into the conservative social language of Vichy.

Within twenty years the term was transformed. In the 1950s it designated the engineers and managers who revolutionized business organization. Since many of these went on 'productivity missions' to the USA, worked for American companies, or emulated the techniques of the latter, *cadres* signified enthusiasm for transatlantic norms of efficiency, competitiveness, and modernization. The word also suggested a more relaxed, egalitarian lifestyle that subverted conventional bourgeois status and was fuelled by soaring living standards. It described the goal of high consumption that became characteristic of the 1960s, with a combination of democratic elitism and hedonism epitomized by holidays with the Club Méditerranée (founded in 1950, half a million members by 1968). Another club aimed explicitly at the *cadres* became one of France's largest retail chains for books and electronic gadgetry—the FNAC (Fédération Nationale des Achats des Cadres). In effect, the prevalence of the term *cadre* (and its use in post-war censuses) denoted the professionalization of the salaried middle classes and the rise of the industrial manager. The complexity of the process was indicated by the subcategories of *cadres*, from upper to lower, and by diverse professional and political affiliations (winning the *cadres* was as vital to the socialists in the 1980s as to the Gaullists in the 1960s). Overall, it signalled the reinvention of a crucial element of the *classes moyennes*.

The middle classes acted as a social leaven in post-war France. They recruited both internally and from the children of small farmers and to a lesser extent industrial workers. Professional qualifications regulated entry to private and public bureaucracies and this favoured subaltern social groups and also women, who from the 1960s increasingly entered the labour force. Access to secondary and higher education was the condition of this mobility, which is why the apparent overproduction of graduates in poor conditions caused an explosion of student protest in May 1968. Subsequent university reforms and the creation of a mass secondary school system nonetheless ensured that the *classes moyennes* continued to be a pivot of society. Yet this did little to reduce the concentration of non-salaried wealth in the upper bourgeoisie. Income from this source (property, shares, dividends), which grew dramatically in the post-war boom, concerned a small proportion of families. In 1977 the richest 10 per cent of households owned 50 per cent of national wealth. Inherited capital correlated closely with entry to the *grandes écoles*, so that the administrative elite was still recruited largely from the privileged bourgeois.

An exceptional trajectory?

How 'peculiar', or at least distinctive, was the development of French society after 1880 by comparison with that of the country's near neighbours? Precocious low population growth, the stability of peasant farming until the 1950s, the sizeable and heterogeneous *classes moyennes*, a limited but important industrial working class, combined in a pattern of change that probably altered society less radically or swiftly than was the case with mid-nineteenth-century Britain or late nineteenth-century Germany, though if a 'moment' of transformation has to be identified, it is 1945–75. Yet the broad convergence of the three societies by the end of the twentieth century— in terms of demography, productive base, urbanization, and living standards—shows that the French path ultimately resulted in a comparable level of development.

It is right to emphasize the continuities in this process—the adaptability of small businesses and farms, for example, or the relatively high per capita growth rates achieved by French manufacturing for much of the period. Simplistic judgements on French 'backwardness', commonplace during the 1950s but going back to the emergence of industrial modernizers during the First World War, were symptoms of frustration at resistance to change more than accurate portrayals of reality. Yet the opposite judgement, that there were few blockages or handicaps to the French path, is no truer. Small farms and small businesses, in retail and production, did not always favour development. The logic of subsistence or family preservation frequently limited mechanization, the division of labour, and fuller engagement in the market, with conservative effects on economic growth and social evolution. This was shown both by the depth of the 1930s depression and the resistance to change in the 1950s and early 1960s. The French path may have been gradual but it was not smooth, as indicated by successive waves of workers' unrest (1906, 1917–20, 1936, 1947–8, 1968) and violent protest by other groups.

Equally, French industry, farming, and retailing had large-scale units from the 1880s and these increased in number and size, if less so than elsewhere. Renault, Michelin, Saint-Gobain, and others were European giants, and much of the dynamism of French economic growth came from such production. Moreover, if it can be argued that small businesses and farms cushioned the shocks of industrialization (limiting mass unemployment in the 1930s, for example), it might also be argued that more dynamic population growth down to the Second World War or fuller industrialization earlier would have produced a more populous or prosperous country. Though unprovable, such counterfactual suggestions serve to nuance judgements.

There was, then, a particularly French process of social transformation that occurred when post-revolutionary society met the challenge of accelerated industrialization from the 1890s in ways that involved radical shifts as well as seamless adaptation. Above all, it required new languages of social representation that seemed at times to threaten the very sense of what it meant to be French. Perhaps it was this drama of contested social identity that was really distinctive. The type of society France should be was the underlying question posed by the political antagonisms of Boulangism and the Dreyfus Affair. Various answers emerged over the following century, ranging from technocratic modernism to the Marxist reductionism that saw France polarized between opposed industrial classes. But balanced progress, with individuality and inventiveness prised above conformity and imitation, and underpinned by property ownership, constituted the ideal for many. Not surprisingly, stagnation in the 1930s and intense change after 1945 brought doubt over whether this ideal was compatible with economic modernity and fed complex feelings towards America, which operated as both a model and a warning for the future. One of the most acute socialist observers of the post-war scene, André Philip, saw socialism's role as the recreation of the sense of community that was disappearing with the advent of 'mass society' (*Le Socialisme trahi*, 1957). Even such an apologist of the *trente glorieuses* as Jean Fourastié felt nostalgia for the world he had lost: 'The adolescents, the women of my youth still sang along the way as they went to and from their hard [rural] labour' (*Les Trente Glorieuses* (1979), 28).

The state and politics were integral to the resolution of this conflict of identity. By the way it constructed the census or defined naturalization, the state influenced the very terms by which society represented itself. Politics provided a medium for the expression of social values and economic interests, though it cannot be reduced to these. The crucial issue is how a modernizing republicanism from the 1880s, whose project was defined above all in political terms (citizenship, the nation), understood social change. Although a pessimist might judge that the Third Republic failed to meet the challenges posed by an industrial working class, recent scholarship has emphasized that a kind of social modernism did emerge, though one reflecting moderate republican views. While the standard welfare provision (old-age pensions, sickness and unemployment insurance) by which the British and German states addressed the insecurity and poverty of industrial workers was not introduced until after 1945 in France (and the late 1950s in the case of unemployment), France pioneered welfare provision for the family. Considerable emphasis was placed on voluntary action—whether the flourishing friendly society movement (*mutualisme*) by which many insured themselves, or the initiatives of reforming municipalities. In the latter case, attempts were made to deal with the interwar housing crisis in socialist and communist-controlled suburbs in Paris and Lyon (e.g. Henri Sellier's garden city at Suresnes, in Paris, or the 'skyscrapers' of Villeurbanne, in Lyon). The 1937 World Fair in Paris celebrated the social reforms of republican France.

Yet the fate of the Popular Front shows how the parliamentary system turned a social consensus by much of the peasantry, *classes moyennes*, and social elites into resistance against reform advanced on behalf of the 'working class'. Parliament continued to supply a framework of opposition to change by elements of the same groups during the Fourth Republic. It was the conversion of the state bureaucracy to the cause of economic growth under the shock of the Second World War that began to furnish a new language—and consensus—for social change after 1945. Only with the advent of the Fifth Republic in 1958, however, under first Gaullist and later socialist hegemony, did the political system begin to catch up with the transformation of French society.

6

Women: distant vistas, changed lives

Siân Reynolds

If one of the indexes of modernization is an increase in women's rights, France has seen remarkable moves in this direction since the *belle époque*, when the formal rights of women—whatever their unofficial power and weight in society—were extremely restricted. There are several possible ways to approach this history. A list of key dates would have all the virtues of clarity, charting every barrier broken down, every 'first' achievement such as Marie Curie's becoming the first woman professor at the Sorbonne in 1906, and every anti-discriminatory law, as so many milestones on the road towards women's emancipation. In this perspective, French women would not have so very different a history from women in comparable European countries: the milestones would not be identical, but the outline would still be recognizable.

A variant on this narrative would instead lay the emphasis on discrimination, on the obstacles in the path of emancipation—and in this version, the Frenchness of France might have a higher profile. The long-standing presence of the Catholic Church, the Napoleonic Code Civil of 1804, which placed restrictions on the rights of the married woman until well into the twentieth century, and the Third Republic's prolonged resistance to women's suffrage before 1944, have all been the centrepieces of accounts of the battle of the sexes in France. If the first kind of narrative would view the story of women's rights as a worldwide long march, the second would chart a particular French variant of misogyny or anti-feminism.

Both approaches can be defended and illustrated. But they tend to isolate 'the woman question'. This chapter aims instead to contextual-ize French women's changing status, by dividing the overall period since 1880 into three sections and relating power relations between the sexes to events affecting French society as a whole. From 1880 until the First World War, it will argue, women's rights were not a particular priority, and organized feminism was in its infancy. Yet economic and social changes gradually affecting the whole of France had the effect of starting a steady but irreversible alteration in the position of women. The second period—the long stretch from the end of the First World War until about the mid-1960s—saw France go through a series of dramatic political and economic upheavals: first the economic depression and the rise of communism and fascism in the 1930s, then the Second World War, followed by the so-called *trente glorieuses* which changed France from a largely rural to an industrial-ized society. Women's rights were now often in the forefront of impassioned debate, but powerful contradictory pressures, political and social, could send apparent changes into reverse. Finally, during the third period, from the mid-1960s to the present day, a new explicit awareness and self-awareness of women as full participants in French society (*des citoyennes à part entière*) has been part of a seismic shift of consciousness in a modernized, partly post-industrial French soci-ety. The argument is intended to open rather than close debate about *l'exception française* in this context.

A precautionary note: inevitably in a survey of societal change, one tends to concentrate on the generation most active at any given time: the age group of say 20 to 50. But in every period there were overlap-ping generations of women with very different experience of what it was like to be female: bicycle-riding girls in 1900 could hold conversa-tions with their grandmothers who might have been born not long after the death of Napoleon (1821).

1880–1914: peasants into Frenchwomen?

In 1896, a young bride broke with tradition in a parish in the Beauce, by refusing to accept the distaff offered to her on her wedding day. Eugen Weber used this as an illustration of change in the countryside in his seminal book *Peasants into Frenchmen*, a study in which the emphasis is firmly on men, but where women are not entirely neglected. In nineteenth-century France, most people still lived in the countryside or in small rural communities. In the 1881 census, 36.8 per cent of all economically active women in France were in small family farms. Put simply, Weber's argument was that the years between 1870 and 1914 formed a key period in the modernization of rural France, creating a new sense of national identity. As agencies of change, he singled out education, individual mobility (through modern transport), the decline of religious observance, and national military service. The fourth of these did not apply to women, and Weber's overall thesis has been contested in some respects. But it may be instructive to see how the factors he identified relate to women.

To begin with education, the Jules Ferry education laws (1879–82) were in part designed to remove primary education from control by the Church. They ushered in what Robert Tombs has called a 'struggle for the soul of France and its votes'. Only male souls could vote of course, but for the first time every village had to provide obligatory, free, and secular primary school education for both boys and girls. Their education was not identical—girls had a dose of domestic arts—but all children aged 6 to 13 learnt to write correct French, to do elementary calculations, and had the principles of hygiene and patriotic republicanism dinned into them. State schools needed trained teachers, for whom special colleges (*écoles normales*) were extended or created. All this was potentially of more importance to girls than to boys (who were more likely to be attending school already). The biggest change of all was the number of state-trained women primary teachers (*institutrices*). Whereas there had been only a handful of training colleges for women before 1870, by 1887 there were 81, compared to 90 for men. Within a period of about two generations of schoolchildren, girls as well as boys were acquiring the *certificat d'études*, changing the sexual geography of illiteracy for ever. At the same time, a new avenue of social and intellectual promotion opened up for women of comparatively humble background. The logic of 'who shall teach the teachers' led to the hierarchical creation of all-girl *lycées* and higher normal schools, making the emergence of the female intellectual a real possibility in time: the generation of Simone de Beauvoir (b. 1908) and Simone Weil (b. 1909), both of whom trained as secondary school teachers in the 1920s, revealed this development most strikingly.

Creating well-educated women philosophers was not top of the reformers' agenda. Ferry himself made it clear that by opening republican education to girls, he had the more political aim of preventing the Catholic Church from winning their souls and turning them into enemies of the Republic inside the home. As a journalist attending prize-giving at a girls' state school in the 1880s remarked: 'How clear it is that the young girls whom Madame H. is preparing for the struggle of life will one day be valiant citizens (*de vaillantes citoyennes*) who will be able to bring up their children in respect for justice and hatred of prejudice.' It would be some time before sexual dimorphism within education entirely vanished. Many girls, especially in the countryside or from bourgeois homes, continued to be sent to private Catholic schools, while their brothers were more readily sent to the 'godless' state sector; comparatively few girls went to state *lycées* at first. But this particular clock would never be put back.

A second factor identified by Weber was increased mobility, geographical and social. The key textbook of republican education, *Le Tour de la France par deux enfants* (1877), was written pseudonymously by a woman, Augustine Fouillée, but the children who travel round France in the story are both boys: to make one of them a girl would probably have caused narrative problems. Young male artisans had traditionally travelled the country (in a ritual also known as the *tour de France*) looking for work. Individual migration and mobility might not seem to apply to women in this period, if we assume that most women left their parents' home only to get married. But young couples were already moving to urban areas, while young women from the country could find positions with bourgeois families in town as domestic servants or wet-nurses: in 1906 about 8 per cent of the entire Parisian population consisted of female domestic servants. If they lived in the industrial belt in north-east France, women could also be recruited to the textile factories. Many urban occupations, such as the garment trade, amounted to sweated labour, to say nothing of the risk of drifting into prostitution, out of poverty. This was not exactly emancipation. Nevertheless leaving the village altered, if it did not necessarily expand, the mental horizon.

For women of the middle and upper classes though, mobility could indeed mean a form of escape. The newly perfected bicycle is often taken as a symbol of emancipation in this period, though only for those young, fit, and well-off enough to ride one! Bicycles made their breakthrough in the 1890s. While for men they quickly became the focus of sporting competition, for women they meant a comparatively safe and unmolested way of getting around town. A Scottish art student in Paris reported in 1897: 'I bike *à l'américaine*, as the nicest French people do: a short skirt, about 4 or 5 inches below the knee and long gaiters which go right to meet the knickerbockers in case of one's skirt blowing up. I always strap mine down.' The railway network had been expanded since the Second Empire, and in 1900 the first line of the Paris Metro was opened, in time for the great Exhibition of that year. Motor cars and aeroplanes were, if not plentiful, at least visible in the 1900s, and several pioneer women aviators even acquired their pilot's licence before the outbreak of war. The end of dependence on the horse freed women even more than it did men. For women in the cities, as cultural historians have noted with much picturesque detail, the big department stores (safe, under cover, anonymous, full of temptation) offered another way to leave home. Recognizing this in his novel on the subject of shopping, Émile Zola changed the name of the real Bon Marché store to 'Au Bonheur des Dames' or Dames' Delight. For the privileged few, international travel was becoming quite possible: foreigners of both sexes flocked to Paris, and the first international associations of women had their earliest meetings around this time.

The third factor, the decline of religious observance, was certainly more observable in town than in country, and in men more than women. This gendered difference should neither be denied nor exaggerated: only some 30 per cent of *all* French people were practising Catholics in 1900. True, older women would mostly have attended Catholic schools before the Ferry laws. But the outlook of the following generation had altered. After the law on associations of 1901, and the separation of Church and state in 1905, the religious vocation was hardly a serious option: it had in the past afforded certain women some quasi-professional independence from male control (in teaching, nursing, and charitable works such as running orphanages). Since society found it hard to function without some substitute for the services of now-abolished or banned religious orders, the professions of lay teachers and nurses, to take the most obvious examples, became established within a state framework. Charitable or welfare-directed activities, still strongly identified with women, were now viewed in a non-religious light. They were laying the foundations of what would eventually become the modern welfare state. This was a long process, continued over many years, but in the end it greatly altered the social landscape. Women had not been socialized by military service as men were, but by 1914, rising generations of girls had been offered a patriotic, secular republican education and increased opportunities for paid work, where once there had only been a voluntary sector. To some extent then, it might be argued that Weber's modernization thesis is as relevant to women as to men.

We should not however exaggerate the degree of change, or underestimate the opposition to it. French society was going through other transformations which initially marginalized women at least as much as in the past, or sought to tie them even more closely into the family. This was the age when the trade unions were flexing their muscles, but women were mainly outside the movement, being only 10 per cent of trade unionists in 1914. Women factory hands often worked in segregated, non-unionized workshops and certainly for less pay than men. Protective legislation of the 1880s and 1890s, part of a wider movement to alter working conditions, was as much to keep women out of the labour market as to protect them. In private life, childbirth remained risky, infant and maternal mortality was high especially among the poor, and contraception was still unscientific and unreliable—although in practice the French birth rate remained low. Tuberculosis and venereal diseases were major killers in urban areas, and 'the family' was seen as the site of health intervention. Hygienists and doctors sought to improve children's health, and deplored mothers going out to work. There was already concern about the French birth rate, although not yet at levels of anxiety reached in later years, and this resulted in the early legislation on maternity leaves and child welfare. Creches, first introduced in France, were seen initially as last-resort protection for children's health. Pioneering contraceptive propaganda however was frowned on.

One arena where comparatively little changed before the First World War was political life. In this France differed from Britain or the United States, where women were quite energetically engaged in civic responsibilities and pressure group politics by the late nineteenth century, and where early feminist movements had sporadic but often spectacular support. Comparable movements were not entirely lacking in France, but the taboo on allowing women into most of the Republic's political structures, even at local level, meant

they were either diverted into philanthropic channels, or that feminists were fairly isolated (like Hubertine Auclert, who campaigned for
the vote from within the early socialist movement). The history of
French feminism has plenty to report on, if we go by conferences and
campaigns, or articles published in feminist periodicals, and it was
undoubtedly building up steam in the 1900s, culminating in the
unfortunately timed demonstration of July 1914. One should neither
exaggerate nor underestimate the feminist movement: vociferous and
in some cases well connected, it was not yet very widespread. There
was a basic cadre of committed and articulate individuals, but at this
stage comparatively little grass-roots support, especially outside Paris.

On the other hand, some women were being drawn into national
politics, if only indirectly. There was much overlap between feminism
and support for the Dreyfusard cause. Both were chiefly urban phenomena, associated with liberal-progressive political milieux. The
early feminists in France came, like the Dreyfusist militants, in disproportionate numbers from Protestant, Jewish, and freethinking
families, sometimes the same ones. It is surely no coincidence that the
Conseil National des Femmes Françaises—which saw its function
largely as a coordinating one for moderate reform and philanthropy,
and in which Protestant women were prominent—was founded in
1901, just after the end of the Dreyfus Affair. On the other side of the
political (and religious) divide, the Ligue Patriotique des Françaises
was founded in the wake of the nationalist *ligues* in the same year, and
long remained the largest women's organization in France.

Did *belle époque* France therefore see the rise of the 'New Woman',
in the sense that the term was used in Anglo-American society after
its launch by Ouida in 1894? The women who attended feminist meetings might be 'New Women', but the label is perhaps misleading.
Were the journalist Séverine (1855–1929), the sculptor Camille Claudel (1864–1939), or Marguerite Durand (1864–1936), founder of the
all-women newpaper *La Fronde* (1897–1905), 'New Women'? They
were all certainly determined women, of unprecedented initiative, yet
the term was never in widespread use in France: it was a foreign
import (like the bicycle, but less successful), and viewed with some
suspicion. Paris in 1900 was full of adventurous young artists and
intellectuals of both sexes, but it was more of a host to a series of
foreign bodies, American, British, German, Russian, than a melting
pot. The women art students in Montparnasse were probably less

integrated into French life than coal miners from Poland were in French mining villages. If one analyses the life histories of those Frenchwomen of forward-looking views who joined the committees of the Musée Social, *the* reforming think-tank of the age, one finds that they correspond more closely to the philanthropic model than to that of the New Woman, whether Bohemian or suffragette.

To hazard some generalizations about this period then, it produced measurable change in the status and experience of French women, in the shape of increased literacy for girls, more mobility, and some expansion of paid employment for women. This age began to raise the consciousness of women, rather as the eighteenth-century Enlightenment had for educated men in the eighteenth century: it brought a shift in mentalities and horizons, both at elite level (the international artistic avant-garde), and for ordinary girls who left school armed with the *certificat d'études*. The *belle époque* was however more in the nature of a slow burn than a revolution. Few girls yet had enough education or experience to challenge a patriarchal society. And the force of the clerical question in the wake of the Dreyfus Affair made the Republic extremely unlikely to consider extending political rights to women. While Dreyfusard feminists were staunchly republican, not many male republicans were sympathetic to feminism, a contradiction which was to bedevil the question of women's suffrage for a long time. But feminism and women's rights were words people recognized even if they didn't all like them, and the sight of young ladies on bicycles did not lead to riots in the street, only to mild clucks of disapproval. Marcel Proust (b. 1871) has his narrator express nostalgia for Odette de Crécy, the ageing *demi-mondaine* in her victoria in the Bois de Boulogne, while he finds slightly scary the sight of the teenage Albertine wheeling her bike along the prom at Balbec. Compared with what came afterwards, this was a period of gradual change. But that change was irreversible.

1914–1964: one step forward, two steps back—dramatic but reversible changes

It is against this background that we should read the more dramatic transformations that took place during the First World War. The integration of more women into paid work in peacetime, in the years before 1914, meant that they could be drafted to replace men, in ways that would have been quite out of the question only forty or so years earlier, during the Franco-Prussian war. As regular nurses near the front, they witnessed appalling sights and had charge of large numbers of wounded and disoriented men. As more men joined up, young women were recruited into munitions factories, or to act as street-car conductors and ticketing clerks. They replaced men as schoolteachers and in office jobs. If the bicycle had made mobility easier, and the sewing-machine had been a two-edged weapon, tying women more firmly to low-paid garment trades, the typewriter offered them so-called white-collar jobs. By 1914, nine out of twelve government ministries *already* had a female typing pool. Looking back on it now, we might reflect that this locked women into yet another subordinate profession, in France as elsewhere. At the time though, it was seen as social promotion for the daughters of farmers and workmen, providing them with a modest living wage.

It might seem as if women's emancipation was set on a progressive course. In retrospect however, the following fifty years look like a sort of roller-coaster ride for gender relations. Expectations had unquestionably been raised during the war about the future role of women. But there were also fears and misgivings about that future. The pendulum swung back and forth as women became more (or less) active, men more (or less) anxious. War factories closed down swiftly after 1918, giving female workers very little redundancy pay; men took back many of their former jobs. On the other hand, the French National Assembly expressed itself in favour of women's suffrage in May 1919, doing the same as its German, British, and American equivalents. But confirmation of that decision was repeatedly blocked both by the Senate and later parliaments, until after the Second World War. The 1919 resolution had come from an outgoing wartime parliament, soon to be replaced by the right-wing Chambre Bleu Horizon, containing many ex-soldiers. The new Chamber was unsympathetic to women's rights and particularly alarmed about France's demographic profile: it introduced stricter penalties for abortion and forbade contraceptive propaganda altogether (1920, 1923). That particular anxiety, fuelled by the loss of life during the war, continued throughout the interwar period, leading to the set of measures known as the Code de la Famille (Family Code) in 1939, which contained incentives for larger families and strengthened the 1920s laws. Since most French people continued to have small families until after the Second World War, the measures tell us more about elite anxiety than about people's actual behaviour. But they are indicative of the climate at a time when the French electorate was particularly 'patriarchal': all-male and older than at any time before or since.

Going by outward appearances though, many taboos were being broken in the 1920s, as the lifestyle of the younger generation was spectacularly redesigned. Young women bobbed their hair and wore shorter skirts. This was not confined to Paris or even big cities, but swept the country. Christine Bard, in her book on *les garçonnes*, as 'flappers' were known in France, shows a photograph of her grandmother, a shop assistant, standing in a working-class street in northern France in 1926 with a perky shingle cut, knee-length pleated skirt, and strappy shoes—she hid the haircut from her father for six months by wearing a wig. But as Mary Louise Roberts observes, 'to look emancipated was not to be emancipated'. She argues that the aim of the fashions was to 'scandalize and infuriate', and detects in the early years after the war a latent fear and anger in men faced by women's potential freedom.

If we look below the surface, to examine what was happening in the economy, we find another complex picture. In the interwar period, the women who had colonized white-collar office jobs might stay *in situ*—but did not advance much. Men were appointed to senior posts, while the expansion of low-grade occupations mopped up the qualified women. They had jobs, which was something new, but not 'careers', a still all-male concept. Secondary education for girls did improve, and some women acquired advanced paper qualifications to become lawyers, doctors, and even university professors (five in 1934)—if only in tiny numbers. These pioneers were more important symbolically perhaps than in changing anything within their professions. They often had a hard time, as pioneers do, but they showed that it was possible to breach the male monopoly.

For large numbers of women in this period though, especially after marriage, the census does not record any continuous employment. Apart from those who remained as family partners in the small farms and shops which still provided the bedrock of the French economy, most women were only sporadically employed: in new light industries (food manufacture), as casual staff in service trades, and in various forms of the 'unofficial economy', which still included domestic labour. The census is thus only of partial help in providing a picture of women's employment, which was often irregular and discontinuous. When the depression hit France in the early 1930s, women also became the unofficial unemployed, since they did not usually qualify for the dole, payable to the male head of household. Catherine Rhein's interviews with women who were young during the depression reports that it affected them less dramatically than men.

[Women] were already familiar with seasonal lay-offs, economic fluctuations, being hired and fired at short notice. Despite the rising tide of unemployment among women, reaching its peak in the late 1930s, the crisis did not take them by surprise . . . they had always had a precarious status.

Men and women were clearly still not in the same labour market, as was revealed in the 1936 strike wave, which involved disproportionate numbers of women as non-unionized labour in light industry, department stores, and catering. In fact, French men and women remained very largely in segregated social groups until as late as the 1960s or so. Schools were mostly single sex until the 1970s, though girls could now take the same baccalauréat as boys; and occupations were largely gender recruited. The major institutions of society—the Church, the army, the diplomatic and higher civil service, the trade unions, politics—remained virtually all male, while health care, social work, primary education, and the lower civil service were largely female; trade union branches and youth movements were generally segregated by sex. This could be a source both of strength and weakness for change in relations between the sexes. It meant that when they did meet it was easy for stereotypes to persist, even in avant-garde circles like those of surrealism or existentialism, which would seem extraordinarily sexist to a young woman today. On the other hand younger generations of women could develop greater confidence without reference to men, in *lycées* and youth movements for instance.

The jerky character of change was exacerbated by the political context. Politics in the 1920s was affected by the financial and moral fallout of the Great War: politics in the 1930s was largely devoted to trying to avert another war. Women, as disenfranchised citizens, have been deemed outside politics by many historians of the period. In fact, the interwar period was a time when more women were *more* politically active than before (or for many years after), across the political spectrum. The causes which mobilized them most in the 1930s were pacifism, which sometimes mutated to anti-fascism, and various forms of feminism, not all connected with the vote. Peace organizations in France, only fairly recently studied in any depth since they were retrospectively if indirectly blamed for the defeat in 1940, were among the biggest pressure groups of the age and there is ample evidence of both mixed and all-women peace groups. On the feminist front, the intermittent struggle for suffrage, though never mobilizing really large numbers, was a sporadic spur to activity. As Paul Smith points out, the question of women's suffrage was hardly ever *off* the agenda in France between the wars. From Christine Bard's encyclopedic work, we know that feminism took many forms during this period—from radical lesbianism to patiently negotiating modest improvements in the rights of married women (1938). From the Maitron dictionary, we know that a younger generation of women was drawn into trade union or radical politics during the Popular Front, or to supporting the republican cause in the Spanish Civil War; and we are starting to discover that they were also to be found on the right and extreme right. The different models of politics could vary from the communist party's initial attempt to ignore gender by building a 'sexless' workers' party, to the more general model of special branches for women. During the Popular Front in 1936, as noted, many women went on strike for the first time in their lives. Léon Blum appointed three women ministers, a surprisingly well-received move, given the difficulty of obtaining women's suffrage. Significantly, two of them were in the area of child welfare and social work, a domain steadily co-opting women to posts of responsibility in this hygiene-conscious age. An 'alternative politics' of women's associations of all kinds, charitable, political, cultural, could be said to have taken root.

The Second World War however brought apparent reversal of the story so far. Alongside some continuities in family law—the Code de la Famille foreshadowed Vichy's policies on the family—the Vichy regime (1940–4) seemed emphatically to reverse progress towards emancipation, at least in its discourse. Gender differentiation lay at the heart of Pétain's regime, which viewed feminism as an alien force.

In a 'return to the Dark Ages', Vichy dumbed down the curriculum in girls' schools: one authoritative spokesman for the regime affirmed: 'We should think twice about educating girls. . . . A girl should be the exact double of her mother, at home and in the family.' Discriminatory laws, enacted simultaneously with those against Jews, theoretically banned married women from state employment such as schoolteaching, and the regime launched a barrage of propaganda about family values. In practice, with so many men in prison camps, many women had to carry on working, some even being recruited for forced labour in Germany. Civilians had to choose whether to collaborate with the occupiers, to accept Vichy, or to resist more or less actively. Women's wartime experience was as varied as that of men, and equally burdened with choices for which they could be held politically responsible after the war, whether as Vichyite social workers, resisters, or collaborators. Consorting with German soldiers for example was seen as national betrayal and punished by public humiliation at the Liberation.

With the trauma of war and occupation over, it might be thought that the Liberation would see a fresh start. But the age of paradoxes was not over. One momentous decision was that all women were enfranchised and enabled to stand for election by the decree of 21 April 1944, a measure passed by the (virtually all-male) consultative assembly, advising de Gaulle's provisional government in Algiers. This important change was not necessarily a major preoccupation for those who enacted it: they were chiefly concerned with restoring some form of democratic government in France to prevent the allies taking over from the Germans. The measure was justified in official discourse by the role women had played in the resistance, and was backed for various reasons by both Gaullists and communists; the anticlerical radicals who most opposed it were in a minority. It was received matter-of-factly by the French population, without either protest or jubilation. To women at the time, 'it just seemed obvious', as Lucie Aubrac and others put it.

So the final achievement of universal suffrage in France, a hundred years after male suffrage, occurred in a slightly anticlimactic fashion. Christine Bard describes pre-war feminism as having run out of steam, in a premature 'strange defeat'. When it came, the pioneer generation of feminists was not around to see it, while younger women, having survived some turbulent years, were not initially drawn into politics, many of them starting families in the post-war baby-boom. The birth rate now rose to 21.3 per thousand, unprecedented in the twentieth century, with live births reaching their all-time peak in 1964. The years from 1945 till the mid-1960s have been described by Clare Duchen as feminism's 'Bermuda triangle', while Charles Sowerwine sees women as 'accepting the ideal of home and motherhood they had rejected in the 1920s'.

Looked at in context, the pause in pressing on with unfinished business is not so hard to understand: as historians we need not necessarily indulge in retrospective finger-wagging. Generation has a great deal to do with it. Young men and women in 1945 had been deprived of a normal youth, but were still able to rescue their private lives, as many autobiographies testify. What is more, the landscape in which they found themselves was very different from that of the 1920s. The rural exodus saw many young French people move to better living conditions in town, but maintaining a household with young children in it still entailed a great deal of domestic labour. The economic miracle of 1945–75, retrospectively baptized *les trente glorieuses*, was primarily an industrial boom, arising out of the Monnet and Marshall Plans which foregrounded heavy industry, gave jobs to all able-bodied men, and drew in thousands of male immigrant workers. It did not primarily affect the sectors where most women might have been employed—nor did it immediately provide such helpful consumer goods as washing machines.

The baby-boom therefore reflected at least in part a certain optimism about industrial *male* employment, recreating faith in the traditional family economy. Add to that a dash of the kind of idyllic domesticity that appeared in a hundred popular American films which played to the cinema-loving generation of the 1940s. The washing machine was round the corner, or rather as Kristin Ross puts it, the 1950s was the decade when the dream society consisted of 'fast cars, clean bodies'. Arguably the middle years of the twentieth century, from the 1920s to the 1960s, were not so much a time when 'nothing happened' in terms of women's status, as when 'too much happened' to be readily combined with radically rethinking gender relations. And the woman question was, after all, deemed to have been settled in 1944 by the vote.

Accordingly, when Simone de Beauvoir published *The Second Sex* in 1949, it was at first greeted with incomprehension and boredom.

With hindsight, we can now see that this key book is rooted in the difficult and contradictory anthropology of relations between the sexes in France that had emerged in Beauvoir's lifetime (b. 1908). She was retrospectively providing a theory of patriarchy that the first generation of feminists, operating with limited education and experience, had not been in a position to formulate, and which many of her contemporaries, in war and peace, had been first too harassed and then too relieved to contemplate.

c.1964–2000s: Beauvoir's adopted daughters? Change dramatic and irreversible

Simone de Beauvoir herself was surprised by the later developments of French feminism. For her peer group in the post-war years, the issues were left and right, communism and anti-colonialism, and despite her having formulated a particular feminist theory at the age of 40 ('One is not born but rather becomes a woman'), it is arguable that she did not identify with feminism in practice until later in life. Her own trajectory as a freelance intellectual, rejecting marriage or children, seemed enviable, indeed heroic to later readers. But it was out of step with most of her contemporaries in the 1940s and 1950s, who were married and did have children.

It is the historically unprecedented concern with *reconciling* reproduction, education, and employment which makes this third period of French history the time when things changed most radically. The 1960s witnessed a further serious decline in churchgoing, which cannot be unconnected with several changes in the reproductive economy: the arrival of the contraceptive pill, followed by decline in the overall number of births, in family size, in rates of marriage, and a rise in the age at which women had their first child. This period would also see the large-scale move of women, whether married, or mothers, or not, into the full-time labour market, as the tertiary sector expanded. Lastly, it saw an explicit rise in feminist consciousness among the many *lycée*-educated women who had at least a secondary education behind them, and who challenged many of the legal, social, and cultural forms of sexism they now detected in French society.

One of the root causes of the 1968 cultural revolution—when effervescence in the universities spilled out on to the streets, launching a strike wave and political crisis that brought France to a standstill and jolted the consciousness of a generation—was the changing nature of higher education. Baby-boomers of both sexes had great expectations of education, and in days of full employment expected to find jobs. By the 1960s, they were flooding (comparatively speaking) into universities previously frequented by a mostly male bourgeois elite. The events of 1968 themselves contained relatively few signs of gender-based protest, being massively male dominated and directed mainly by the young against the old—but when fuses blow, other wires may get crossed.

It was the generation of women young (or youngish!) in 1968 that started the French women's liberation movement known as the MLF (Mouvement de Libération des Femmes) shortly afterwards. This might not have taken the philosophically charged form that it did in France if a number of women intellectuals had not already been drawn into the critical analysis of French society, during the Algerian and Vietnam wars, and again in 1968. On the other hand, if the MLF had confined itself to the debates about sexual equality and difference which have raged in intellectual circles ever since, it would not have touched such a nerve in society. The greater sexual freedom of the later 1960s removed inhibitions about mentioning sex-related problems. For a few years in the 1970s, women of all ages and social classes actively joined campaigns on issues relating to sex and reproduction which had long been a source of muted controversy. Family-planning clinics, run by an earlier generation of women's rights activists, had had only semi-legal existence in France. De Gaulle's government had belatedly been obliged, under pressure from the left, to introduce the Neuwirth law in 1967, recognizing the existence of the new contraceptive pill and rolling back some of the 1920s legislation. Next the laws on abortion were challenged, starting in 1971 when 343 women signed a manifesto claiming to have undergone illegal abortions; a spectacular defence campaign was mounted during an abortion trial at the Paris suburb of Bobigny. The incoming administration of President Valéry Giscard d'Estaing in 1974 responded by passing legislation to legalize abortion. Piloted by the new health minister, Simone Veil, the bill allowing IVG (Interruption Volontaire de Grossesse) was a temporary five-year measure, which owed its passage to opposition support. Further demonstrations were later held before it became permanent in 1980.

It is perhaps hazardous to connect too closely the downturn in France's demographic profile and the revolutionary influx of women to the full-time labour market, but modern birth control meant that women could choose more freely when, or whether, they had a first child. The birth rate began to drop in 1964, then more steeply in the mid-1970s. (Latest statistics suggest that the rate for *completed* families will not lag so far behind that of the earlier generation: but their parents will be older, with many first-time mothers being over 30.) The gender balance of the full-time labour force also shifted decisively from the 1970s on—despite (and/or because of) the oil crisis and its impact on the French economy and employment. The crisis years saw the expansion of the tertiary or service sector, plus new industries like electronics, which employed women, and the decline of overwhelmingly male heavy industries, such as coal and steel. The tertiary sector included both well-paid professions (teaching, medicine, etc.) and also very low-paid unqualified work (catering), and women were found at all levels, though still with a tendency to be in lower-paid or unpromoted jobs. This pattern was observable in other countries too, such as Britain. What was different about France was that the majority of women now worked full-time, rather than part-time, even after having children. This may in turn be partly explained by the very full provision of childcare in France, from creches to *colonies de vacances*, put in place essentially by a pronatalist state, not to encourage women to work, but to persuade them to have larger families despite working. (French men are still reported to contribute rather little to housework and childcare.) But if access to full-time regular employment, with equal pay for equal work, and a good system of childcare, is an index of progress, then the *trente glorieuses* for French women could be said to have occurred roughly from the mid-1960s to the 1990s, rather than earlier, and to have been relatively independent of the economic crisis.

The change in biographical experience this would bring can be strikingly illustrated by the pension profiles of three generations of women, based on real individuals, as reported in a recent survey (*Données sociales* (1999), 429). In some ways they are representative of our three artificially categorized periods. Madame A, born in 1915, was never employed. Married very young in the 1930s, she brought up four children. On reaching 65 in 1980, she was entitled only to the state minimum pension in her own right. Her eldest daughter, Madame B, was born in 1932. She worked between the ages of 18 and 20, then married and stopped work until she was 37 in 1969, having had three children. Thereafter she worked full-time until the age of 65, in 1987. Her state pension (including six years' worth of contributions for having had children) was 38 per cent less than that of her husband but well above the minimum. Her own daughter, Madame C, born in 1954, remained in full-time education until the age of 23 (that would make it baccalauréat + five years), and could expect statistically to put in 37 years of full-time employment, with generous maternity leave for having children, stopping at age 60 in 2014. Her pension will still be less than that of her husband, but twice her mother's and three times that of her grandmother.

Changes took place in the political arena too. The Giscard administration was the first which really had to respond to pressure from the MLF to alter the law. Other 1970s reforms included liberalization on divorce and contraception, regarded as overdue since the Catholic-influenced 'moral order' of the early Fifth Republic had been unsympathetic to moves on these matters. Giscard also innovated at government level, not only by appointing Simone Veil, an outsider who became a popular career politician, but by creating a junior ministry 'for the condition of women'. Like Blum's ministers, this post, first held by the journalist Françoise Giroud, had more symbolic than practical importance. But when François Mitterrand became president in 1981, he kept his promise to create a more solidly based ministry 'of the Rights of Woman' (in the singular, which did not please everyone), and appointed the active feminist politician Yvette Roudy. Ironically, by this time the MLF was no longer a mass-based movement. What did happen, thanks to Roudy's commitment, was a series of well-publicized measures during the first legislature, 1981–6, relating to employment, health, reimbursement of abortion, family law, and so on, that effectively removed most of the remaining discriminatory legislation against women. The ministry was well regarded abroad as a pioneering influence on other countries. It never entirely regained the high profile it had during these years, being only intermittently revived by successive governments of right and left thereafter. The 1990s did, however, see further legislation in the area of sexual politics: not only a law on sexual harassment, but also, in 1999 an innovative measure, reflecting change in society, which allows 'cohabiting couples, whatever their sex' to register a civil union or PACS (*pacte civil de solidarité*). Most PACS unions to date have been of same-sex couples.

The creation of the ministry of women's rights had fitted into a wider policy developed in France only after de Gaulle (but using a mechanism of his constitution) of promoting non-elected women to ministerial office, despite their low representation in the National Assembly. High-profile ministers were sometimes outsiders in politics, at least in their early days. This initiative was two-edged—it provided prominent role models for women, but at the same time their promotion was interpreted as the result of patronage, however competent they might be. This process was dramatically illustrated by the appointment of France's first woman prime minister, Édith Cresson, by Mitterrand in 1991. Lacking the support of the socialist party, she was viewed (as indeed some male premiers have been), as the president's poodle. Her tenure, not helped by some mistakes of her own making, was to some extent 'booby-trapped' from the start and proved to be a false dawn.

This unsatisfactory attempt to promote women from above may have been a factor in the development of the novel campaign for political 'parity' launched in France shortly afterwards. This sought to ensure that women were equally represented in the elective assemblies of the Republic. Originating in a proposal from the former socialist politician Françoise Gaspard and others, it was launched with a manifesto in the press in November 1993, signed by 577 people, the same number as there are deputies in the National Assembly. Unlike that body, where the proportion of women has never risen above 12 per cent, the manifesto was signed by equal numbers of men and women, chiefly intellectuals, artists, and politicians. The campaign for 50:50 representation was viewed as utopian by many, and was challenged by others, including some feminists, as contrary to the republican principle of equality of opportunity. Critics argued that if the group 'women' was written into the constitution, ethnic or regional minorities might claim similar rights, leading to what in French is described as *communautarisme*, the fractioning of the national body into separate communities. Despite this opposition, the campaign made surprising progress in the late 1990s, partly as a result of comparisons within Europe. In June 1999, under the presidency of Jacques Chirac and the premiership of Lionel Jospin, both of whom supported some form of change, the Senate and National Assembly meeting together at Versailles amended the constitution to guarantee 'equal access' for citizens of both sexes to elective office. The word 'parity' was not employed. When the first steps were taken towards implementing the change, in the spring of 2000, the National Assembly went further than expected in insisting that where elections were by proportional or list representation (i.e. in European, senatorial, regional, and municipal elections), equal numbers of men and women should be included throughout the lists.

The National Assembly itself, arguably the most important body in the Republic, was however still to be elected by single-member constituency, and still is at the time of writing. Instead, financial incentives were introduced to encourage parties to achieve gender balance there. The first parliamentary elections after the law was introduced were held in June 2002, in the wake of the rather unexpected result of the presidential election, which saw Lionel Jospin eliminated in the first round, and Jacques Chirac re-elected against Jean-Marie Le Pen on the second. Partly as a result of the collapse of the left, the percentage of women elected to the new Assembly moved up only marginally. There were indeed more women candidates overall in the first round (38.8 per cent as against 23 per cent in 1997), but this figure fell to 23 per cent on the second, and finally only 71 women entered the National Assembly (12.3 per cent of the 577 députés, as against 10.9 per cent in 1997). This reflected the lower percentage of women candidates (under 20 per cent) put forward by the winning parliamentary group, the right-of-centre Union pour la Majorité Présidentielle. Women ministers did, however, account for 25 per cent of the first cabinet of the new prime minister, Jean-Pierre Raffarin (10 out of 39).

Finally, as France has moved into the twenty-first century, one can point to two new areas of potentially significant change concerning women which are still evolving. In the creative sphere—literature, fine art, cinema, music, and so on—while French women have certainly been present throughout the whole period under review, their role has often been confined to performance rather than creation (actresses, film stars), or to less highly valued forms of art (pot-boilers). Partly because of the construction of the 'canon', most histories of literature take note of only occasional women writers before

about the 1960s—though they have made up for it since: Marcelle
Marini argues that the real breakthrough came in 1970–90. Virginia
Woolf in *A Room of One's Own* (1929) had remarked that there were
plenty of books *about* women. The novelty of recent years is that far
more women, in France as elsewhere, are visible themselves as creators, writers, theatre directors, film-makers, and so on. To cite one
example from many, one pioneer role-model since the 1970s has been
the inspirational theatre director Ariane Mnouchkine (b. 1934).

The second area concerns women born abroad but resident in
France, particularly in the families of immigrant workers. The early
generations of immigrants were mostly young single men. From the
1970s on, immigration allowed family reconstitution, which meant
that many adult women from former French colonies especially in
north Africa, came to live in France, often without speaking French
or having much education. Cultural factors too have kept this generation of older women to some extent isolated within French society, a thoroughly underestimated silent presence, rarely consulted by
policy makers. Then when young second-generation immigrants
began to make their presence felt within French society, it was
young men rather than young women who were most visible,
whether in political movements, world music, or the cultural field
such as film-making. In various ways this is now changing. Arguably the gender divide within the different immigrant cultures in
France, something still understudied by sociologists, is the area
where one might find both innovation and conflict at the turn of
the new century, prefigured by the 1990s headscarf affair.

Conclusion

This chapter has been addressing two underlying questions. To what
extent has change in the status of women in France been substantial,
irreversible, and positive? And to what extent has change taken a
different course in France from that in comparable countries? This
account suggests that it makes sense to view the latter question in the
context of French history as a whole. On doing so, one finds that
France is partly typical of western Europe, partly distinctive. Changes
in women's status have been great but not complete. The rise in

educational opportunities for girls has been a widespread phenomenon throughout Europe. But in France as elsewhere, numbers tell only a partial story: girls are more likely than boys to study arts and vocational subjects, being under-represented in science, engineering, and business, which are all paths to good careers. And those uniquely French elite institutions, the *grandes écoles*, in particular the ENA (École Nationale d'Administration) have remained rather male dominated down to the present.

In terms of employment, the main distinctive feature about France is that women work full-time, whether or not they have children (although during the 1990s economic crisis there was an increase in women's part-time work). French women still have a higher unemployment rate than men (14 per cent compared to 10 per cent in early 2000), and their average earnings remain 24 per cent less than those of men. The range of jobs they occupy, while expanding, is also much smaller than for men, indicating that the labour market is still somewhat segregated. Some of these features are shared with women in Europe as a whole.

Politically it can be argued that French republicanism carries distinctive ideological baggage which has worked against women in the past. I argued some time ago that the Republic was created not just without women but against them during the French Revolution, and that that model was reinforced during the nineteenth century. The Church was a significant but not the only factor in that rejection, which was also a matter of expediency for Third Republic politicians. One effect was the delay in creating truly universal suffrage. But to 'allow' women to vote in 1945 was like inviting people to play the political game by rules that had been made up without their consent. The same could be said about the appointment of women ministers. It took some time before these flaws in republican universalism were seriously challenged. But it could be argued that, somewhat paradoxically, France's republican universalism itself has made it possible to come up with the concept of 'parity'—despite opposition from some ultra-republican quarters. In other countries, gender balance has been a matter for informal and incremental change. In republican and centralized France, as in so many other respects, once a decision has been taken, across-the-board change is implemented at a stroke. On the other hand, the key elective body, the National Assembly, has yet to be seriously affected by the move towards parity.

It will be interesting to see what difference 'parity' makes: French exceptionalism has not yet spoken its last word.

One last historical conclusion is that when we look at the big picture, change in women's status has had its own rhythms, which are only intermittently linked to the major articulations of French history, and then sometimes in contradictory ways. If we had taken that list of 'key dates for women', they would form a sort of counterpoint with other dates, such as the founding of the Fifth Republic in 1958, which was of course of *significance* to both men and women but made no particular *difference* to women as a group. It has been suggested here somewhat provocatively that over the last hundred years or so, French women have witnessed their own particular versions of the Enlightenment, the Dark Ages, and the *trente glorieuses*, that their historical experience has necessarily been different from that of men, while taking place in a historical context shared with men. Recognition that all history is 'enacted on a field of gender' as Joan Scott puts it, is another way of looking at the figures in the French landscape.

7

Culture and the intellectuals

Robert Tombs

Introduction

However dazzling the transformations of the last century, French cultural life has continued to bear enduring hallmarks. One is the centrality of the state as patron and policeman. Linked to this is the public prominence of intellectuals. Third is a sense of national cultural exceptionalism (if not superiority) though paradoxically this often accompanies a pessimism in the face of perceived threats from inferior yet overwhelming foreign influence. Finally, the concentration of political and cultural life in the capital after the eclipse of courtly Versailles in 1789 has given French intellectual life an unparalleled intensity. Indeed, its history is largely a Parisian story, and, because of the attractions of Paris to outsiders, a cosmopolitan one.

States have always used the arts to glorify their power. In most countries, private patronage and a free market for books, paintings, and music have tended to balance or even replace the state's dominance. But in France, shaken by political conflict since 1789, old and new regimes have sought legitimacy through cultural intervention to influence the masses as well as the elite. Republicans, Bonapartes, Bourbons, and Orleanists manipulated architecture, music, festival, literature, sculpture, and painting as propaganda, and they censored dissidence. After 1870, the democratic Third, Fourth, and Fifth Republics, while conceding greater freedom, never considered culture a private matter. They continued the regalian function of self-glorification, and greatly extended the didactic function of shaping the ideas and values of the 'one and indivisible' nation. Very broadly, these two functions connect respectively with elite or high culture and mass or popular culture. The former was influenced through official institutions: the Institut de France and its five member Academies (above all the Académie Française of forty sword-bearing 'immortals'), higher education institutions (including art school and conservatory), the state-sponsored Salon exhibitions, prestigious state prizes (such as the Prix de Rome for music and art), appointments, and commissions. It has been commonplace to criticize this system of patronage for promoting mediocre 'academic' art and ignoring original talent: this was often true, and probably inevitable. On the other hand, defenders regarded it as a bulwark against commercial vulgarity and foreign contamination. And few people carried criticism to the point of disdaining membership: Émile Zola tried twenty-four times to get into the Academy, Marcel Proust was gasping to be asked, and even the arch-rebel Charles Péguy was making approaches.

The various Republics tried to bridge the gap between the regalian and didactic functions and reach out to the masses. Statues, public museums, design training, murals in public buildings, and great public festivities such as the Universal Expositions of 1889 (for which the Eiffel Tower was built), 1900, and 1937 were all intended to have aesthetic, moral, economic, and political benefits. In the words of a parliamentary report of 1875, the aim was to 'elevate the public spirit, ennoble popular imagination [and] develop . . . love of the beautiful, which no nation can ignore with impunity, whether for the progress of its civilization or for its glory'. The state vastly increased its cultural activity during the twentieth century, and moreover acted directly through its own bureaucracy rather than through autonomous official bodies such as the Academies. The Popular Front government set up a department of leisure and sport in 1936 as part of an all-embracing popular cultural policy. The Vichy regime saw an authoritarian attempt to regenerate national culture. The Fifth Republic—especially under its two dominant presidents, Charles de Gaulle and François Mitterrand—made culture a more conspicuous state activity than at any time since the Bonapartes.

Writers, artists, academics, musicians, publishers, and producers have had to respond to the state, whether to exploit, resist, subvert, or simply avoid it. The Third Republic had a lighter hand than its predecessors. The written word was largely free: prosecution of writers almost ceased, except for insulting the army. Even theatre censorship (though not that of songs and films) was abolished in 1906. Official-dom still posed as defender of cultural rectitude, as when in 1900 an arts administrator tried to prevent the president of the Republic from entering a modern art exhibition with the cry 'Keep out, this dis-honours France!' But they were powerless to silence writers or artists. Indeed official hostility provided invaluable publicity: how better to attract paying customers than to be officially stigmatized as mad, bad, and dangerous to know?

By intervening in cultural life, the state gave the arts and artists a greater political significance than in other countries. Many resisted: *l'art pour l'art* was a familiar slogan. But others relished a platform. So illustrious had their public role been since Montesquieu, Voltaire, and Rousseau that it had affected writers' and artists' conception of their function, and the public's expectations. This was displayed when Victor Hugo died in 1885: he had participated in politics since the 1820s, had also been an innovative and popular dramatist and novelist, and—'alas!' lamented André Gide—was France's greatest modern poet. His funeral and 'Pantheonization' (burial in the Pan-theon, France's temple to her 'Great Men') was the apotheosis of the artist as prophet, and one of the great spectacles in Paris's history.

This role of prophet and preacher not only to France but to the world draws on two fundamental assumptions. First, that French culture uniquely embodies universal intellectual, aesthetic, moral, and historic values, even if there may be disagreement as to precisely which: the Graeco-Roman classical heritage, 'Cartesian' rationalism, clarity, elegance, Catholic spirituality, or the capacity for revolution-ary innovation. Second, that those steeped in it have special insight into human affairs, by superior intelligence or knowledge, or by a sort of moral and spiritual osmosis. Hence they have the right and duty to express these insights not as mere individuals, but as representatives of *l'intelligence française* itself.

This public mission was one that modern French intellectuals were tempted or doomed to take up. Consequently, the ideological mes-sages of art, literature, and philosophy were publicly argued out and labelled: avant-garde or traditional, French or foreign, Catholic or atheist, left or right. Was such public engagement 'a strict duty', as the pioneer sociologist Émile Durkheim asserted, or could it become, in Julien Benda's famous phrase, 'la trahison des clercs', intellectual treason? In either case, the prominence of intellectuals was a major reason for the prestige of French culture in countries where the opinions of the intelligentsia were treated with less reverence.

Despite (or because of?) their aspiration to global leadership there has been a recurring belief among French intellectuals that their culture is threatened by barbarous foreign innovations, at different times German, Jewish, or 'Anglo-Saxon'. These have been associated with intellectual obscurity, linguistic debasement, commercialism, and vulgarity. This cultural pessimism often reflects perceptions of more general decline arising, for example, from a falling birth rate, political instability, economic stagnation, or military defeat. It has been seen as the duty of the state, in alliance with the intellectuals, to protect national culture. From 1901, the Opera was required to produce a quota of French works to keep Wagnerism at bay, and a century later radio and television have comparable quotas against American products. Paradoxically, therefore, assertions of universalism can lead in practice to insularity.

The *belle époque* and the birth of the intellectual, 1890–1914

The *belle époque*, as it was nostalgically called later, saw the beginnings of a familiar cultural world: of an increasingly standardized, even international, mass commercial culture of entertainment; and— in conscious reaction—an avant-garde with a mission to disrupt and shock. The setting was one of economic and technological acceleration. Cities and their suburbs grew, increasing their existing cultural leadership. People had more money and leisure. Traditional thrills like the corpses in the Morgue and (until 1939) public executions were supplemented by waxwork chambers of horrors. There was a vogue for spectacular painted panoramas, especially of battles. Technical innovations created ever more spectacles. Some criticized these as crass, vulgar, and anti-French—'a fairyland of the ugly, the obscene and the grotesque', wrote the novelist Anatole France. Lunapark, established in Paris in 1909, was the first in a long line of 'entirely mechanical' American imports that were lambasted and then adopted.

Newspapers became 'Americanized', dropping their prices, changing their format and content, and adopting illustrations. The Paris papers—over fifty titles—quintupled their daily print-run between 1870 and 1914 to five million. Commentators of right and left denounced the new press as sensationalist and corrupting, to no effect. New publications catered to new readerships: sports enthusiasts, women, children. Serialized stories—*feuilletons*—had long been a leading attraction, and new genres of science and detective fiction had large followings across the conventional mass/elite boundary. They influenced cinema, and later radio and television.

Another foreign novelty—arguably the greatest cultural import from Britain—was sport, promoted from the 1880s as a healthy and moral outlet for the urban masses and a promotor of character and military virtues. Football, rugby, boxing, tennis, athletics, cycling, and rowing were at first amateur and upper-class activities. But the growing demand for entertainment modified them to suit French tastes. Competitive professional cycling became a French speciality. The Tour de France (1903), the first sport popularized by the press, became an instrument of patriotic integration as its cyclists travelled the provincial highways and byways.

Music and dancing, especially in the hundreds of popular *cafés-concerts* such as the still existing Bataclan, and in the bigger, plusher British-influenced *music-halls* such as the Folies Bergères, began to create nationally famous singers and entertainers and a music industry producing thousands of tunes for sale as sheet music and later phonograph records. Henri de Toulouse-Lautrec's 1890s posters of singers such as Aristide Bruant and dancers such as La Goulue captured their raffish glamour. A variation was the Montmartre cabaret, a mixture of working-class bar and intellectual club. The most famous was Le Chat Noir (1881), which provided an unpredictable and sometimes uproarious mixture of food and drink, poetry, theatre and music. These soon became profitable attractions, drawing mainstream critics and writers and foreign tourists, including the prince of Wales; so many performers were lured to big commercial venues in Montmartre such as the Moulin Rouge (1889) and more respectable boulevard music-halls such as the Olympia (1893).

The theatre was still the pre-eminent commercial and fashionable entertainment. Alongside the subsidized state theatres—the Théâtre Français, the Odéon, and the Opéra—was the commercial 'boulevard' theatre, with a diet of gritty dramas about sex, power, and money, such as those of Henry Bernstein, enlivened by comedies on the same subjects, notably those by Georges Feydeau. Leading writers and performers became stars, promoters of fashion as well as art. The biggest star of all, Sarah Bernhardt, combined classical and boulevard theatre and later cinema. In protest against the commercial theatre, which the young novelist Romain Rolland criticized as sex obsessed and 'Jewish', an experimental drama movement started in the late 1880s, asserting serious, non-monetary artistic values. Here it certainly succeeded, losing money with magnificent indifference: even the Odéon ran out of cash under the uncompromising realist director André Antoine. Some productions were provocatively avant-garde (most famously the uproarious production of Alfred Jarry's *Ubu roi* in 1896), but the great successes were achieved with Shakespeare, the French classics, and Ibsen. An artistic sensation of a different kind was the arrival of Diaghilev's Ballets Russes in 1909, which became the main channel of artistic innovation to the mainstream audience. However, the biggest triumphs were patriotic costume dramas, most memorably the young Edmond Rostand's Napoleonic saga *L'Aiglon* (1900) and his *Cyrano de Bergerac* (1897), a celebration in verse of French gallantry, wit, and *panache* that appealed across the boundaries of classical, boulevard, and avant-garde.

Drawing on the theatre, the music-hall, the waxwork, and the newspaper *feuilleton* came cinema, surely the great French innovation of world importance. Invented by the Lumière brothers and first demonstrated in the Grand Café in Paris, it had a shaky start, not least when a projector caused a disastrous fire in 1897. It was consolidated by the theatre director Georges Méliès, who first made films with stories. Early cinema was peripatetic, with travelling projectionists taking mobile screens to halls, barns, and the open air. Success brought rapid investment. Led by Charles Pathé, entrepreneurs opened permanent cinemas, and by 1908 there were 10,000; Léon Gaumont's Paris studios were turning out a film a day.

Paris, then, was a wonderful seedbed for a profusion of cultural blooms. The liberty of the Third Republic, especially in the tolerant atmosphere of its capital, with its training schools, universities, patrons and galleries, relative cheapness, and of course established prestige and glamour, attracted provincial and foreign artists and writers and made it the world's cultural centre from the 1880s to the

Second World War. Despite the traditional rows and riots (most notorious, those for *Ubu roi* and Stravinsky's *Rite of Spring*), it was open to experiment, indeed eager for novelty. It enjoyed an unparalleled range of cultural networks and vectors. At one end of the social spectrum were the Académie Française and the salons of aristocratic ladies; at the other, the cafés of Montmartre and Montparnasse. There were great establishment newspapers and reviews such as the *Revue des deux mondes*; the principal avant-garde organ, the *Revue blanche*; and countless ephemeral newsheets. If there was constant intellectual, ideological, and political strife—duels were frequent—there was nevertheless remarkably fluid interaction. For example the Chat Noir's patrons included not only musicians and writers such as Claude Debussy, Guy de Maupassant, Paul Verlaine, Stéphane Mallarmé, but also leading politicians and France's most senior philosopher, Ernest Renan. The avant-garde composer Eric Satie worked there as a pianist and one of its *chansonniers*, the playwright Maurice Donnay, was later elected to the Académie Française. Similarly, the avant-garde Théâtre de l'Œuvre had the support of established cultural figures such as the novelist Maurice Barrès and the leading critic Jules Lemaître. Though it was a male-dominated world, women were a vital presence as cultural entrepreneurs through their salons, and also as creators. Bernhardt was a global celebrity; the young Colette was one of several best-selling women novelists; painters such as Berthe Morisot and poets such as Anna de Noailles were recognized figures; while in science, the Polish-born Marie Curie (winner of two Nobel prizes) was internationally renowned.

The Dreyfus Affair had superficially no connection with innocent cultural activities. But really it did: its impact was connected with the popular press, with the intense patriotism of urban culture, and with the expansion of the academic profession as universities were modernized. It expressed conflicting conceptions of Frenchness amid social, economic, and cultural changes that gave rise to xenophobia and anti-Semitism. The affair seemed to reveal the existence of 'two Frances', separated by opposing traditions and loyalties: one democratic, secular, progressive, and cosmopolitan; the other authoritarian, Catholic, traditionalist, and nationalist. People were forced to reconsider cherished values and take sides. Would left-wing anti-Semites defend a bourgeois Jew or would they ally with the right? Would patriotic republicans oppose the army? Forcing these issues into the open in 1898 was the novelist Émile Zola's 'J'accuse', a published attack on the right, the army, and the Catholic Church. This individual stand by a leading writer was in the tradition of Voltaire and Hugo. But it precipitated a new phenomenon, the collective mobilization of little-known academics, scientists, artists, and writers. Hundreds signed petitions and joined new organizations: the Dreyfusard Ligue des Droits de l'Homme, or the anti-Dreyfusard Ligue de la Patrie Française (led by the critic Jules Lemaître, the poet François Coppée, and the novelist Maurice Barrès) and the Ligue de l'Action Française, led by the young nationalist philosopher Charles Maurras.

The term *les intellectuels*—which always implied involvement in politics—was popularized by Barrès, who defined them scornfully as people who believe that 'society must be founded on logic'. What motivated the intellectuals in the first, and probably most intense, confrontation in their history? It has been suggested that recent cultural modernization, such as the growth of the press and the universities, had decreased their status while increasing their numbers, and that involvement in the affair was a collective attempt to reassert their influence. As for choice of sides, anti-Dreyfusards broadly represented the cultural 'establishment' and Dreyfusards those outside it. Hence, senior scholars in traditional disciplines such as law and established writers and artists tended to accept the court's verdict and so be anti-Dreyfusard. Newer scientific or quasi-scientific disciplines such as history and sociology were more likely to conclude that Dreyfus's guilt had not been established. The artistic avant-garde tended to be anti-establishment and so pro-Dreyfus; Méliès made a Dreyfusard film—probably the first ever on a political theme. But no generalization wholly fits: the Académie Française, pinnacle of the establishment, was fairly evenly divided. Pre-existing political or religious loyalties were crucial, but personal conscience, the influence of friends, and even accident could also be decisive. For example, the iconoclastic playwright Jarry stayed neutral, as did the leading composers Debussy and Maurice Ravel; the rising young poet Paul Valéry was strongly anti-Dreyfusard; while the hugely successful patriotic playwright Rostand was, surprisingly, Dreyfusard. Among artists, Auguste Renoir was probably Dreyfusard, while Paul Cézanne, patriarch of the avant-garde, was anti-Dreyfusard. Among writers, Zola's old-fashioned republicanism and trust in science led him one way;

the younger Barrès's fashionable critique of rationalism and individualism and his interest in national cultural identity led him the
other.

The Dreyfusards won the political battle. But the deeper intellectual contest was undecided. From about 1890 there was a
Europe-wide 'revolt against Positivism' (the rationalist quasi-
scientific philosophy that posited that the only knowable reality was
what could be observed). Positivism underpinned the secularist,
democratic, and moderate values of late nineteenth-century French
republicanism. The new trend stressed the non-rational, mystical,
and subconscious, and was far more alien to the world of Zola than to
that of his antagonists such as Barrès or the young poet Paul Claudel,
newly converted to Catholicism, who wrote 'at last we are leaving that
hideous world . . . of the nineteenth century, that prison camp, that
hideous mechanism governed by laws that were completely inflexible
and, worst of all, knowable and teachable'. The ambivalence of the
new trend is demonstrated by Georges Sorel, who in *Réflexions sur la
violence* (1908) stressed the importance of intuition, myth, and hero-
ism, and was admired by, and himself admired, extremists of both
right and left.

This 'revolt' raised problems that have concerned French intellectuals and artists ever since. Drawing on German thinkers, especially Nietzsche, Freud, and later Husserl and Heidegger—when
French intellectuals think, it has been said, they think in German—
they sought a deeper meaning and reality than that contained in
surface appearance or the conscious mind. This encouraged an
artistic avant-garde (the term itself coined in these years), often
associated with anarchism or later Marxism, which was erupting in
painting, poetry, theatre, and music; but it also nourished a powerful
current of mysticism that renewed the French Catholic and national
traditions in literature and music, still flowering in the 1950s with
Francis Poulenc and in the stupendous inventiveness of Olivier
Messiaen up to his death in 1992.

Hence, artists wanted to go beyond the superficial subjective
description they associated with the Impressionist painting of the
1870s and 1880s and realist and naturalist writing such as that of Zola.
In poetry, the symbolism of Mallarmé, reflected in the music of
Debussy, sought unconscious symbolic meanings in words, images,
and sounds. In painting, Cézanne laboured to represent space,

volume, and texture, both in landscape and the human body, by carefully contrived colours and forms; while Paul Gauguin, Vincent Van Gogh, the 'Nabis', and the 'Fauves' ('Wild Beasts') used colour not to mimic nature but to represent emotion—'colours became sticks of dynamite', wrote the painter André Derain. This was sufficiently shocking for President Loubet to refuse to open the 1905 Autumn Salon containing thirty-nine works by Matisse, Gauguin, Derain, Maurice Vlaminck, and others. But 'Cubist' and 'Futurist' artists regarded this as still too subjective and simplistic. Influenced by the philosophy of Henri Bergson, philosophical star of the 1900s who was interested in the nature of creativity and processes of change, a range of artists wanted to represent the dimension of time, and also to increase the intellectual content of art. The Cubists, led by Georges Braque and Pablo Picasso, congregating round an old factory in Montmartre, the Bateau-Lavoir, aimed to deconstruct surface appearance, particularly to show Bergsonian connections between space and time—in short, to show not how things looked, but how they were.

The *annus mirabilis* of French—or Parisian—experimental creativity is often said to have been 1913, which saw among other works Igor Stravinsky's *Rite of Spring*; Proust's *Du côté de chez Swann*; the avant-garde poet and critic Guillaume Apollinaire's *Alcools*; Alain-Fournier's poetic and dreamlike novel *Le Grand Meaulnes*; the first season of the seminal Théâtre du Vieux-Colombier; and new novels by the nationalists Barrès and Ernest Psichari. Arguably, this culmination of the *belle époque* was the peak of French artistic influence for the whole twentieth century, before the irreparable damage of war.

The First World War and its aftermath

The immediate effect was disruption as 3,700,000 men were called up. As the war progressed cultural life was further affected by a range of controls, including censorship and paper rationing, combined with patriotic determination to rally to the national defence. Although the left unhesitatingly accepted the duty to defend democratic and republican France, war inevitably pushed the views of the nationalists into the ascendent. Barrès, in articles, books, and as a member of parliament, was the most prominent of those writers who threw themselves into what the novelist Paul Bourget called 'maintaining the war spirit'. Their heroic and optimistic portrayal of war ('Gaiety reigns in the trenches') was dominant for the first two years, and it was widely shared: even Apollinaire wrote the famous line 'Dieu que la guerre est jolie!' and the view of war as a source of regeneration and purification, voiced before 1914 by writers such as Charles Péguy and Ernest Psichari (both killed in the first months), was widespread.

From 1916, a different tone was heard. Men serving in the trenches (where some 500 French writers were killed), angered by the unreality of what they called *bourrage de crâne* ('head cramming'), published realistic accounts based on experience. Henri Barbusse's *Le Feu* (serialized in 1916) and George Duhamel's *La Vie des martyrs* (1917) and *Civilisation 1914–17* (1918) were the most read. Both won the Prix Goncourt and caused huge public reaction, not least from soldiers. However, although they condemned the horror of the war, these were not calls to surrender; indeed, knowledge of the horrors already suffered could be a reason for continuing to victory. Maurras's nationalist paper *Action Française* gained readers among the cultural elite, and in 1917 subscribers included Proust and the novelist André Gide, the sculptor Rodin, and the poet Apollinaire, who wrote admiringly of Maurras.

Outright rejection of the war remained marginal, for the presence of German troops on French soil made national defence seem an inescapable necessity; defeatism would anyway have been censored. The principal critical voices were those of Barbusse, the last chapter of *Le Feu* calling forlornly for the unity of nations, and Romain Rolland, resident in Switzerland, whose 1915 book *Au dessus de la mêlée*, called for reconciliation. He was revolted by the use of colonial troops—'savage hordes'—against 'a great European people', and argued that the war was a consequence of an economic, political, and social system for which the allies shared responsibility. However, neither Rolland nor Barbusse advocated French defeat, which placed them in a logical dilemma. Although Rolland was awarded the Nobel Prize for Literature in 1916, his influence was limited. Nevertheless, tensions were increasing, and once the war was over, horror at the appalling human cost, resentment against political and cultural leaders, demands for social and political change, and determination to prevent any future war, caused political and intellectual radicalization on both left and right.

The effect of war on the avant-garde was profound and lasting. Many of its leading figures fought—including Apollinaire (who was seriously wounded) and the painters Braque, Derain, and Léger; others painted camouflage or designed helmets. Even those not directly involved, such as Picasso (a Spanish citizen), were affected by the changing atmosphere. Influenced by wartime nationalism, a consensus emerged that pre-war art had been cosmopolitan, self-indulgent, and decadent; and that the war showed the need for a 'purer', more 'serious' art that expressed French and Latin cultural values against the menace of German *Kultur*. The Cubists (or 'Kubists', as their critics preferred) were accused of being un-French. In painting, music, and literature there was a profound and lasting revival of 'classical' values, associated with the supposed French inheritance of Graeco-Roman characteristics of rationality, elegance, and control. The young poet and impresario Jean Cocteau, in a pamphlet illustrated by Picasso, called for 'French music for France', criticized Debussy for imitating Wagner, and praised Satie for his classical simplicity, clarity, and proportion. Much avant-garde art, Cubism in particular with its emphasis on intellect over sentiment, was amenable to this interpretation, and its practitioners were now eager to stress their Latin roots: 'Cubism was a classicism after the Romanticism of the Fauves,' asserted Cocteau. Picasso, Juan Gris, Robert Delaunay, and Gino Severini now produced portraits that they liked to compare with those of the nineteenth-century arch-classicist Ingres, and used 'Latin' themes such as the *commedia dell'arte* harlequins. This did not always have the desired affect: Cocteau's ballet *Parade* (designed by Picasso, with music by Satie), though intended to bring the pre-war avant-garde into the social and intellectual mainstream (his supporters included a bevy of countesses, Barrès, and the Italian nationalist poet d'Annunzio), was given a hostile reception. But in general, the pre-war avant-garde were becoming more integrated into a society that always had an appetite for radical chic. A new avant-garde of outsiders, the Dadaists (in Switzerland, well away from the patriotic pressures of Paris) condemned the likes of Picasso for selling out, and even rejected the war itself.

It is often said that the war engendered cultural radicalization, a rejection of tradition in favour of 'modernism'. This was not so. War inspired familiar patriotic art—such as the brightly coloured *images d'Épinal* (which influenced work by Picasso, Dufy, Braque, and Léger), cartoon strips showing French children beating the Boches, patriotic novels, poetry, and music. Furthermore, suffering and loss expressed themselves above all through traditional cultural forms. There was a poignant need to find a spiritual dimension in the war, to make sacrifices seem worthwhile, and to maintain a link with those who had died. Conventional religious practice revived, and a strong spiritualist current emerged, not confined to any one ideological or intellectual level. The theme of an apocalyptic return of the dead was strong in literature and in films such as Abel Gance's *J'accuse*, seen by over a million people. Artists and writers trying to express the experience of the trenches usually chose conventional means—the realist novel, representative painting and sculpture, and regular verse. Severini's bold 1916 Futurist paintings of war drew no response; later war memorials drew on familiar figurative art. Above all, traditional artistic forms were intended, and were able, to comfort and heal.

The physical sufferings of industrialized war, present in the minds and bodies of millions of soldiers, widows, orphans, and *mutilés*, and its moral hideousness, had inevitably profound effects after the fighting ended. French intellectual life took on a darker intensity, and this was to be compounded by the Second World War. The bustle of the *belle époque*, with its coteries, duels, anarchism, and absinthe (now banned), seemed frivolous: 'How happy seem the days when we seriously discussed the future of Cubism, or the respective merits of free or regular verse!' The experience of war convinced many intellectuals, for whom it was the crucial event of their lives, that violence and irrationality ruled, and that European society was (as many had already suspected) in crisis: in Valéry's words, 'We realized that a civilization was just as fragile as a life.' More than ever it was their duty to witness and 'engage'; but on which side? The war had created an often apocalyptic yearning for the coming of a new age. For some, the Russian Revolution was its dawn—what Rolland called 'the great glow in the East'. On the other hand, regeneration of national cultural traditions had been stimulated by war; classicism and Catholicism, sometimes in combination, offered a different remedy.

Between the wars: from the *années folles* to the *années noires*

A no less important response to the end of war was the desire to return to normality, forget suffering, and have fun. France as elsewhere saw an explosion of commercial entertainment using new technologies, and the promotion of new forms of consumption, for example through new illustrated magazines such as *Marie-Claire*. These were linked with alluring images of modernity, individual freedom and enjoyment. For those very reasons, they were attacked by cultural critics of both right and left, such as George Duhamel, who condemned cinema audiences as 'drunken helots'.

The cinema, the gramophone, and the radio were the great new cultural media. France was a few years slower to adopt them than the United States, Britain, or Germany: the new technology had largely to be imported, and hence represented *foreign* mass culture that was treated with some suspicion. Nevertheless, by 1931—only four years after the first 'talkie' in the United States—a quarter of French cinemas were equipped for sound. In Paris, the cinema overtook live entertainment in importance during the 1930s: in 1925, the cinema drew 31 per cent of box-office receipts, in 1939, 72 per cent. The neighbourhood cinema, with regular Saturday night customers, provided a new form of sociability, and further advanced national cultural homogenization, though Hollywood was already a popular presence. By the late 1930s, France's 4,000 cinemas registered 250 million entries per year. Though undeniably a mass phenomenon, this audience was relatively and absolutely smaller than in America or Britain, a perennial problem for the industry, which suffered chronic economic problems from 1933 onwards. Yet this was the golden age of the French cinema, which made some ambitious and thoughtful films that were both popular and critical successes in a style that has been called realist populism or (in Marcel Carné's own phrase) 'le fantastique social'. Among them were Jean Renoir's *La Grande Illusion* (1937)—the First World War as the end of the Old Regime—and Carné's *Hôtel du Nord* (1938)—love and death in working-class Paris.

Radio advanced at the same time as cinema, with the number of TSF ('wireless') sets increasing from 500,000 in 1929 to 5 million in

1938, with dozens of state and private stations. Although its products—games, serials, news reports—were ephemeral, they too were a means of national cultural integration. Radio, the gramophone, and the cinema made stars both of new music-hall performers such as Maurice Chevalier (influenced by British and American styles) and, in the 1930s, of a new generation of more intimate microphone crooners such as Tino Rossi and Charles Trenet. They also rejuvenated the popular *café-concert* tradition, represented from the late 1930s by Edith Piaf. Some critics deplored 'Anglo-American morals, tastes and pleasures,' but popular entertainment was still largely French in form and theme, centred on the comedy or tragedy of the lives of 'the little people'. Jazz remained a Parisian speciality, its singers and dancers—such as Josephine Baker, famous not least for her miniscule costumes—an exotic curiosity.

The excitement of the *années folles* evoked stern disapproval from those artists and intellectuals who, marked by the war, wanted cultural and moral regeneration, not escapist hedonism. The Catholic writer Georges Bernanos wrote that 'the prevailing atmosphere was that of a brothel'; and the war novelist Duhamel urged every European to 'reject what he sees as American in his house, in his clothing, in his soul'—a sentiment that won the plaudits of the Académie Française. Many intellectuals believed that the hard-won victory was being squandered. Some were drawn towards the purifying extremes of communism or fascism, and not a few oscillated somewhere between the two, such as the architect Le Corbusier and the Catholic philosophical guru Emmanuel Mounier. Barbusse joined the communist party, becoming a loyal acolyte of Stalinism. Some, notably the young avant-garde writer Pierre Drieu La Rochelle, were attracted by the dynamic youthfulness of fascism; and the novelist Céline, the most brilliantly original as well as the most sinister talent of his generation, found in fascism a vehicle for his nihilism. Many intellectuals on left as well as right were impressed by the authoritarianism of Maurras's Action Française, so vigorous in its assertion of the uniqueness and universality of French culture, the heir of Greece and Rome, and so withering in its denunciation of liberals, democrats, foreigners, and Jews.

The younger generation of Dadaist poets and artists, the founders of surrealism in the early 1920s, were drawn to communism because of its attacks on bourgeois society and culture. Their principal concern was to explore and liberate the unconscious mind, 'freed from the control of reason', using such means as analysis of dreams, automatic writing and painting, collages, photography, and film to disturb conventional perceptions of reality. Surrealism attracted a cosmopolitan galaxy of new talent—to name but a few, the poets André Breton, Louis Aragon, and Paul Eluard, the painters Max Ernst, Juan Miró, and Salvador Dali, the photographer Man Ray, the film-maker Luis Buñuel—and by the late 1930s it spread both internationally and intellectually, influencing new fields such as anthropology and psychiatry. But relations with the communist party were turbulent: militants tended to regard surrealist artistic activities as self-indulgent, 'bourgeois', obscure, and useless for propaganda purposes. Many surrealists had their own intellectual and political objections to Soviet communism as well as rejecting cultural dictation. The result was fragmentation.

Much of France's cultural activity lay between these warring extremes. Paris, a relative haven of tolerance, diversity, freedom, and fun, had an Indian summer between the wars as the West's cultural capital. It was enlivened by refugees such as the Russians Stravinsky, Vasily Kandinsky, and Marc Chagall. American cultural pilgrims frequented the artistic cafés of Montparnasse, the Latin Quarter, and Montmartre. However, it was not bohemian or pseudo-bohemian iconoclasm that predominated. In the theatre, in striking contrast to pre-war taste, the brilliant reworkings of classical mythology by Jean Giraudoux dominated serious drama. The novel remained the major literary form, maintaining a preoccupation with psychological and moral analysis. The Catholic writers François Mauriac and Georges Bernanos were powerful voices; while secular moral issues were pursued by André Gide. Poetry maintained prestige and creativity: over 300 poets were published, and writers such as Paul Valéry, Paul Claudel, and Saint-Jean Perse (all diplomats) wrote in a grand tradition of intellectual elevation and linguistic fastidiousness, employing Chinese and Japanese as well as Ancient Greek motifs.

French influence was to prove of lasting importance in social sciences, which shared the general desire to go beyond Positivism. Drawing on recent advances in sociology, geography, and psychology, the historians Marc Bloch and Lucien Febvre pursued a new approach to historical explanation, stressing the importance of durable structures of landscape (mountains, rivers), society and mentality (such as myths), and reducing political events—the focus of conventional history—to secondary importance. Their journal *Annales* (1929) attained and retains worldwide influence, and the changes they brought about in understanding the past have been profound and probably permanent.

The 1930s saw economic crisis, rising fascism, and the approach of war. All affected cultural life and caused intellectuals again to take a stand, even those like Gide who had previously avoided politics. At the same time, the state, under the left-wing Popular Front, expanded cultural intervention. These phenomena were connected, for as so often in France, political events proved cultural catalysts. In February 1934, riots in Paris raised the possibility of a right-wing coup. Both right- and left-wing intellectuals were galvanized, the latter supporting a new alliance of radical republicans, socialists, and communists, the Popular Front. They won power in 1936 to save France from both fascism and economic depression. For reasons of idealism and propaganda they introduced an unprecedented range of initiatives to democratize culture as a way of educating and uniting the nation: from youth hostels and paid holidays to scientific research; from commissioning cantatas to subsidizing films; from opening the Louvre in the evening to creating regional folklore museums. Communists were enthusiastic, for this recalled the USSR; moreover, their new populist strategy featured a cloying show of patriotism: 'My party has given me back the colours of France,' gushed the surrealist poet Aragon, 'my blue-eyed France, my France of Joan of Arc and Maurice Chevalier.' Time and money were short, but the Popular Front's cultural plans influenced every subsequent government, including Vichy, the Liberation government, and the Fifth Republic. The most lasting works produced under Popular Front auspices were films by Carné and Renoir, though the former was criticized by communist critics for showing the proletariat in a bad light, while the latter's *La Marseillaise*, the Front's flagship film, combined revolutionary fervour and patriotism, but showed the French Revolution in so rosy and expurgated a manner that critics and the public found it worthy but dull.

The International Exposition of 1937 provided the last great showcase for Paris as world cultural capital: participants included Le Corbusier, the composers Arthur Honegger and Darius Milhaud, and Miró and Picasso. His *Guernica*, in the Spanish pavilion, was not the only reminder of the threatening world outside: the Soviet and German pavilions, crushing monuments of totalitarian cultural bluster, squared up to each other beside the Seine, brutal symbols of the alternative facing French intellectuals, and of their helplessness.

Julien Benda, in *La Trahison des clercs* (1927), had posed a recurring problem: how could intellectual honesty survive political activism? Benda, formerly a Dreyfusard, did not oppose engagement. But he defined the duty of what he called *les clercs* as defending unchanging, rational, and disinterested ideals. He believed they betrayed this duty—he named the nationalists Barrès, Péguy, and Maurras among others—by subordinating pure ideals to political causes. However, younger intellectuals rejected Benda's argument: for them 'the terrible *trahison des clercs* [was] idealist cowardice'; the intellectual must be prepared, as Sartre put it later, to have dirty hands.

The Popular Front and the events of the late 1930s, especially the Spanish Civil War, intensified intellectuals' dilemmas. Many saw a choice only between communism and fascism. Some found that choice repugnant, as both communism and fascism bared their fangs. Two leading right-wing intellectuals, the Catholic writers Bernanos and Mauriac, broke with fascism in protest against atrocities in Spain. On the left, a visit to Russia led Gide to withdraw from the communist-backed peace movement. Breton and some surrealists condemned Stalin's show trials; but others—notably Éluard and Aragon—became the party's house intellectuals, the latter robustly declaring that 'to claim innocence for [Stalin's victims] is to adopt the Hitlerian thesis'.

The prospect of another war created crises of conscience for intellectuals. Many on the left saw war as the ultimate evil: how then to oppose fascist aggression? Others looked to the Soviet Union as their second, or perhaps their first, loyalty: but in 1939 it signed a treaty with Hitler, the great enemy. The right was nationalist by definition, but many admired fascism and refused to contemplate a war against Germany and Italy: who, asked Brasillach, wanted to die for Danzig? The picture is one of general disarray and pessimism.

The dark years: escapism and engagement

The German invasion in June 1940 fragmented cultural life physically and mentally. Intellectuals were scattered. Many were in prisoner-of-war camps (where the historian Fernand Braudel, for example, was drafting from memory his great work *La Méditerranée*). Many fled to the unoccupied south, giving provincial towns, particularly Marseille, an unwonted burst of cultural activity. Some gravitated to Vichy, the new seat of government. A few followed de Gaulle to London. Most remained in, or soon returned to, occupied Paris. Intellectual and moral divisions were no less marked. Was it a patriotic duty to support the new regime of Marshal Pétain and work for moral and intellectual regeneration, and not least spare France further bloodshed? Was it a duty to oppose reaction and fascism? But how, given that the war seemed over and the Soviet Union was an ally of Hitler? Should cultural life continue or should artists remain silent? If the former, would it signal the unconquerability of French culture, or acquiescence in French defeat? If the latter, would it be a sign of defiance or impotence?

Most people for a time saw Pétain as their best hope. They wanted a return to some kind of normality, intellectuals included. A few left France or remained silent, but most decided that getting back to work was not only a way of earning a living but also a duty. This fitted in with German plans for a pliable France. Not a few cultural celebrities were willing to get into bed with the Nazis: some literally, like the film star Arletty and the designer Coco Chanel. Others spiritually, such as the delegations of scientists, academics, musicians, writers, entertainers (including Chevalier, Trenet, and Piaf), actors and artists (including Derain and Vlaminck, though Matisse and Braque refused) who were willing to visit Germany in 1941 and 1942. Artists and critics flocked to the Paris exhibition of Hitler's favourite sculptor, the overblown neoclassicist Arno Breker. Febvre and Bloch had a dispiriting quarrel about whether to bring out *Annales*; Febvre insisted, and Bloch, a Jew, had to step down. Such was the price of normality.

For the right, who had scorned the pre-war Republic and opposed war, France's defeat seemed a bitter vindication. Maurras spoke of 'the divine surprise' of Pétain's policy of regenerating France along

Action Française lines: authoritarianism, nationalism, and Catholicism. His influence was clear in the new government's 'National Revolution', which combined anti-democratic reaction with boy-scoutish team spirit, and drew inspiration from Sorel, Péguy, Barrès, and Maurras himself. Most of the intellectual right, including Valéry, Claudel, and Mauriac, joined the cult of Pétain, as did not a few of the left as well as hybrids such as Mounier, whose Jeune France movement started programmes of popular arts and theatre to regenerate French youth. However, more extreme right-wing intellectuals led by Drieu and Brasillach found this 'revolution' too tame: they wanted a fascist France allying with Germany to build a new Europe, and they stayed in Paris, with their base the extremist press such as *Gringoire* and *Je suis partout.*

There was an understandable taste for cultural escapism from the surrounding gloom. So occupied France was to prove artistically fertile: if it was a huge prison, at least that guaranteed a captive audience and facilities for concentrated work. Established writers vied with new talents. Jean-Paul Sartre finished his thesis, his classical drama *Les Mouches* (1942), and his experimental play *Huis clos* (1944). Albert Camus published a philosophical essay and two novels, including *L'Étranger* (1942). The theatre had new neo-classical tragedies by Montherlant and Anouilh, and Claudel's vast historical fresco *Le Soulier de satin*, produced by the brilliant young Jean-Louis Barrault. The film industry too was remarkably active, producing among many others Henri Clousot's *Le Corbeau* (1943), Carné's *Les Visiteurs du soir* (1942), and his masterpiece *Les Enfants du paradis*, often considered the best French film ever made, begun in 1943. Did such works contain hidden political messages? If so they were enigmatic; most people probably enjoyed them for their bitter-sweet sentiments of love, sacrifice, and loss.

True cultural dissidence came in other forms, and eventually drew on every intellectual current from Catholic to communist. The underground review *Les Lettres françaises* and the clandestine publisher Les Éditions de Minuit emerged in 1942. From opposite ends of the ideological spectrum, Mauriac (soon disillusioned with Pétain) and Aragon (once the USSR was invaded) were important figures, though the masterpiece of resistance literature was *Le Silence de la mer* by 'Vercors' (Jean Bruller), published by Éditions de Minuit in 1943. Many intellectuals engaged in physical resistance too, and inevitably some paid with their lives, among them the historian Marc Bloch. But the uncertainty many felt is exemplified by the *engagé* left-wing novelist André Malraux, who only became active in 1944.

The Liberation brought triumph or nemesis to engaged intellectuals. Many who had committed themselves to Pétain and collaborationism were blacklisted, prosecuted, or (like Céline) exiled. Drieu La Rochelle killed himself. Maurras, shouting 'It's Dreyfus's revenge', was sentenced to life imprisonment. Brasillach was condemned to death. A group of prominent intellectuals (including some on the left, notably Camus) argued that people, especially if talented, should not be killed for their words. But the role of the intellectual was shown to carry risks as well as rewards: Brasillach was shot. The whole intellectual current of the nationalist right was discredited. Even before the Liberation, many right-wingers had changed sides and renounced—or more often denied—their previous allegiances. Although many Catholic and nationalist intellectuals had been genuine resisters, it was the left that now held intellectual and moral ascendency. Communist ambivalence before 1941 was forgotten, as they assumed the title of 'le parti des 100,000 fusillés', leaders of the patriotic anti-fascist struggle and the largest post-war political movement.

The time of the intellectuals, 1945–1989

The 'thirty glorious years' from the end of the war to the Arab oil crisis saw France change from a society of small towns, small firms, small incomes, and small families to an expansive, wealthy, and mobile industrial society. Its politics also eventually became more stable after 150 years of division and rupture. These were not easy or painless transitions. The Cold War and its domestic repercussions; the violent process of decolonization; the onrush of capitalism and the mini-revolution of May 1968; the posthumous political triumph of de Gaulle as creator of a stable political system; the long delayed but ultimately hollow victory of socialism under Mitterrand—all provided intellectuals with ample matter for debate. France lost what has been called its political 'exceptionalism'—the perennial conflicts stemming from the great divide of the Revolution; but it also lost its cultural pre-eminence.

The Cold War and decolonization—in particular the atrocious struggle in Algeria—kept intellectuals deeply involved in politics after the Liberation. Since 1917 the communist party had benefited from the revolutionary propensities of some intellectuals, but relations had often been tense. Its role in the resistance—backed up by the prestige of Soviet power—now magnified its attractiveness. Picasso and the old surrealist circle joined or rejoined (though Picasso's 1953 portrait of Stalin displeased the party). Rising young intellectuals such as Sartre, the philosopher Maurice Merleau-Ponty, the novelist Marguerite Duras, and Catholics such as Mounier and his disciples gravitated towards communism, even if most did not actually 'take their party card'. Marxism had become in Sartre's words, 'the unsurpassable philosophy of our time,' though it served more as a progressive label than as a serious theory. Marxist intellectuals set the terms and agenda of public debate; their influence in the media and teachers' and students' unions meant that openly hostile voices faced an uphill struggle. Thus it remained for some thirty years.

In the 1940s and 1950s, there was also a new intellectual lifestyle. Left Bank cafés near Saint-Germain-des-Prés were the focus of a culture of philosophy, politics, literature, music, and self-discovery whose influence—or at least whose image—was global. Jean-Paul Sartre, philosopher, novelist, and playwright, and Albert Camus, resistance fighter, novelist, and playwright, were the stars, along with the musician and writer Boris Vian, the singer Juliette Gréco, and the leading female intellectual Simone de Beauvoir, author of *Le Deux-ième Sexe* (1949), communist, and inseparable partner of Sartre. Existentialism was the fashionable philosophy and literary theme, notably in Sartre's *L'Être et le néant*, influenced by the German philosophers Husserl and Heidegger. This was about finding meaning in an 'absurd' world without God or Reason—a problem intellectuals had been grappling with since 1880. The answer now was to assert one's freedom by choosing to act in a great cause: in practice, for many this meant communism.

The avant-garde theatre showed some of these preoccupations vividly. Rejecting the olympian classicism of the interwar period, the 'theatre of the absurd'—pioneered by Samuel Beckett, in *En attendant Godot* (1947) and Eugène Ionescu—confronted audiences with meaninglessness and irresolution. Ideas of authenticity and identity were explored, often violently, in former surrealist Antonin Artaud's 'theatre of cruelty' and the plays of Jean Genet. More straightforward Marxist politics appeared in the works of Brecht and his followers, especially powerful in the new state-subsidized provincial theatres.

Very different cultural changes were taking place with which intellectuals had little sympathy. Hollywood films, *le jazz, le rock, le jean, le coca, le chewing*, and eventually *le macdo* were imported into culture and language. As in the 1930s, popular singers adopted American names—most famously Johnny Hallyday (born Jean-Philippe Smet) and Eddie Mitchell—and often tried to sing in English. Similar things happened in other countries, but in France they had not only the usual attractions of association with liberty, modernity, youth, and wealth, but also carried the special glamour of transgression: Saint-Germain's leading jazz club was aptly named Le Tabou. For nowhere else in western Europe was Americanization treated with such hostility by cultural elites as a pollution and a threat, even when they consumed its products. This too was not new, and objections combined the voices of nostalgics (as in the films of Jacques Tati in the 1950s and 1960s, which showed the passing of old France with a lucidity both hilarious and depressing), cultural conservatives, and the political left. As in the 1930s, it was communists who led the attack, particularly on the 1946 Blum–Byrnes trade agreement giving American cultural products access to the French market. A 1949 law excluded American cartoon strips, which, among other things, replaced Mickey Mouse with the Belgian-produced Astérix le Gaulois. However, here the intellectuals were isolated from public opinion, which, polls showed, liked America more than any other country.

Despite American competition, French artists have been highly successful in at least certain areas of modern global culture. Once decried as vulgar, French cinema was proclaimed the 'seventh art', and the most fashionable one at that. Influenced by American and Italian directors, a brilliant generation of critics and film-makers— François Truffaut, Eric Rohmer, Jean-Luc Godard, and others—first expressing their views in *Les Cahiers du cinema* (the sort of intellectual review so important in French culture since the 1880s), revolutionized the style and content of the cinema in the 1950s and 1960s. In different ways, they moved away from conventional theatrical polish towards intimacy and spontaneity, linked with the political and philosophical concerns of the time. However, intellectual values did not reign supreme: these were the years of Brigitte Bardot, embodiment of a quite different cultural revolution.

After returning to power in 1958, de Gaulle appointed the formerly left-wing intellectual André Malraux to head a new Ministry of Cultural Affairs, the first in a democratic country. Novelist, airman, veteran of Spain, the Popular Front, and the resistance, Malraux epitomized the intellectual as man of action. One aim was didactic: as during the Popular Front and Vichy, decentralizing culture was to integrate the nation. Maisons de la Culture, local cultural centres (since largely abandoned), were to be the outposts. The other aim was regalian: exalting France through its culture as part of de Gaulle's 'policy of grandeur'. So the *Mona Lisa*, with Malraux in attendance, was dispatched on a tour of the United States in 1963, and the *Venus de Milo* to Japan in 1964. Boasted Malraux, 'four million Japanese saw the French flag behind that statue'. A law, widely imitated abroad, was enacted in 1962 to protect urban conservation areas. Acres of blackened Paris buildings were washed and repaired—Malraux's most remembered and most permanent achievement, though at the expense of making old Paris a gentrified museum.

However powerful in the 1940s and 1950s, Marxist intellectual and moral ascendency slowly crumbled. It was shaken in 1956 by Khrushchev's partial disclosure of the Stalin Terror and by Soviet crushing of the Hungarian uprising. Some intellectuals protested or broke with communism. But opposition to the Algerian war in the 1950s and 1960s remobilized a broad spectrum of intellectuals on an issue reminiscent of the Dreyfus case: patriotism and support for the army again conflicted with human rights. After the Algerian war ended, hostility to America and imperialism in South America and Asia, a desire to be on the same side as the proletariat ('we mustn't upset Billancourt', as the catchphrase went), and an instinctive feeling that an intellectual had to be opposed to 'bourgeois-capitalist society' delayed serious ideological rethinking. Hence, new utopias—Cuba, Vietnam, Cambodia, and especially China—were successively discovered as the promised lands of communism.

The 'events' of May 1968 were primarily a cultural festival, an unstable mixture of Marxism and libertarian hedonism, made up of heady aspirations, speeches, posters, and memorable slogans

('Prohibitions prohibited'; 'Under the pavement the beach'). Rapid university expansion mirrored wider socio-economic change, and both caused discontent with an arrogant 'technocratic' system. These resentments were heightened by a widespread feeling, linked with events elsewhere, that revolutionary change—political, social, and cultural—was in the air. Events took characteristically French forms, particularly a self-conscious emulation of revolutionary tradition— 1944, 1936, 1871, 1789. For several years there were cultural aftershocks: continuing *gauchiste* excitement reflected in the arts (a characteristic example being Ariane Mnouchkine's Théâtre du Soleil and its impro-vised, audience-involving *1789*); the accelerating abandonment of orthodox communism; and the spread of post-Marxist theories. Especially significant was the emergence of the most important politi-cal and intellectual feminist movement since the 1840s, first focusing (as in other countries) on issues such as abortion and legal rights; in recent years, focusing on psychology, linguistics, philosophy, and lit-erature in the works of writers such as Julia Kristeva, Hélène Cixous, and Luce Irigaray.

But in the long run 1968 proved more an end than a beginning: the culmination of an intellectual fantasy of revolution. The long eco-nomic recession that began in 1974 posed a greater threat to the political order, but ultimately a more serious one still to the main-stream left (which was forced to try, unsuccessfully, to solve the crisis in the 1980s) and a fatal one to 1960s-style student radicalism as a preoccupation with finding a job replaced that of changing the world.

In 1981, what has been called 'the long march of the French Left' reached its destination: power. The election of François Mitterrand heralded further cultural and ideological changes. Some prominent intellectuals became part of the governing elite. Mitterrand himself had intellectual leanings, and arguably embodied the definition by Ory and Sirinelli of the intellectual as 'the man of culture . . . placed in the situation of a man of politics'. But the intellectual left was inevitably largely neutralized by its links with the government. More-over, its cultural ascendency was waning. During the 1970s, the fading prestige of the Soviet Union collapsed: Alexander Solzhenitsyn's *L'Archipel du goulag* (1974) was the *coup de grâce*. Third-world vari-ants of *les lendemains qui chantent* ('singing tomorrows') also proved disappointing. Consequently, most intellectuals dropped Marxism— which 'links us with the hangmen'—altogether. This was a worldwide development, but in France it was self-conscious and dramatic: like Clovis, first baptized king of the Franks, French intellectuals learnt to 'burn what you have adored and adore what you have burnt'. Historians, philosophers (led by youthful 'new philosophers' such as André Glucksmann and Bernard-Henry Lévy), social scientists, and political analysts needed new tools of analysis. A generation of ex-Marxist historians, led by François Furet and Maurice Agulhon, began reinterpreting the past. Some looked to the *Annales* school; others discovered liberalism or disinterred traditional republicanism; many turned to a new kind of cultural history in which language replaced socio-economic struggle as the thread of history.

The most influential novelties were structuralism and its successor post-structuralism, developed from the 1960s and 70s. In a sense, this was a return to origins, a postmodernism that drew on the post-positivism of the *belle époque*, especially Freudianism and the linguistics of Ferdinand de Saussure, combined with the 1920s writings of Heidegger. As before, the intention, pioneered by the anthropologist Claude Lévi-Strauss in the 1950s, was to deconstruct appearances to discover underlying realities—'structures' of language, psychology, culture, and hence of power. Post-structuralism was less a reversal than a development—or complication—of this trend, stressing uncertainty of meaning and changeability of language, identity, and thought. The most famous names were Roland Barthes, Jacques Lacan, Jacques Derrida, Michel Foucault, and, more radically, Jean Baudrillard. Arguably no French intellectuals since Bergson and Sorel have had such influence among social and literary theorists, especially in English-speaking universities where, more than in France, they came to embody a new orthodoxy. A remarkable range of work emerged: ethics from Emmanuel Levinas and Jean-François Lyotard, social theory from Pierre Bourdieu, and feminist theory from Kristeva, Cixous, and others. Critics have accused many of them of obscurity, of incoherence, of political misjudgement, of garbling scientific concepts, and, most fundamentally, of promoting a postmodern relativism that undermines rationality. But these were precisely their attractions: they offered a new source of intellectual radicalism to undermine the validity of 'Western' cultural orthodoxies, and are thus the heirs of the surrealists.

Under Mitterrand, cultural policy became literally spectacular, a mixture of idealism, nationalism, politics, and megalomania. Jack

Lang, a theatrical administrator and charismatic publicist, became the new Malraux. As always, one aim was to democratize culture. However, where the Popular Front had aimed to 'raise the masses to culture [but] not to vulgarize culture', in a more relativistic and hedonistic age the theme was 'le tout culturel'—everything was culture. Famously, rock music and tagging attracted Lang's subsidies. As he told *Playboy* in 1981, 'I would like people to think of culture as pleasure, enjoyment, not as duty, pedantry, privilege or social obligation.' Another aim was to defend French popular culture—especially cinema, television, and pop music—against Anglo-Saxon 'cultural imperialism'. Most spectacular were Mitterrand's dozen 'Great Cultural Projects', a regalian extravaganza that overshadowed even the vast Centre Georges Pompidou and Giscard d'Estaing's Musée d'Orsay: they included a music and science 'city', a renovated Louvre with a glass pyramid, a new opera house, a new arc de triomphe, and a new national library. They aimed to make Paris again the world's cultural capital and, cynics accused, leave eternal monuments to the greatness of François Mitterrand. Like Louis XIV or Napoleon III, the president took a personal hand, choosing the seats for the opera house and the architects for the Louvre and the library. Total cost was fabulous. Cultural centralization in Paris was strengthened. Aesthetic reactions were mixed. Results are debatable.

The new monuments were shown to the world amid nationwide celebrations of the bicentenary of the French Revolution in 1989, when history and culture were mobilized to serve the state: as Mitterrand revealingly put it, France was 'the third military power in the world, the fourth or fifth economic power, and as a cultural force, its place was without equal'. The centrepiece—a festive parade down the Champs-Élysée—was organized after many difficulties by an American-trained publicity specialist, Jean-Pierre Goude. This demonstrated that France could outdo the world in exuberant postmodern kitsch: hardly a public celebration anywhere is now without its Goudist carnival. But it also showed that the Revolution had lost its meaning. This was underlined as the bicentenary was outshone by the collapse of the revolutionary regimes of the communist world, ending a historical cycle begun in 1789. The old political language, much of it made in France, no longer made sense.

Where did that leave the intellectuals, whose language it was? As Pascal Ory and Jean-François Sirinelli neatly put it, a spokesman has to have something to say. The 'silence of the intellectuals' has been lamented (usually by intellectuals themselves), though as the two most stentorian specimens have probably been Maurras and Sartre, reticence may not be devoid of advantages. Instead of posing as prophets, intellectuals have tended to adopt the humbler roles of expert, critic, adviser, and, in some cases, media personality.

French culture and the world, since c.1990

Writing on modern French culture is often elegiac, an account of golden ages, Indian summers, and decline. Certainly, neither France, nor Paris, nor French intellectuals, enjoy their old cultural primacy. One reason is that freedom and tolerance have become the norm throughout Europe, so Paris no longer needs to act, in Tony Judt's phrase, as a 'clearing house for modern thought'. The other, less palatable, reason is of course the ascendency of 'Anglo-Saxon' culture, both in mass commercial entertainment and intellectual communication.

So French culture can no longer be universal, but it remains important and certainly distinctive. Two examples of distinctiveness are an ingrained ambition to achieve quality—which in popular culture has often produced work of imagination, intelligence, and enduring appeal; and the instinct of applying general principles to practical problems—a valuable corrective in a postmodern, post-ideological, and perhaps even post-democratic world of relativism, 'spin', and pragmatism.

What relationship is emerging between a France that is no longer the centre, and the outside world? It is marked at the political level by protectionism. Recent examples have been the Loi Toubon (1994), requiring the use of French for certain purposes, and the enlisting of the European Commission to limit imported material for television and radio. What now is the purpose of such protectionism? The original justification was to defend French culture from inferior foreign products and supply the nation with wholesome cultural and ideological fare. But since Lang, culture has been packaged for fun and profit—the 'heritage economy'. French-made imitations of the much-decried American commercial culture—rap, rock, tagging, cartoon strips, soap operas, theme parks—have been supported and promoted. Disneyland Paris has become France's biggest cultural attraction. So defence of culture has turned into mere defence of market share.

More positively, we have noted the state's vast efforts since 1936 to create a sort of NHS of the mind. This commands a consensus, brings political benefits, and is widely envied abroad. Has it been successful in its aims of protecting, fostering, and democratizing French culture, and helping to integrate society? These are controversial questions. The problems of protectionism and subsidy are that, in the long run, they risk nurturing mediocrity. They insulate artists from their audience and from new developments. State patronage tends to benefit insiders. It is easy to identify these symptoms in areas long reliant on state protection: the theatre (where audiences stagnate, established directors rule, and there has been little new independent writing); music (the composer and conductor Pierre Boulez, dominant since the 1970s, is said to have controlled well over £100 million in public funds, while Olivier Messiaen, France's greatest composer, was a church organist writing a quite different kind of music); cinema (the audience share of French films within France has now fallen below 30 per cent). In contrast, the Paris Opera Ballet, its technical standards raised in the 1980s by Rudolf Nureyev with the aid of fabulous subsidies, is internationally admired for its lavish productions of the classics; but this is hardly cultural democratization. Television, the truly democratic medium, remains the poor relation, dross for the masses, embarassingly poor.

Defenders of the system dismiss arguments about quality as reactionary elitism, and point to material achievements: budgets, buildings, output. Policy has concentrated on building a large institutional framework with little attention to demand, assuming that an audience would appear for what was provided. Defenders point to the huge numbers visiting the Pompidou Centre and the Louvre pyramid. Critics reply that these have become mere tourist attractions, whose artistic contents receive cursory attention. Despite colossal expenditure, the core audience and those actively participating in cultural activities remain relatively small, and disproportionately composed of the middle-aged middle class and schoolchildren. Particular beneficiaries from state largesse have been culture professionals (including 14,000 administrators) and middle-class Parisians (who, for example, benefit from subsidies of some £100 per ticket at the Bastille Opera). These are powerful lobbies, who invoke patriotism and democracy in justification of the system. If there are shortcomings, defenders argue that without protection the situation would be still worse, and that therefore even more state action and funding is needed.

However, the very principles of policy since Malraux have been condemned by the cultural historian Marc Fumaroli. He argues that creativity has been harmed by reducing culture to a branch of the tourist industry; that the state has created a dependency culture in the arts, making them unable to respond to the outside world; and that the marketing of 'ready-to-wear culture' requiring no knowledge or effort prevents genuine aesthetic experience. Even critics less radical than Fumaroli fear that artistic activity has become too subordinate to state projects and marketing.

It may be that, as electronic media multiply, cultural protectionism will resemble the decrees of King Canute. Technology and cultural relativism might dissolve the distinctions between centre and periphery, national and foreign, elite and mass. This would indeed be cultural democratization, but not the sort that politicians and intellectuals have tried to create. We might interpret such changes as the latest round of what Apollinaire called 'the long quarrel of tradition and invention, of Order and Adventure'. But there has certainly been one cultural revolution in the last generation that is unprecedented and profound: the widespread acquisition of English as a bridge with the world outside. For a younger generation, the cultural frontier of the Hexagon is no longer a barrier.

8

Religion, anticlericalism, and secularization

Maurice Larkin

Religion and secularization are commonly viewed as having a night and day relationship, in which the growth of one entails the symmetrical waning of the other. Yet the history of France since 1880 showed each as having a trajectory of its own, which periodically seemed like a reflection in reverse of its counterpart, but which in reality was shaped by sharply different if related forces. The matter was further complicated by the fact that the secularization of society proceeded at a different pace from that of politics. Social secularization had the massive yet stealthy movement of the night tide, while state policies of secularization displayed the violent but sporadic force of a water cannon, the vehemence of one government being followed by the easy-going indifference of another.

That said, the contrast needs some softening. The tide of secularization did not move evenly. Not only were some regions submerged more rapidly than others, but extraneous factors, such as foreign invasion and unexpected changes of regime, intervened like offshore winds, periodically pushing back the tide but without reversing its overall direction. Conversely, the much more chequered pattern of state policies concealed a greater consistency of principle than the surface might initially suggest. One must distinguish the hostile anticlericalism of major segments of the left from the more broadly based programme of *laïcité*, aimed at disentangling public institutions from the involvement and influence of the Catholic Church, or any other body that might claim a moral mandate to prescribe to society how it should live.

Although the anticlerical campaigns of the militant left had a direct and damaging impact on the Church when the militants were in a position of power or influence, the wider process of *laïcité* commanded a much greater degree of consensual support among republicans than did the crusades of the *mangeurs de curés*. Indeed it is arguable that Napoleon's Concordatory system (extended to include Protestants and Jews, as well as Catholics) embodied the same principles as the regime of Separation that replaced it in 1905–6—despite the obvious differences that have tended to obscure the lines of continuity. In the same way, it is currently claimed that the granting of state aid to denominational private schools after 1959 did not necessarily violate the principles of state neutrality that had traditionally been invoked to prohibit such aid during the 170 years since the Revolution.

The vehemence of religious issues in French political debate largely stemmed from the fact that the principal protagonist of religious interests was the highly disciplined and doctrinally monolithic Catholic Church, with its worldwide commitments and complex diplomatic concerns. Royal repression of Protestants under the *ancien régime* had left them numerically weak. Even in the 1880s, there were only some 650,000 baptized Protestants in France, of whom 80,000 belonged to the Lutheran Église de la Confession d'Augsbourg, while most of the others belonged to the Calvinist Église Réformée. To complicate matters further, the Église Réformée itself was split between an 'orthodox' majority and a 'liberal' minority, each holding separate synods until the two wings eventually came to a formal agreement in the 1930s. This disunity allowed a much greater diversity of opinion among Protestants, which rendered them less hostile towards the aims and ethos of secular republicanism than their Catholic counterparts. Indeed the 'liberal' wing of the Église Réformée was to provide the Republic with some of its leading exponents of *laïcité*. The Jewish community, like most Protestants, had more to gain than lose from *laïcité*, and the arrival of east European refugees, swelling their numbers from some 50,000 to 80,000 in the next twenty years, was to confront them with renewed anti-Semitism, exacerbated by economic recession and the repercussions of the Dreyfus Affair.

As explained in the Introduction, the Catholic Church in the 1880s openly sympathized with the various monarchist opponents of the Third Republic—believing them to be the only hope of stemming the secularizing programme of the current government. The prime purpose of this programme was the formation of future generations of citizens who would think rationally and find fulfilment in the betterment of society and the nation. In varying degrees, republicans saw Catholic teaching as a major potential obstacle to these objectives, with its appeal to non-rational sources of guidance such as Revelation and the authority of the Church. Many thought it sufficient to exclude Catholic or other denominational religious instruction from the formal curriculum of state schools, while others wished to go much further and prohibit members of religious orders from teaching in either state or private schools—especially in view of the hostile attitude of most of the clergy towards the republican establishment. The fact remained, however, that well over 90 per cent of the French population were baptized as Catholics; and political prudence, as well as republican respect for freedom of conscience, urged restraint, even among militant anticlericals.

Yet perhaps only a quarter to a third of French adults—most of them women—went regularly to mass on Sundays, even though deliberate non-attendance was traditionally regarded by the Church as a grave sin. Churchgoing was most evident in the pastoral regions, remote from the principal centres and arteries of economic change and secular attitudes, with the Breton peninsular, the Massif Central, and the eastern uplands as the prime examples. Yet religious observance was also strong in those industrial districts that were adjacent to the German Rhineland and Belgium, where Catholic practice was traditionally high and relatively unscathed by the brief experience of annexation to revolutionary France. Although in France itself the Revolution was relatively short-lived, its more vehement persecution of the Catholic Church stripped out lukewarm parishioners; and the habit of churchgoing, once broken, was not easily mended—even under the more benevolent regimes that followed. Then, in subsequent decades, the growth of industry and commerce took job-seeking villagers from their families and settled them in communities where social conventions had no traditional roots, and where there was little social incentive to go to church. And for those who remained in the countryside, the progressive widening of military service in 1872 and 1889 condemned a large proportion of them to three dreary years of drill and kit-cleaning, with little to enliven it except the bars and brothels of garrison towns. Thereafter the next test of their religion came with marriage, overshadowed by the Church's condemnation of *coitus reservatus* and any form of birth control other than abstinence. The rural population in particular had strong reasons for limiting the size of their families, since the revolutionary and Napoleonic inheritance laws stipulated the division of land between heirs, with the inherent danger that farms would become smaller and less viable with the passing of each generation. If then, as now, a large proportion of couples shut their minds to church teaching on these matters, the strain on their religious allegiance was more deeply felt in the nineteenth century than in the early twenty-first, especially in small villages, where going to confession was often a precondition of receiving Easter communion. Fear of close questioning by an overzealous priest, who knew all his parishioners, could easily lead by extension to avoidance of church altogether.

At the same time the intellectual currents that eroded religious belief in post-Enlightenment France were not confined to the educated public. Railways and newspapers put the rural provinces in increasing contact with the secular attitudes of the main centres of population; and even the illiterate listened willingly or otherwise to the loud disputes of the local luminaries in the market-place bars. Church leaders sought consolation in the rising popularity of the various Marian pilgrimages and devotions that had sprung up in the course of the nineteenth century; but these displays of popular piety mainly involved people who were already part of the diminishing total of churchgoers—counter-currents of enthusiasm within a receding tide.

1880–1914: confrontation

By 1879 government was safely in the hands of committed republicans; and the way was clear for a programme of *laïcité*. Any deliberate attempt to uproot religious belief in the minds of the young was precluded, both in principle and practice, by republican respect for the individual conscience, and by fear of offending the personal beliefs of a sizeable segment of the electorate. But denominational religious instruction was now formally banished from all state primary schools (law of 25 July 1881)—this now being a matter for the parish priest outside normal teaching hours, for pupils whose parents wanted it—and the new classes of 'moral and civic education' were expected to observe a strict neutrality on religious issues. In his famous letter to state primary school teachers of November 1881, the architect of these measures, Jules Ferry, told them 'you are in no way to be the apostles of a new gospel'. A teacher's duty was to convey by example and moral influence 'this good, deep-rooted morality that we have received from our parents . . . without attempting to discuss its philosophical foundations'. There was ongoing debate as to whether 'duties to God' should remain part of the programme. They were omitted from the relevant legislation, but were included in official circulars—although what happened in practice depended greatly on individual teachers and prevailing attitudes in the local community. A subsequent law (30 October 1886) provided for the phased removal of Catholic nuns and brothers from state primary schools—and half had gone by the early 1890s.

Despite the abolition of fees in state primary schools in 1881, well over a fifth of this age group of pupils continued to attend private schools, mostly Catholic. The proportion was even higher in the secondary sector—which admittedly catered for a privileged elite of merely 5 per cent of the adolescent population—where nearly half the boys went to private schools. Given the hostility of the Church to the new Republic, it was feared that these Catholic schools would produce further opponents of the regime whose education and social advantages would give them influential positions in the professions, the army, and the civil service. Jesuit colleges were among the most prestigious of these schools, with their stress on character building and their high proportion of successful entrants into the mainly state-run *grandes écoles*, which were the tertiary sector gateway into the fast lane of public and private employment. The Jesuits' return to France in the early nineteenth century had never been legally authorized, and the government took advantage of this to order their expulsion in 1880, together with a number of other unauthorized orders. In practice, these measures were observed very loosely, and many schools continued much as before under the nominal control of laymen. Indeed, within a few years, the exiled clergy were back in greater number, with the result that by the late 1890s nearly 20 per cent of the entire male secondary school population were taught in schools belonging to the religious orders, while a further 22 per cent attended other Catholic private schools.

Despite left-wing calls for the abolition of the Concordatory regime with its state salaries for bishops and parish priests, no French government in the nineteenth century contemplated abandoning these convenient means of keeping the Church on a tight leash. The increasing reliance of the clergy on their modest state income meant that suspension of salary was an effective way of disciplining outspoken clerics who criticized government policy, while the prime role that the Concordat gave to the government in choosing episcopal candidates was a guarantee against the appointment of firebrands. When anticlericals claimed that the Concordatory regime was incompatible with republican ideals of state neutrality in religious matters, Ferry pointed out that the principle of ecclesiastical state salaries, agreed in Napoleon's Concordat of 1801 with Pius VII, had been rapidly extended to rabbis, as well as to the pastors of the two principal Protestant denominations.

The pope of these times, Leo XIII (1878–1903), was a realist and a man of intellect, who realized more than most senior churchmen that a Church without sympathy for the aspirations of modern society would forfeit much of its influence. This was apparent not only in his encyclical on social justice, *Rerum novarum* (1891), which inspired a whole generation of committed Catholics to concern themselves much more directly with the predicament of the industrial working classes, but it also informed much of his dealings with France. The collapse of Boulangism in 1889 confirmed his belief that the current republic was there to stay—and that until the bulk of French Catholics accepted the fact, the Church could not expect better treatment from the government. Percipient Catholics and many disillusioned monarchists shared this view, especially those who believed that their own material interests would best be served by joining forces with conservative Republicans against left-wing demands for social reform. They therefore welcomed Leo's encyclical of February 1892, *Aux milieux des sollicitudes*, advising a Catholic *ralliement* to the de facto regime. Even so, it created resentment among many with traditionalist loyalties; and, of those who grudgingly complied with the papal request to move onto republican terrain, a sizeable proportion did so merely to stand on firmer ground in their fight against republican policies. Leo's encyclical had also been partly motivated by the less realistic hope that a grateful French government might reward him by putting pressure on the Italian government to restore Rome to the pope and remove its baggage to the former if short-lived Italian capital, Florence. Successive French foreign ministers kept a polite silence on the many occasions when the Vatican raised the matter with them; but if France had no interest in worsening its relations with Italy, it was glad enough to accept the pope's help in creating a conservative republican alliance against the growing if modest electoral successes of the socialists.

But this welcome détente in Franco-Church relations was rapidly put in jeopardy by the repercussions of the Dreyfus Affair, with its attendant rumours of clerico-military plots to overthrow the Republic. In fact only three of the generals who had expressed a cautious interest in these schemes had significant personal links with the Church, while even the Assumptionists—owners of the violently anti-Semitic, wide-selling newspaper, *La Croix*—had cautioned Catholics against becoming involved in the projected coup of 23 February 1899, despite their strong sympathy for its quixotic leader, Paul Déroulède. In private audiences, Leo XIII left the Assumptionists in no doubt as to his extreme displeasure with their conduct during the Dreyfus Affair. He regarded the nationalists and anti-Semitic leagues as disreputable adventurers, and had long since discarded the possibility of a royalist or Bonapartist restoration, despite rival claims from the entourages of both pretenders that the Church would receive generous new privileges when the Republic fell.

As widely expected the first ecclesiastical victims of Waldeck-Rousseau's campaign against political subversion (June 1899–June 1902) were the Assumptionists, duly declared dissolved in 1900. Although the Jesuits had behaved very cautiously during the crisis—through a mixture of experienced prudence and fidelity to the pope's wishes—the fact that their colleges provided 15 per cent of the intake into the military academies put the less resourceful of them on the road to exile once more, in accordance with the government's pledge to guarantee the republican loyalty of the army. Waldeck-Rousseau's successor, Émile Combes (June 1902–January 1905) was an obsessive anticlerical, embittered by his own early experience as a *séminariste manqué* and personally convinced that the unnatural celibate life of the cloister unfitted members of religious orders for teaching the young. By the end of his ministry, tens of thousands of monks, friars, and nuns had been evicted from their communities, and as a result of his measures, a third of the schools run by religious orders were closed down. The survival of others depended on their nominal take-over by laymen and on an exhausting variety of semi-legal manoeuvres, while classrooms and corridors continued to be haunted by a flitting spirit world of supposedly dispersed regular clergy, conceal-ing their presence in a strange assortment of lay attire. To complete the cull, a law of 7 July 1904 ordered the phased exclusion of author-ized as well as unauthorized orders from teaching in any school, however owned or administered.

Parallel with Combes's comb-out of the congregations was a renewed vigilance in the recruitment and promotion of members of the civil and armed services. In the technical ministries, requiring professional expertise rather than loyalty to the government's overall intentions, committed Catholics had relatively few difficulties of entry and advancement. But in the *grands corps d'état* and in those ministries concerned with implementing government directives with quasi-political implications, especially in matters of internal security, Combes re-emphasized the need to exclude anyone whose whole-hearted commitment to government policies was in doubt. The evic-tion of the religious orders was a prime case in point, which had already triggered the resignations of a number of Catholic officials. Much more controversial—and fatal to Combes's government—was the insidious scheme to prevent the promotion of committed Catho-lics in the officer ranks of the army, regardless of their political convictions, which emerged in the *affaire des fiches*.

Like his predecessors in government, Combes regarded the Con-cordatory regime as too valuable a means of controlling the bishops and parish priests to merit annulment. Indeed it was his clumsy efforts to browbeat the new pope, Pius X (1903–14), into accepting his increasingly rigorous interpretation of the Concordat—especially in the matter of episcopal appointments—that paradoxically led to its abolition, contrary to his wishes. Threatening the Vatican with uni-lateral destruction of the Concordat, he unwittingly gave the anti-clericals in parliament the opportunity to take him at his word and insist that it become a reality—as it did under his equally reluctant successor, Maurice Rouvier (January 1905–March 1906). The resultant Separation law (9 December 1905) abolished the state salaries of Protestant pastors and rabbis as well as those of bishops and parish clergy. Jews accepted the situation with little demur. Their recent suffering during the Dreyfus crisis reinforced their inclination to keep a low profile, and the financial burden of providing for rabbis was offset by the political weakening of the Catholic Church, many of whose members had been prominent in the campaigns against them. Protestant attitudes to the law were mixed, some sanguinely seeing it as an opportunity to recruit members from an enfeebled Catholic Church and possibly make competitive bids for Church property when the question of future legal ownership came up. Now that the state no longer officially recognized the bishops as the legal embodiment of the authority and the orthodoxy of the Church in France, the Separation law stipulated that parish property should be given to *associations cultuelles*, representative of the body of the Catholic citizens in each parish. Other Protestants noted that ministers were giving unofficial assurances that property would be transferred only to those associations that accepted the authority of the Catholic hierarchy; and a significant segment of informed Protestant opinion saw the Separation law as insufficiently libertarian in its detail to compensate for the financial losses that it would entail.

If many Protestants thought the government oversolicitous for the orthodoxy of the proposed *associations cultuelles*, the Vatican alleged that these guarantees were worthless, as long as the letter of the law failed to designate obedience to the Catholic hierarchy as the main criterion of orthodoxy. On this pretext, Rome forbade French Catholics to form *associations cultuelles*—overriding, and indeed deliberately misconstruing, the formal recommendation of a majority of French bishops that they should be created. The outcome of the Vatican's intransigence was that the Church in France had no legal embodiment to which the state was prepared to transfer church property. It was not until 1924 that the realism of later popes settled the issue; but in the interval most of the unclaimed property had been given by default to sundry secular semi-charitable bodies and was beyond recovery. Political prudence decided the government to make a concession over the cathedrals and parish churches, which were left in the hands of the clergy as unofficial non-paying tenants until the eventual resolution of the issue in 1924.

In reality, Rome's prime reason for this self-mutilating sacrifice imposed on the French clergy was the fear felt by the new papal secretary of state, Rafael Merry del Val, that compliance with the terms of the Separation law, unilaterally destroying the Concordat, would signal to other anticlerical governments that the Church had lost the will to defend itself and that they could take similar measures with impunity. At the same time Merry del Val and his master, Pius X, were determined to make use of their new-found freedom to appoint bishops who were sympathetic to their own hardline policies. And lest the residual majority of Concordatory bishops were resistant to what this fresh leaven would bring, the Vatican refused to allow the French bishops to make use of their similarly new-found freedom to hold national assemblies. The outcome was that the French Church continued to be little more than an agglomeration of dioceses, out of touch with each other, dominated by Rome, and deprived of the means of taking vigorous collective action to coordinate their policies and rationalize their hard-pressed resources. With the abolition of the Concordatory regime, the Church was now theoretically free to redeploy its parish clergy to match the demographic changes of an industrializing society, without having to seek the permission of an unsympathetic government. But, without a national collegial leadership, the vision and will to take advantage of the positive aspects of the Separation law were dismally lacking; and such changes as occurred in the way of amalgamating parishes, etc., were weary responses to financial necessity rather than part of any national strategy.

Rome's suspicion of collective initiatives in France was matched by a parallel suspicion of French intellectuals, resulting in a witch-hunt of innovative thinkers among the clergy—the so-called modernist crisis—which lasted for most of Pius X's pontificate. These were depressing times for the French Church, saddled with responsibility for finding an income for its parish clergy and bishops. Unlike the English-speaking countries, French Catholics had no tradition of having to provide for their own priests; and although the initial sense of solidarity, induced by the anticlerical campaigns of the Combes era, encouraged generous contributions to the diocesan collections for the upkeep of the clergy (the *denier du culte*), the momentum was hard to sustain. The Concordatory salary, though meagre, had at least been secure—giving their recipients a certain modest standing in village life as part of the national establishment. Although the post-Separation Church learned to cope, the uncertain future discouraged recruitment to the priesthood, and within a decade annual ordinations had dropped to a half of what they had been at the turn of the century. Even the firmer legal footing, achieved by the settlement of 1924, was to reverse the trend only slowly, with the annual level in 1939 still a quarter below that of 1900.

1914–1940: a compromise of sorts

War, as always, led to an initial softening of domestic animosities in the face of foreign invasion. It also saw a rapid rise in churchgoing—most notably at times of particular crisis and in the regions where danger was greatest. Conversely the weary stalemate reached on the western front by 1917 saw the national level of religious practice back to peacetime norms—even if it stayed high in battle zones and in German prisoner-of-war camps, where many French soldiers, who had abandoned religion in adolescence, found in Sunday mass a tacit expression of mutual support and patriotic identity. And a large number of the captive priests celebrating these masses had been serving as foot-slogging, rifle-carrying soldiers in the trenches, since only those priests who had been part of the pre-1905 Concordatory establishment were confined to non-combatant roles. One in six of the uniformed clergy was killed—a third of these losses consisting of members of congregations, including many who had rallied to the nation that had sent them into exile ten years earlier.

All these factors helped to lessen anticlericalism, especially when combined with a growing awareness that the sweeping legislation of the pre-war decade had created great hardship for the clergy whose financial survival was now dependent on how the population valued their services. Already in 1914 the archetypally anticlerical Louis Malvy, minister of the interior, called a temporary halt to the process of shutting down Catholic schools that contravened the anti-congregation laws of the Combes era; and although the later years of the war heard a truculent recrudescence of anticlerical accusations in left-wing circles, partly triggered by Benedict XV's attempts to foster a negotiated armistice, the French Church entered the post-war period in a strong position to profit from the right-of-centre victory in the 1919 elections.

The French recovery of Alsace-Lorraine at the peace settlement immediately posed the question of whether this territory should remain immune from the *lois laïques* which had been established in the rest of France during the German occupation of the lost provinces. Their relatively high level of religious practice persuaded the government to adopt a policy of immunity, lest dissident particularism be encouraged; and the good sense of this decision was to be demonstrated in 1924–6, when Édouard Herriot's Cartel des Gauches government ill-advisedly set about preparations for extending the *lois laïques* to Alsace-Lorraine, only to find that anticlericalism was now a divisive issue instead of the rallying banner that radicals had successfully waved in the pre-war days of *concentration républicaine*. The survival of the Concordatory regime in Alsace-Lorraine was a major factor in deciding the government in 1920 to re-establish diplomatic links with the Vatican, which had been broken off by Combes in 1904. This enabled the continuation of the traditional Concordatory system by which the government proposed episcopal candidates for the sees of Strasbourg and Metz. By extension there followed an informal arrangement in 1921 permitting the government to voice any misgivings it might have concerning the Vatican's choice of bishops in the rest of France. The Vatican would listen to, if not necessarily act on, these objections; but, in the thirty years to come, the Vatican did in fact substitute a more acceptable candidate on the dozen or so occasions that government unease was expressed.

There still remained the crippling fact that the intransigence of Pius X over the Separation laws had left the Church in France without legal representatives to which former ecclesiastical property could be given. Both Benedict XV (1914–22) and Pius XI (1922–39) recognized the self-defeating nature of this policy, but a settlement of the issue had been delayed by the filial devotion of Pius X's episcopal appointments who did not share the older bishops' realism in these matters. In obeisance to the dead pontiff and his vociferous votaries, a compromise form of legal structure was devised which did not change anything of substance but allowed the creation of *associations diocésaines* in 1924—putting the French Church at last on a stable legal footing.

A similar willingness to shed the attitudes of his eponymous predecessor—and those of his stubborn legacy of episcopal think-alikes—prompted the pope in 1926 to prohibit Catholics from joining Action Française. Before the war, Merry del Val had firmly believed that one should not spurn fellow-opponents of what he called 'the forces of evil and international freemasonry ranged against the Church'; and this had made Pius X reluctant to condemn Charles Maurras's neo-pagan movement of the extreme right, despite its seduction of priests who naïvely saw it as the French Church's most effective potential ally. Unfortunately the third Pius of the century—Pius XII (1939–58)—lost no time in lifting the ban, in response to a finger-crossing declaration of submission by a calculating but unrepentant Maurras.

The political defence of church interests in France had been a continuing problem for both the Vatican and French Catholics. Leo XIII had counselled mutual cooperation with 'moderate' socially conservative Republicans rather than the formation of a specifically confessional party, with all the risks of marginalization. Even when the anticlerical measures of Waldeck-Rousseau provoked into being an unmistakable party of Catholic defence, it was careful to take the innocuous title of Action Libérale (1901). Admittedly when Édouard Herriot's Cartel des Gauches government seemed to threaten a renewal of anticlericalism, General Édouard de Castelnau responded by creating an unashamed Fédération Nationale Catholique (FNC) in February 1925. But this was a nationwide extra-parliamentary move-ment, rather than a Chamber party; and although its demand for a radical review of the Combes legislative legacy received the support of nearly half of the new parliament of 1928, the failing fortunes of Herriot's anticlerical alliance saw a corresponding decline in the pro-file of the FNC. Among the actual parliamentary parties themselves, the only ones specifically committed to Catholic interests were the Parti Démocrate Populaire (PDP)—a small group of less than twenty Christian democrat deputies, favouring moderate social reform—and the tiny Union Populaire Républicaine from Alsace-Lorraine. While one member of the PDP did succeed in achieving ministerial rank in the interwar period, the only other three committed Catholics to do so typically belonged to secular parties with no specific Catholic con-nection. Indeed it was conservative parties like the Fédération Répub-licaine and Alliance Démocratique that were the Church's main hope of sympathetic support in parliamentary debate. Nor did the rise of the Popular Front in the mid-1930s call into being a party or movement of Catholic defence as in 1901 and 1925. If Catholics were sceptical of the 'main tendue' proffered by Maurice Thorez, anticlericalism did not seem to be part of the Front's agenda.

Although defence of the Church was no longer the prime concern of parliamentary Catholics in the 1930s, Pius XI was determined to make the expansion of church influence the priority at ground level. He had inaugurated his pontificate with a stirring call for 'the organized participation of the laity in the hierarchical apostolate of the Church, transcending party politics for the establishment of Christ's reign throughout the world' (encyclical *Ubi arcano dei*, 1922). Foremost among the Catholic action bodies that spearheaded this offensive were the Belgian-born Jeunesse Ouvrière Chrétienne (JOC), which spilled into France in 1927, and the Jeunesse Agricole Chrétienne (JAC) of 1929. Their aim was to challenge the secular world on its own terms by combining progressive professionalism with a social concern that would transform society, letting their actions and achievements in their particular socio-occupational milieux convey the Christian message through the force of their example and their results. The trade union movement, Confédération Française des Travailleurs Chrétiens (1919), which numbered 400,000 in 1936, came to rely heavily on JOC as a source of members and articulate representatives. Moreover, many of the influential Catholic politicians of post-war France—notably the members of the Mouvement Républicain Populaire (MRP)—initially cut their teeth in the pre-war debates and activities of JOC, JAC, and the Jeunesse Étudiante Chrétienne (JEC). The 1930s also witnessed important developments for French Protestants. After decades of desultory negotiations, the two wings of the Calvinist Église Réformée de France came together in 1938 to form the Église Réformée de France under the presidency of Marc Boegner, bringing with them the bulk of their members. On the level of Protestant spirituality, the most significant development of the period was the growing influence of the austere Swiss theologian, Karl Barthes, with his emphasis on scripture. For many young French Catholics, on the other hand, the growing appeal of the Personalist philosophy of Emmanuel Mounier and the review, *Esprit*, lay in its combination of spirituality with a firm commitment to social and political progress. Among Jews, parallel and divergent currents of religious thought in the 1930s were inevitably overshadowed by the arrival of tens of thousands of refugees from Nazi persecution, swelling the overall Jewish population to 300,000 by the outbreak of war in 1939.

1940–1960: a narrow escape—and unexpected prizes

Devastated by the defeat of 1940, a large number of French Catholics were prepared to seek consolation in what the papal nuncio notoriously called 'the Pétain miracle'. Even so, the Vichy regime was not the clerical Valhalla that its critics have frequently claimed. Its ministers included relatively few committed Catholics, despite the patricianly presence in 1940–1 of a cohort of *comme-il-faut* churchgoers for whom the Church was principally a serviceable pillar of conservatism. Catholic commitment was strong, however, in segments of the secondary echelons of government, especially those concerned with harnessing youth to the hastily crafted ideals of the National Revolution; and the entourage of the Marshal had its collection of 'soft-cheeked altar-boys'—as Admiral Darlan contemptuously called them. For a Church still bearing the scars of the Combes era, the secular clergy were understandably, if short-sightedly, very well disposed to a regime that formally legalized the interwar government's tolerance of regular clergy in private schools, and which subsequently abolished Combes's legislation against the religious orders (April 1942). Yet although the bishops pressed hard for government financial aid for Catholic private schools, the best they got was government permission for municipal authorities to give support if they chose to do so. As a result of these measures, the proportion of primary school pupils in the private, predominantly Catholic sector, rose from 18 to 23 per cent by 1943. And while the secular nature of the state schools was still in principle preserved, off-premises religious instruction was permitted in school hours for children whose parents requested it (March 1941). With Darlan's accession as head of government (February 1941–April 1942)—and Germany demanding yet more of the French economy—government benignity rapidly cooled, while Pierre Laval (April 1942–August 1944) had even less desire to spend favours and scarce resources on an institution which he personally despised and distrusted.

The Church's initial enthusiasm for Vichy was increasingly mixed with apprehension. The government's growing involvement in the onslaught on the Jews prompted the nuncio in 1942 to protest to Pétain, while an emissary from the French bishops privately advised Pétain to resign lest he become irretrievably a German puppet. Even so, the bishops' collective expressions of loyal regard for the Marshal continued unabated until the early months of 1944, when the rapidly changing course of events increasingly counselled prudence and an end to episcopal claims that Resistance activists were terrorists. The Protestant leadership, on the other hand, had been much more persistent in its criticism of Vichy's treatment of the Jews, albeit within the context of cautiously courteous relations with the regime.

The lessons of past history might have predicted that the Liberation would unleash a tide of anticlerical retribution, as had happened in 1830, 1871, and the 1880s when the Church had been seen as the erstwhile ally of despotism. Although several bishops had publicly denounced Vichy's role in the anti-Semitic campaign—with some of them arrested in consequence—the majority had kept silent. And although a thousand priests had been deported to Germany—either for outspoken criticism, or by personal choice, to help young deportees—self-sacrifice on this scale was not for everyone; and most of the clergy preferred to keep a low profile in conformity with the don't-rock-the-boat pronouncements of their superiors. Yet comeuppance did not come. On the contrary, the Church in France paradoxically entered the post-war world with more political weight than it had had for seventy years. Not only were a third of the main portfolios in de Gaulle's Liberation government held by committed Catholics, but de Gaulle himself was the first practising Catholic to be premier since the Ordre Moral of the 1870s. Indeed eleven of the next twenty-five governments of post-war France were to be led by practising Catholics, while the new parliamentary embodiment of Catholic interests, the MRP was to obtain an average of four to five ministerial seats in the governments of the first decade of liberated France.

The dominance of figures such as de Gaulle and Georges Bidault in Liberation-era politics symbolized the fact that the resistance record of a small but determined minority of practising Catholics threw into sharp relief the distinction that the general public were increasingly making between committed Catholic laymen—who shared their social and professional concerns—and the senior clergy whose celibate, introverted, Romespun world seemed remote from their own. The slackening tension between Church and Republic between the wars had already lessened the need for clergy and laity to stand shoulder-to-shoulder in defence of Catholic interests, while Pius XI's encouragement of lay Catholic activity gave a further fillip to lay independence of outlook and action. The wartime split of attitudes towards Vichy between the bishops and Catholic members of the resistance made strong-minded members of the laity even less disposed to accept episcopal guidance, especially in secular matters. Pius XII, for his part, was expiating his much-criticized low profile of the war years by crouching even lower in the immediate post-war period of recrimination—and the French bishops thought it wise to follow his example. Yet recrimination even against the senior clergy remained surprisingly muted in substantial sections of the non-believing population—largely because many of them secretly recognized in the inglorious wartime record of many churchmen a reflection of their own cautious passivity and self-interest, faced with the perils of the time. Better forgive and forget, lest others remember.

The resistance roots of many of the MRP's leadership was not the only factor which made it the second largest party in the post-war assemblies. The newly established female vote was perhaps the most important, but the temporary eclipse of conservative, Vichy-tainted politicians who would normally have competed for the Catholic vote was a further bonus—even if it increasingly shackled the MRP to a grass-roots clientele who did not share the party leadership's aspirations to be accepted as a progressive movement with a social conscience.

The MRP's electoral successes were also helped by the rise in religious observance that had been triggered by the fears and deprivations of the war years. This rise had been further buttressed by the fact that Vichy had regarded churchgoing as a recommendation, rather than a liability, when it came to seeking entry and promotion in the more politically sensitive branches of the public services. The interwar years had already seen a relaxing of republican vigilance in these matters—with anti-Catholic suspicion becoming largely the perquisite of freemasonry and the socialist teachers' unions. Indeed this may have been a factor in the slight rise in male church-attendance noted during the 1930s in areas where it had been particularly low before the First World War. The euphoria of the Liberation, followed by the anxieties of the developing Cold War, helped to keep many churches fuller than they had been since the early years of the Third Republic—even if this remarkable phenomenon was largely sustained by the middle classes, especially the professional classes, who were enjoying the rehabilitation of Catholicism in republican politics and contemporary culture. French Catholic writing in the Liberation era displayed an adventurous enthusiasm that it had not known since the turn of the century, made all the brighter by the reluctance of Rome to restrain speculative theologians at a time when papal silence seemed the policy of prudence. Moreover its reflection in secular literature and drama reached beyond the religiously committed to a much wider clientele of reader and playgoer.

But this happy period of progressive innovation was short-lived. The onset of the Cold War enabled the Vatican to enter the warm embrace of the western powers, which were happy to welcome an ally with such long-standing anti-communist credentials. Once out of the cold, and with the necessary background warmth of an increasingly powerful Christian Democrat party in Italy—to say nothing of France and West Germany—Rome was ready to gather back the straying sheep and eliminate the goats. The most memorable victim was the worker-priest movement, which Archbishop Suhard of Paris had inaugurated in January 1944 in an attempt to counter the continuing loss of contact between the Church and the industrial working classes; the response of workers to the factors that had recently increased middle-class churchgoing was less marked and of shorter duration. During the next two years permission was given to more than a hundred priests to take full-time jobs in factories and other secular employment in the hope of creating close links, based on mutual solidarity, with a workforce that had grown up with virtually no contact with the Church. Their dedication and education made them attractive candidates for trade union activity, tempting some to become involved in communist CGT committee work. The Vatican responded in January 1954 by severely limiting the total working hours and activities that worker-priests could undertake, making them virtually unemployable in secular industry. The result—

welcome in conservative corners of the Curia—was that the movement ceased to have a meaningful existence.

Further casualties of the Cold War were the initial social ideals of the MRP. The exclusion of the communists in 1947 from the left-wing coalition that had ruled France—and the eventual departure of the socialists in 1951—obliged the surviving government parties to take on board the radicals in 1947 and then the conservatives in 1951, thereby killing hopes for further social reform. The creation more-over of a formal Gaullist party in 1947 pushed the MRP into adopting an increasingly conservative image in an effort to outbid the Gaullists for the old-style Catholic vote. The MRP's fears of Gaullist competi-tion were to prove more than justified—though in a way few of them would have predicted. The Algerian crisis not only brought de Gaulle to power in 1958 but also gave him the opportunity to provide Cath-olic education with the biggest prize that it had received since the *ancien régime*—major state subsidies for Catholic private schools (Debré law of December 1959). Fear of the civil chaos that a weaken-ing of de Gaulle's position might entail induced parliament to swal-low a concession that even its right-wing majority might otherwise have been unable to deliver. The bill was careful to stipulate that subsidized schools could not refuse entry to any child on religious grounds—a provision that arguably kept the bill within the letter of *laïcité*. Paradoxically the very size of the gift—dwarfing the miniscule concessions of the much-contested Marie and Barangé laws of September 1951—gave it a curious fall-of-the-curtain finality that discouraged further debate. Even the monster confrontation of 1984 was triggered by proposed modifications to the law, not by any threat of its removal. Thereafter the rapidly growing control of government by the Gaullists and their allies was increasingly seen by Catholics as the best guarantee of their interests; and within a decade the dwindling parliamentary rump of the MRP was carved up and cannibalized by other parties.

1960–2002: a Christian burial?

The 1960s were a period of ambivalent fortunes for the French Church. On the political front, it enjoyed an apparent security unparalleled since the early years of the Third Republic. Not only were the first three presidents of the Fifth Republic self-proclaimed practising Catholics, but perhaps as many as half of the government ministers under de Gaulle and Pompidou were rumoured to be regular churchgoers. In the civil service there was now no hallowed corner of *laïcité* that was not open to committed Catholics—even if the engrained respect for the established rung-by-rung ladders of promotion meant that the junior appointments of earlier regimes still had a continued advantage over former victims of anticlericalism who were now hoping to profit from the new spirit abroad.

While all of this might seem to exceed by far the wildest hopes of earlier generations of Catholics, it was in some ways an ironic victory. From the Church's point of view, the Catholics now in positions of power had little more to do than defend what had already been achieved—with whatever upward financial and libertarian adjustments their ministerial colleagues and the taxpayer would allow. Few churchmen realistically imagined, or even wanted, a re-establishment of religious education in the state school curriculum or a repeal of the various nineteenth-century laws that had separated religious considerations from the public law and institutions in secular matters. Moreover, the more conservative clergy noted with a wistful eye that Catholics in power behaved little differently from their freethinking colleagues when it came to legislation on contraception and abortion, both of which made their greatest headway when de Gaulle and Giscard d'Estaing were presidents of the Republic. Equally, when stalwart members of the anticlerical rearguard attacked Catholic ministers, it was rarely on religious issues—which featured with decreasing frequency in the politics of the late twentieth century—but rather on their socio-economic or other secular policies.

What was most disturbing to the clergy, however, was that this otherwise gratifying decline in politico-religious conflict was also a reflection of the rapid decline in religious practice that started to affect western Europe in the 1960s. This decade saw the coming-of-age of the 'baby-boomers' of the immediate post-war years—a generation which had no personal memories of the fears and privations of war, and whose attainment of adult independence coincided with a period of unprecedented economic prosperity, when nothing seemed out of reach. The development of the contraceptive pill not only favoured growing sexual permissiveness—in an age still ignorant of

AIDS—but it put women on a closer par with men. All this seemed to proffer a vision of bliss that was a safer bet than that of a heaven without tangible proof of existence. But in the early 1960s, liberal theologians seemed to be suggesting that youth could have much of this, and heaven too; and it was widely hoped that the *aggiornamento* proposed by the second Vatican Council (1962–5) would lead to a softening of the Church's position on contraception. After the death of the much disliked Pius XII in 1958, French expectations of a more sympathetic leadership in Rome were aroused by the advent of John XXIII (1958–63), who as a popular nuncio in Paris had witnessed the euphoric hopes of the Catholic avant-garde in the Liberation era. The language of the Council that he called, and the encyclicals and documents that followed in its wake, seemed to promise a new spirit of collegiality and free choice—albeit subject to the pope's ultimate authority. But the death of the new pope and the election of the cautiously conservative Paul VI (1963–78) permitted, if it did not necessarily cause, the misgivings of traditionalists to exert an increasing influence on the implementation of the Council's resolutions. Various liturgical changes undoubtedly made church services and sacraments more comprehensible to the less-educated sections of society; but the modest structures that were created to allow the voices of the various layers of church membership to be heard depended entirely on the willingness of those at the top to listen and be influenced. The greatest disappointment was Paul VI's re-endorsement of the Vatican's traditional condemnation of contraception other than the optimistically named 'safe period' (*Humanae vitae*, 25 July 1968)—effectively rejecting the majority opinion of his own advisory committee on the matter. The bitter feeling in France was that the Council had resulted in little change, except in rhetoric and surface externals. All this dashed the remaining hopes of those restless Catholics who had lingered in the club to see if relaxed rules and a new management would make for a more comfortable existence, in which corporate effort could be directed to the misfortunes of humanity rather than to mortifying the flesh. (The negative implications for the population problems of the Third World would later be aggravated by the onset of AIDS.)

In the course of the 1960s, weekly attendance at mass fell from well over 20 per cent of the adult population to less than 15 per cent—dropping further from 11 to 8 per cent between 1986 and 1994. A sample survey of 1989 nevertheless revealed a regional pattern of churchgoing that still had recognizable affinities with the patterns of the previous century, even if the levels were much lower and the regional differences less marked. That of the old Vendée (13.3 per cent) was still three and a half times higher than that of the Limousin (3.8 per cent), the traditional fief of landlord-hating peasant anti-clericalism. The pattern of gender differences was also familiar, if less marked, with church attendance in 1994 half as high again among women than among men, and belief in God a quarter higher—despite the increasing secularization of women's professional lives and the disappearance among men of pre–1914 fears that churchgoing might be a liability in certain branches of public service.

The corresponding situation among Protestants and Jews is much more difficult to measure, in that non-attendance at weekly services was not regarded as entailing such draconian divine punishment as conservative Catholic teaching had traditionally claimed. The 1960s had certainly seen a similar defection among the young as had hit the Catholic Church—despite the absence of the *Humanae vitae* factor. Traditional authority in all forms of religion and secular life was being scrutinized and challenged by the young in these impetuous years. Even so, the papal hard line on sexual matters—given yet greater emphasis by John Paul II (1978–   )—led not only to a loss of Catholics but also to a loss of authority over those who remained. By the early 1990s French polls were revealing that over 80 per cent of regular mass-going women were ignoring Vatican views on contra-ception, while it was already evident that only 1 per cent of adult practising Catholics went to monthly confession—compared with 20 per cent in the 1950s. In an age, moreover, when personal problems seemed better treated by the professional world of counsellors and psychiatrists, many priests were questioning their own role as moral advisers, and were joining those who were quitting the priesthood for a variety of other reasons, notably the Vatican's insistence on celibacy. Between the mid-1960s and 1980s, the number of French secular priests fell from some 40,000 to 27,000. Progressive Catholics were bravely hiding their embarrassment by proclaiming a dialectical view of how church doctrine and thinking would develop. They claimed that the Vatican's traditionalist views were the thesis, while their own avant-garde opinions were the antithesis. They cheerfully predicted that the conflict between thesis and antithesis would give rise in

God's good time to a series of mutually acceptable syntheses. Nor did it particularly perturb them that the charismatic, globe-trotting John Paul II did not always seem to appreciate the nature of the role that they had unilaterally bestowed upon him, despite the thespian versatility of his student days in Poland.

Sociologists suggest that the future of religious sentiment is likely to be one of continuing 'disinstitutionalization'—variously described as '*bricolage*', 'do-it-yourself', or '*à la carte*'. Political scientists, for their part, are divided on the extent to which this 'disinstitutionalization' has already weakened religion as a factor in French politics. Those who believe that religion still retains great influence point out that in the 1997 legislative elections, roughly 70 per cent of practising Catholics supported the politics of the right as against 30 per cent who voted for the left. Others reply that this voting preference for the right springs principally from the fact that these Catholics come from socio-economic milieux which favour both conservatism and Catholicism. Conservatism and Catholicism are two distinct entities, whatever their alleged affinities, and should be understood as twin products of a given social situation, rather than as a parent–offspring relationship with Catholicism as the parent of conservatism. The same type of argument underlies conflicting interpretations of the huge demonstration that took place in Paris on 24 June 1984, and which caused the socialist government to drop its relatively modest proposals for closer state involvement in those private schools that were in receipt of public funds. Although religious factors were undoubtedly present, many bishops privately felt that the proposals could have been accepted with only relatively minor modification. In fact only a fifth of the parents with children in the private sector were practising Catholics, most of the others having chosen this sector through dissatisfaction with the local state school, or through fear that if their children went there, they might be graded and streamed in a way that diminished their future prospects. And it was essentially these secular fears that created such strong and successful resistance.

The presence in late twentieth-century France of some four million Muslims gave rise to analogous but more complicated issues of interpretation, where ethnic culture and religion were difficult to disentangle. This was symptomatically reflected in the government's clumsy and inconsistent handling of the matter of Muslim female headdress in state schools during the period 1989 to 1996. The case for prohibition rested on the theoretical grounds that the *foulard* was an affirmation of religious identity, with a proselytizing potential that contravened the principle of *laïcité*. It was also argued by others that the *foulard* was a symbol of the subjection of women, unacceptable in a state school—a claim that partly shifted the debate from considerations of religion to one of culture. The Conseil d'État eventually succeeded in imposing the case for toleration by rejecting the claim of potential proselytism. But the whole episode revealed the greyness of the area between religion and culture.

The Muslim presence also gave rise to a parallel debate on the nature of *laïcité* itself, which generated ambivalent feelings among committed Catholics. On the one hand, French bishops were active in aiding and encouraging the integration of Muslim immigrants into French society, and were critical of the periodic hardening of government immigration policies. But while this programme of welcome entailed respect for immigrants' beliefs and a benign attitude towards unfamiliar practices, it also involved a wary vigilance lest fervent Islamists sought concessions from the state that went beyond what *laïcité* currently allowed Christian and Jewish communities to enjoy. A libertarian minority of Catholics, attracted by the more easy-going attitudes across the Channel, favoured making common cause with Islamists against the more rigorous aspects of French *laïcité*; but the bulk of Catholic commentators were more inclined to put their trust in the existing *système laïque*. After half a century of largely cordial relations between Church and state, *laïcité* no longer held the hostile associations of the pre-1914 era; and although committed Catholics were at one with Protestants and freethinkers in publicly proclaiming the virtues of tolerance and pluralism, they were not immune to the lurking feeling in France that Western and republican values in society and family life needed the protection of existing law, lest they be circumvented by an Islamist minority seeking exemption from those aspects that they found uncongenial—and who in any case might not necessarily understand or appreciate the subtle boundaries that divided the civil and religious spheres in France. Catholic leaders, therefore, found themselves in the ironic situation of appealing to the safeguards of *laïcité* that their grandfathers had so vigorously criticized. In any case, most of them had long since relinquished the hope (and even the concept) of reconverting their freethinking fellow nationals to Catholic practice, and had settled for the more modest aim of encouraging respect for Christian values in society as a whole. For this much gentler game, they were prepared to concede that the *régime laïc* was as level a playing-field as they were likely to get—and, whatever its shortcomings, the goalposts were securely rooted in the well-trodden soil of the past century, and not easily shifted by groups of any persuasion seeking particular advantage for themselves.

Conclusion: France in the twenty-first century

James McMillan

France has come a long way since 1880. If more than a few traces of the France of the *fin-de-siècle* could still be discerned in the France of the Fourth Republic, the France of 2002 bears little resemblance to the France of 1958, or even of 1968. France is no longer a largely rural society but has become a recognizably and self-consciously modern country with a highly developed and expanding economy (the rate of economic expansion in 2001 was just under 3 per cent). In common with all other developed countries France faces the challenges posed by globalization and the free market, but it appears that the protracted period of difficulties and adjustments which the French underwent in the 1980s and 1990s has produced an economy that is more dynamic, leaner, and fitter than ever before in the early years of the new century.

The process of readjustment has been particularly painful in France because the French have had to rethink their distinctive approach to economic management, which, after 1945, assigned a key role to direction by the state. At ENA, *dirigisme* was once an article of faith, but in less than a decade there has been a decisive shift of emphasis, reflected, on the one hand, in the marked decline of applicants (down 30 per cent between 1995 and 1999) and, on the other hand, by the rise of a new generation of managers who seem to relish the challenges of the global economy and have no fear of competition. Their language is that of the international business school, with its accent on flexibility and the need to react swiftly to opportunities, rather than on state direction.

Nevertheless, the state continues to be France's largest employer, directly providing a quarter of the entire job market and indirectly supporting many more. Public expenditure runs at more than 50 per cent of GDP. Big government is still a key feature of the French way of economic management. Economic protectionism has by no means been abandoned completely, notably in the energy sector, where the likes of Electricité de France can exploit the open economies of other countries (for instance in the acquisition of a 20 per cent stake in the Italian electricity company Montedison) while remaining a protected species at home. Other problems remain, as for example in the field of research and development, where the dead hand of centralization is again a significant factor behind a failure to innovate and to produce an adequate supply of scientists and engineers with the capability of operating at the cutting edge of research. France's place in the knowledge economy of the future has still to be decided. Unemployment, too, persists at an unacceptably high level, even if under the Jospin government it was brought down dramatically by one million after 1997.

The positive side of big government can be seen in the state's provision of public services, which for most people, ensure a quality of life that is among the highest in the world. The great change here came after the Second World War: before 1914, the very idea of an income tax was reviled by the liberal bourgeoisie. In the post-1945 era, however, because the welfare services which were established were the product as much of a tradition of right-wing social Catholicism as of left-wing socialism, they have not so far been subjected to the ideological onslaught which characterized the long period of Conservative rule in Britain inaugurated by Margaret Thatcher's electoral victory in 1979. Ownership in France is shared across the entire political spectrum. The French public health care system is second to none, while there are also generous family allowances, excellent childcare facilities, and paid holidays. The Jospin government is likely to be best remembered for its introduction of the thirty-five-hour week, which, contrary to what its opponents claimed, has created rather than reduced jobs while at the same time giving workers more precious leisure time. Whether the state can continue to provide services of the quality and quantity as those which have been available hitherto is likely to form the core of much future political debate.

The role of the state is also fundamental to the politics of national identity, or how the French see themselves and how they wish to be seen by others. The republican vision was a universalist one, predicated on cultural assimilation and the ties of citizenship which bound the nation together in the republican polity. Politics based on difference—whether of language, region, religion, race or class, or gender—were opposed in the name of the Republic one and indivisible. The continuing relevance and viability of the republican model in the twenty-first century has become a highly charged political issue and is likely to generate further controversy as it comes under fire from the apologists for identity politics centred on, say, ethnicity, gender, sexual orientation, or regional diversity.

At the same time, it is a moot point whether the republican vision retains any relevance for French relations with the wider world. In 1880, and despite the debacle of 1870, the French had a strong historic sense of their country as a great European power and as a country with a mission, deriving from the French Revolution, to take its universalist ideas round the world. Few questioned France's moral, political, and cultural superiority, eventually vindicated in the outcome of the First World War. The Second World War produced an entirely new world order centred on the rivalry between the two superpowers, the USA and the USSR, yet after 1945, French policy makers, oblivious to the lessons of 1940 and undeterred by further humiliations such as Dien Bien Phu and the loss of Algeria, continued to believe that France could—and should—be a decisive force in world affairs. That was the message of de Gaulle at the height of the bipolar Cold War era, and it remained the message of Mitterrand and of Chirac in the post-Cold War years after 1989. It is a message which plays well with the French electorate, but whether it corresponds to any kind of geopolitical reality may be doubted.

The fact remains that France is now only a power of the second rank at best and it is far from clear that Gaullist-inspired ambitions to build a multipolar world order will meet with any kind of success in the face of the unilateralist attitudes which prevail in the Washington of George W. Bush Junior. The French belief that 'Europe', headed by France and building on the rock of close Franco-German co-operation, can be a counterweight to American hegemony and a key element in the forging of a new multipolar world order is arguably a delusion, and a dangerous one at that. The vilification of France in general and of President Chirac in particular by the Bush administration and the American media in the wake of French efforts to oppose an American and British sponsored invasion of Iraq in March 2003 suggests that France may not be allowed to indulge in self-deception in foreign policy for much longer. Post-11 September 2001, the security agenda is now dominated by the American (and British) determination to deal with 'rogue states' and terrorism, with or without a UN mandate or any by-your-leave from the French. Where that leaves French defence policy is also a nice question, since the French have since de Gaulle vaunted their nuclear *force de frappe* rather than tried to develop the kind of mobile conventional forces required to act decisively in the world's hot spots.

What is clear, however, is that, in terms of domestic politics, the ideologically driven politics deriving from the French Revolution now appear to belong to a remote past, though they long continued to reverberate, even in the 1990s, when matters such as speculation over Mitterrand's true loyalties under the Occupation and the trials of the likes of Touvier and Papon for crimes against humanity committed under Vichy touched raw nerves and reopened old wounds regarding France's dark years between 1940 and 1944. Religious conflict has likewise abated over the longer term, as Maurice Larkin has shown, though militant supporters of the *idée laïque* still find excuses to protest about the continuing influence of religion in public life. In 1996, the visit of Pope John Paul II to France to celebrate the fifteen-hundredth anniversary of the baptism of Clovis brought demonstrators onto the streets. And, of course, Islam—now the second religion in France—has confronted secularists with a new enemy.

The Fifth Republic has undoubtedly given France real political stability, though before the 2002 presidential and legislative elections many commentators expressed fears that the institutionalization of 'cohabitation', especially as it operated under the Chirac–Jospin cohabitation of 1997 to 2002, would eventually produce political paralysis. Some thought that the time had come to move towards a full-blown American-style presidential system. Others, like the pressure group calling itself the Convention for the Sixth Republic, wanted to revert to a more overtly parliamentary regime. Power sharing between a president of the Republic and a prime minister of a different party was never intended by the framers of the original 1958 constitution and had the presidential and parliamentary elections of 2002 prolonged that situation, the French could easily have been in the business of having to draft yet another constitution—their sixteenth since 1791. In the event, they were spared another constitutional crisis, but subjected to a political trauma nevertheless.

The shock result in the first round of the presidential elections of 2002 demonstrated all too clearly that French politics can still be as volatile as at any time in the past. Just when commentators were complaining about how boring and predictable politics had become under the Chirac–Jospin cohabitation, the bombshell of National Front leader Jean-Marie Le Pen's showing in the first ballot exploded received wisdom about the attainment of consensus. True enough, in the face of the menace to democratic values posed by the far right, the left and centre-left, holding their noses, rallied to Chirac and thereby demonstrated that the Fifth Republic, like the Third, could command overwhelming support when the Republic itself was in danger. The legislative elections which followed in June and which gave President Chirac the right-wing parliamentary majority he had asked for in order to carry out his programme can be seen to have returned France to normality after the excitement of the spring. The regime, in effect, reverted to its Gaullist default position.

Whether the right will once again experience the kind of unbroken ascendancy it enjoyed between 1958 and 1981 will depend in large measure on the left's ability to regroup and refashion itself after the debacle of 2002. The failures of Jospin will not be easily forgotten or forgiven and for the next five years Chirac, with a compliant government headed up by the obscure Jean-Pierre Raffarin, has emerged as the strong man of not only French but of European politics—a remarkable about-turn in the fortunes of a political leader who was widely seen as probably the weakest of all the presidents of the Fifth Republic in his first *septennat* between 1995 and 2002.

Yet the implications of the Le Pen vote cannot be overlooked. It may be business as usual for the great majority, but fully a fifth of the French electorate remains disenchanted with mainstream consensus politics and refuses to identify with the issues prioritized by the political class. As in the *belle époque*, political consensus has its limits. Politics as a beauty contest betweeen Chirac and Jospin, or as a question of the manoeuvres of personalities in vogue with the media, do not address the concerns of those worried by crime, unemployment, bad housing, sink schools, immigration, and questions about race and nationality that go to the heart of people's perception of their national identity.

All of these issues are now subsumed under the heading of 'insecurity', the buzz word of Le Pen's electoral campaign and a top priority for the Chirac government. Yet as long as mainstream politicians and commentators continue to reduce this complex and related set of problems to the single issue of crime on the streets there will continue to be incomprehension on the one side and alienation on the other. Le Pen articulates the fears and emotions of those who feel dispossessed, disempowered, and disoriented by the pace and impact of global change. Millions of French people (more men than women, older rather than younger, poor rather than well-off) reject a world shattered into fragments by the forces of competitive individualism and readily identify with an irrational and emotional style of politics which, like the right-wing nationalism of the turn of the century, promises 'France for the French' and searches for scapegoats— formerly Jews and freemasons, now mainly non-white immigrants— to explain the collapse of communities, the disappearance of small businesses, high unemployment, and the crime wave. In the face of the rise of a new and disturbing version of identity politics on the French far right, the watchwords of the Republic—liberty, equality, and fraternity—retain their relevance. They remain to be fully realized.

Further reading

Consolidating the Republic: politics 1880–1914

The most recent survey of the whole period covered by this book is Charles Sowerwine, *France since 1870: Culture, Politics and Society* (Basingstoke, 2001). Sir Denis Brogan, *The Development of Modern France, 1870–1939* (London, 1967) still sparkles and delights. The best introduction to the political culture of nineteenth-century France is Robert Tombs, *France 1814–1914* (London, 1996). It can be supplemented by Maurice Agulhon, *Marianne au pouvoir: l'imagerie et la symbolique républicaine de 1880 à 1914* (Paris, 1989), and James R. Lehning, *To Be a Citizen: The Political Culture of the Early Third Republic* (Ithaca, NY, 2001). The theme of citizenship and so-called 'universal' suffrage is pursued by Pierre Rosanvallon, *Le Sacre du citoyen* (Paris, 1992), and Raymond Huard, *Le Suffrage universel en France (1848–1946)* (Paris, 1991). On memory and the weight of the past regarding the themes of Republic and Nation, consult Robert Gildea, *The Past in French History* (New Haven, 1994), as well as the monumental and multi-volume *Les Lieux de mémoire*, ed. Pierre Nora (Paris, 1984–92). There are stimulating essays in Robert Tombs (ed.), *Nationhood and Nationalism in France from Boulangism to the Great War* (London, 1991). Other relevant studies include Avner Ben-Amos, *Funerals, Politics and Memory in Modern France 1789–1996* (Oxford, 2000); Rosamonde Sanson, *Le 14e juillet: fête et conscience nationale, 1789–1795* (1976); Olivier Ihl, *La Fête républicaine* (Paris, 1996). On the early Third Republic, see Odile Rudelle, *La République absolue, 1870–1889* (Paris, 1986); Léo Hamon, *Les Opportunistes: les débuts de la République aux républicains* (Paris, 1986), and Francois Furet (ed.), *Jules Ferry: Fondateur de la République* (1985). For the 'culture war', in addition to works cited in the Further Reading for Chapter 8, see also James F. McMillan, 'Priest Hits Girl!: The Front Line of the "War of the Two Frances" ', in C. M. Clark and W. Kaiser (eds.), *Culture Wars: Religious-Secular Conflict in Nineteenth-Century Europe* (Cambridge, 2003), and Herman Lebovics, *True France: The Wars over Cultural Identity, 1900–1945* (Ithaca, NY, 1992). E. M. Acomb, *The French Laic Laws, 1879–1889* (New York, 1941), is good on the legislative culture war. Herman Lebovics, *The Alliance of Iron and Wheat in the Third French Republic, 1860–1914: Origins of the New Conservatism* (Baton Rouge, La., 1988), discusses the reconfiguration of the parliamentary right. Pierre Sorlin, *Waldeck-Rousseau* (Paris, 1966), is an important biography.

On left-wing republicans, see Patrick H. Hutton, *The Cult of the Revolutionary Tradition: The Blanquists in French Politics 1864–1893* (Berkeley,

Calif., 1981), and Judith Stone, *Sons of the Revolution: Radical Democrats in France, 1862–1914* (Baton Rouge, La., 1996). On the Boulangist episode, see especially William D. Irvine, *The Boulanger Affair Reconsidered* (New York, 1989), and Jacques Néré, *Le Boulangisme et la presse* (Paris, 1964). The rise of the new, nationalist right has been extensively studied by Zeev Sternhell: see especially his *La Droite révolutionnaire: les origines françaises du fascisme* (Paris, 1978) and *Maurice Barrès et le nationalisme français* (Paris, 1985). Other key studies are Eugen Weber, *Action Française: Royalism and Reaction in Twentieth-Century France* (Stanford, Calif., 1962), and Michel Winock, *Nationalism, Anti-Semitism and Fascism in France* (Stanford, Calif., 1998). Also valuable are Karen Offen, *Paul de Cassagnac and the Authoritarian Tradition in Nineteenth-Century France* (New York, 1991), and Philip G. Nord, *Paris Shopkeepers and the Politics of Resentment* (Princeton, 1986). The Dreyfus Affair can be approached in Eric Cahm, *The Dreyfus Affair in French Society and Politics* (London, 1996), but the best account remains Jean-Denis Bredin, *The Affair: The Case of Alfred Dreyfus* (New York, 1986). Two important articles are Paula Hyman, 'The Dreyfus Affair: The Visual and the Historical', in *Journal of Modern History*, 61 (Mar. 1989), 88–109, and Nancy Fitch, 'Mass Culture, Mass Parliamentary Politics and Modern Anti-Semitism: The Dreyfus Affair in Rural France', *American Historical Review* (Feb. 1992), 55–95, the latter of which contests some of the views of Michael Burns, *Rural France and French Politics: Boulangism and the Dreyfus Affair, 1886–1900* (Princeton, 1984). The reaction against democracy is the theme of Robert A. Nye, *The Origins of Crowd Psychology: Gustave Le Bon and the Crisis of Mass Democracy in the Third Republic* (London, 1975). For the left, Harvey Goldberg, *The Life of Jean Jaurès* (Madison, Wis., 1962), is a splendid study of France's greatest socialist. Reformism can be approached via K. Steven Vincent, *Between Marxism and Anarchism: Benoît Malon and French Reformist Socialism* (Berkeley, Calif., 1992) while for Marxism there is Robert C. Stuart, *Marxism at Work: Ideology, Class and French Socialism during the Third Republic* (Cambridge, 1992). Tony Judt, *Socialism in Provence 1871–1914: A Study in the Origins of the Modern French Left* (Cambridge, Mass., 1979), is an important study of the appeal of socialism in the countryside, while Bernard Moss, *The Origins of the French Labor Movement, 1830–1914: The Socialism of Skilled Workers* (Berkeley, Calif., 1976), discusses its relationship to the working classes. Charles Sowerwine, *Sisters or Citizens? Women and Socialism in France since 1876* (Cambridge, 1982), is authoritative on the minority of women who joined the socialist movement. Jean Maitron (ed.), *Dictionnaire biographique de l'histoire du mouvement ouvrier français* (Paris, 1974) is a rich source of information on labour militants. On the feminist movement, see the works by Hause with Kenney, Scott, and McMillan cited in the further reading for Chapter 6.

The Republic in crisis: politics 1914–1945

The most important work on political life in this period to have been written in recent times, sadly published in neither French nor English, is Gilles Le Béguec, 'L'Entrée au Palais-Bourbon: les filières privilégiées d'accès à la fonction parlementaire 1919–1939', unpublished thesis for the Doctorat d'État, Paris X Nanterre, 1989, a mine of information on the structures and attitudes of the French political elite. Nicholas Roussellier, *Le Parlement de l'éloquence: la souveraineté de la délibération au lendemain de la Grande Guerre* (Paris, 1997), provides a stimulating discussion of parliamentary politics in the early 1920s. Siân Reynolds, *France between the Wars: Gender and Politics* (London, 1996), discusses the gendered dimension of politics, while Gérard Noiriel, *Les Origines républicaines de Vichy* (Paris, 1999), is a fascinating account of the relationship between national identity, race, social structure, and politics in the Third Republic and under Vichy. The following works provide histories of the major political parties: Edward Mortimer, *The Rise of the French Communist Party 1920–1947* (London, 1984); Stéphane Courtois and Marc Lazar, *Histoire du Parti communiste français* (Paris, 1995); Tony Judt, *La Reconstruction du Parti socialiste 1921–1926* (Paris, 1976); Nathaniel Greene, *Crisis and Decline: The French Socialist Party in the Popular Front Era* (New York, 1969); Peter Larmour, *The French Radical Party in the 1930s* (Stanford, Calif., 1964); Serge Berstein, *Histoire du Parti Radical*, 2 vols, (Paris, 1980); W. D. Irvine, *French Conservatism in Crisis: The Republican Federation of France* (Baton Rouge, La., 1979); Jean-Claude Delbreil, *Centrisme et démocratie chrétienne en France: le Parti démocrate populaire des origines au M.R.P.* (Paris, 1990); Donald G. Wileman, 'L'Alliance républicaine démocratique: The Dead Centre of French Politics, 1901–1947', Ph.D. (York University Toronto, 1988). A comprehensive account of the Popular Front can be found in Julian Jackson, *The Popular Front in France* (Cambridge, 1988), while the vexed question of French fascism is discussed in Philippe Burrin, *La Dérive fasciste: Bergery, Déat, Doriot* (Paris: Seuil, 1986); Jacques Nobécourt, *Le Colonel de La Rocque (1885–1946), ou les pièges du nationalisme chrétien* (Paris, 1997); Robert Soucy, *French Fascism: The Second Wave* (New Haven, 1995); and Kevin Passmore, *From Liberalism to Fascism: The Right in a French Province, 1928–1939* (Cambridge, 1997).

Robert Paxton's groundbreaking *Vichy France: Old Guard and New Order* (New York: Columbia University Press, 1982) remains essential, but has at last been superseded by Julian Jackson, *France: The Dark Years* (Oxford, 2001). On the ambiguities of the Occupation, the best study is now Robert Gildea's original and stimulating *Marianne in Chains: In Search of the German Occupation 1940–45* (London, 2002). One of the best insights into Vichy political ideology is Francine Muel-Dreyfus, *Vichy et l'éternel féminin* (Paris, 1996). H. R. Kedward's two books on the resistance remain unbeatable: *Resistance in Vichy France* (Oxford, 1978) and *In Search of the Maquis: Rural Resistance in France 1942–1944* (Oxford, 1993). Miranda Pollard, *Reign of Virtue: Mobilising Gender in Vichy France* (Chicago, 1998), demonstrates the centrality of gender to Vichy policy, while Paula Schwartz's important article 'Partisanes and gender politics in Vichy France', *French Historical Studies*, 16/1 (1989), 126–51, remains the most important study of women and gender in the resistance.

The Fifth Republic as parenthesis? Politics since 1945

Still very useful is Philip Williams, *Politics in Post-war France. Parties and the Constitution in the Fourth Republic* (London, 1954). Richard Vinen, *Bourgeois Politics in France 1945–1951* (Cambridge, 1995), deals with part of the political spectrum for part of the life of the Fourth Republic. Vincent Auriol, *Journal du Septennat* (1947–1953 7 vols.) (Paris, 1970–80), probably provides the most detailed insights into the working of the Fourth Republic. Jean-Pierre Rioux, *The Fourth Republic, 1944–1958* (Cambridge, 1987), provides a good overall summary. Irwin Wall's *French Communism in the Era of Stalin* (Westport, Conn., 1983) is good on Cold War communism. On Poujadism see Dominique Borne, *Petits-bourgeois en révolte? Le mouvement Poujade* (Paris, 1956) as well as Pierre Poujade, *J'ai choisi le combat* (Saint-Céré, 1957). Very little of the vast outpouring of recent work on the Algerian war is concerned with its specifically political aspects. There is, however, much to be learned from general accounts such as Alastair Horne, *A Savage War of Peace. Algeria 1954–1962* (London, 1977), or Jean-Pierre Rioux, *La Guerre d'Algérie et les Français* (Paris, 1990).

The most interesting book on the early years of the Fifth Republic is Jean Charlot, *The Gaullist Phenomenon: The Gaullist Movement in the Fifth Republic* (London, 1971). See also Serge Berstein, *The Republic of de Gaulle, 1958–1969* (Cambridge, 1993): Institut Charles de Gaulle, *De Gaulle et ses Premiers Ministres 1959–1969* (1990); and G. Pilleul (ed.), *L'Entourage et de Gaulle* (Paris, 1979). On the political impact of television see Jean-Pierre Guichard, *De Gaulle et les Mass Media: l'image du Général* (Paris, 1985). Annie Kriegel, *The French Communists: Profile of a People* (London, 1968), describes the social basis of the party. There is a vast literature on 1968. See especially Richard Johnson, *The French Communist Party versus the Students: Revolutionary Politics in May–June 1968* (New Haven, Conn., 1972), and Henri Weber, *Vingt ans après: que reste-t-il de 68?* (Paris, 1988). On the 1970s see Jean-Pierre Rioux and Serge Berstein, *The Pompidou Years, 1969–1974* (Cambridge, 2000): J. R. Frears, *France in the Giscard Presidency* (London, 1981): David Bell and Byron Criddle, *The French Socialist Party: The Emergence of a Party of Government* (Oxford, 1984 and 1988). The Mitterrand years have already generated a good deal of writing. See Pierre Favier and Michel Martin-Roland's four-volume account of *La Décennie Mitterrand*; i: *Les*

Ruptures, 1981–1984; ii: *Les Épreuves (1984–1988)*; iii: *Les Défis (1988–1991)*; and iv: *Les Déchirements (1992–1995)* (all republished Paris, 1995). On Chirac's career so far, see Annie Collovald, *Jacques Chirac et le gaullisme: biographie d'un héritier à histoires* (Paris, 1999).

France, Europe, and the world: international politics since 1880

For a recent overview, see J. F. V. Keiger, *France and the World since 1870* (London, 2001). On the French Empire, a good starting point is Robert Aldrich, *Greater France: A History of French Overseas Expansion* (Basingstoke, 1996), while the *mission civilisatrice* is examined by Alice L. Conklin, *A Mission to Civilize: The Republican Idea of Empire in France and West Africa, 1895–1930* (Stanford, Calif., 1997). For perceptions of colonial peoples, consult Pierre Brocheux and Daniel Hémery, *Indochine: la colonisation ambiguë* (Paris, 1995), on Indochina, and Patricia Lorcin, *Imperial Identities: Stereotyping, Prejudice and Race in Colonial Algeria* (London, 1995), on Algeria. The latter's history is also surveyed by Charles Robert Ageron, *Modern Algeria: A History from 1830 to the Present* (London, 1991).

French diplomacy in the period preceding the First World War is analysed by J. F. V. Keiger, *France and the Origins of the First World War* (London, 1983), and the same author has also written a biography of a key figure, *Raymond Poincaré* (Cambridge, 1997). Military aspects are covered by Douglas Porch, *The March to the Marne: The French Army, 1871–1914* (Cambridge, 1981), and by Jean Doise and Maurice Vaïsse, *Politique étrangère de la France: diplomatie et outil militaire 1871–1991* (Paris, 1992). Douglas Porch also studies the intelligence dimension in *A History of French Intelligence from the Dreyfus Affair to the Gulf War* (New York, 1995). An excellent survey of Franco-German relations is Raymond Poidevin and Jacques Bariéty, *Les Relations franco-allemandes 1815–1975* (Paris, 1977), while P. M. H. Bell, *France and Britain: Entente and Estrangement, 1900–1940* (London, 1996) is a lively account of Franco-British relations. For the line taken by Clemenceau at Versailles, see David R. Watson, *Georges Clemenceau: A Political Biography* (London, 1974). The foreign policy of France between the wars can usefully be pursued in Anthony Adamthwaite, *Grandeur and Misery: France's Bid for Power in Europe 1914–1940* (London, 1995), and in Robert J. Young, *France and the Origins of the Second World War* (London, 1996), while the shortcomings of French policy in the 1930s are dissected at greater length by Jean-Baptiste Duroselle in *La Décadence, 1932–1939* (Paris, 1979). Martin Alexander, *The Republic in Danger: General Maurice Gamelin and the Politics of French Defence 1933–1940* (Cambridge, 1992), is an important monograph, and no student of the fall of France should ignore the moving personal testimony of Marc Bloch's *Strange Defeat: A Statement of Evidence Written in 1940* (New York, 1968). On the post-Second World War period, the standard work by

Alfred Grosser, *La IVe République et sa politique extérieure* (Paris, 1961), can be supplemented by John Young, *France, the Cold War and the Western Alliance, 1944–1949: French Foreign Policy and Post-War Europe* (Leicester, 1990), and William I. Hitchcock, *France Restored: Cold War Diplomacy and the Quest for Leadership in Europe, 1944–1954* (Chapel Hill, NC, 1998). F. Roy Willis, *France, Germany and the New Europe, 1945–1963* (Stanford, Calif., 1965), still repays reading. On the difficulties of the disengagement from empire, see, for Indochina, R. E. M. Irving, *The First Indochina War: French and American Policy, 1946–1954* (London, 1975), and, for Algeria, Martin S. Clark et al. (eds.), *The Algerian War and the French Army, 1954–62: Experiences, Images, Testimonies* (Basingstoke, 2002). On de Gaulle's foreign policy, consult Philip G. Cerny, *The Politics of Grandeur: Ideological Aspects of de Gaulle's Foreign Policy* (Cambridge, 1980), and Maurice Vaïsse, *La Grandeur: politique étrangère du général de Gaulle, 1958–1969* (Paris, 1998), and for his legacy Philip H. Gordon, *A Certain Idea of France: French Security Policy and the Gaullist Legacy* (Princeton, 1993). The important topic of Franco-American relations can be pursued in Frank Costigliola, *France and the United States: The Cold Alliance since World War II* (New York, 1992), and Irwin M. Wall, *The United States and the Making of Post-war France 1945–1954* (Cambridge, 1991). M. Wise, 'France and European Unity', in R. Aldrich and J. Connell (eds.), *France in World Politics* (London, 1989) is a good introduction to its theme. For a stimulating collection on the situation of France in the post-Cold War world, see Gregory Flynn (ed.), *Remaking the Hexagon: The New France in the New Europe* (1995).

The transformation of society

For the economy, see François Caron, *An Economic History of Modern France* (London, 1979). On economic growth in general, Patrick Fridenson and André Straus (eds.), *Le Capitalisme français, 19–20e siècle: blocages et dynamismes d'une croissance* (Paris, 1997) and for the role of the state Richard F. Kuisel, *Capitalism and the State in Modern France: Renovation and Economic Management in the Twentieth Century* (Cambridge, 1981) as well as, more broadly, Pierre Rosanvallon, *L'État en France de 1789 à nos jours* (Paris, 1990). The economics of wartime is one of the topics covered in Patrick Fridenson (ed.), *The French Home Front, 1914–1918* (Oxford, 1992) while post-Second World War expansion is the subject of Jean Fourastié, *Les Trente Glorieuses ou la révolution invisible de 1946 à 1975* (Paris, 1979; new edition, 2000). Employers are studied in Maurice Lévy-Leboyer (ed.), *Le Patronat de la seconde industrialisation, Cahiers du Mouvement Social*, no. 4 (Paris, 1979). For an exemplary history of a particularly important firm, Patrick Fridenson, *Histoire des usines Renault: naissance de la grande entreprise, 1898–1939* (Paris, 1972), and for the culture of the factory Robert Linhart, *The Assembly Line*

(London, 1981). Mixed reactions to the American model are discussed by Richard F. Kuisel, *Seducing the French: The Dilemma of Americanization* (Berkeley, Calif., 1993).

For longer-term perspectives on French society, see Yves Lequin (ed.), *Histoire des français, XIXe–XXe siècles* (Paris, 1983), 2 vols. The standard work of reference on demographic structures is Jacques Dupâquier (ed.), *Histoire de la population française* (Paris, 1988, 4 vols.), vol. iii: *De 1789 à 1914*; vol. iv: *De 1914 à nos jours.* On particular social classes, Eugen Weber, *Peasants into Frenchmen: The Modernization of Rural France 1870–1914* (London, 1977) is always stimulating, while Gordon Wright, *Revolution in Rural France: The Peasantry in the Twentieth Century* (Stanford, Calif., 1964), and Annie Moulin, *Peasants and Society in France since 1789* (Cambridge, 1991) are good surveys. Also valuable is Michel Debatisse, *La Révolution silencieuse: le combat des paysans* (Paris, 1963), while Ephraïm Grenadou and Alain Prévost, *Grenadou, paysan français* (Paris, 1966) is a rarity, the autobiography of a peasant. Gérard Noiriel, *Workers in French Society in the 19th and 20th Centuries* (Oxford, 1989), is important on the development of class consciousness among workers and Edward Shorter and Charles Tilly, *Strikes in France 1830–1968* (Cambridge, 1978), on cycles of militancy. Tyler Stovall, *The Rise of the Paris Red Belt* (Berkeley and Los Angeles, 1990) and Annie Fourcaut, (ed.), *Banlieue rouge, 1920–1960* (Paris, 1992), chart the rise of the red suburbs of Paris, while Norma Evanson, *Paris, A Century of Change, 1878–1978* (New Haven, 1979), describes the capital's evolution more generally. Steven Zdatny, *The Politics of Survival: Artisans in Twentieth Century France* (New York, 1990) examines a key stratum. Immigrant workers are the subject of Gérard Noiriel, *Le Creuset français: histoire de l'immigration XIXe et XXe siècles* (Paris, 1988), and Laurent Gervereau, Pierre Milza, and Emile Témime (eds.), *Toute la France: histoire de l'immigration en France au XXe siècle* (Paris, 1998). Antoine Prost (ed.), *La Résistance: une histoire sociale* (Paris, 1997), offers new insights on change during the 'dark years', while André Philip, *Le Socialisme trahi* (Paris, 1957) is a contemporary account of the disappointment of working-class hopes after the Second World War.

For the bourgeoisie, a good starting point is Adeline Daumard, *Les Bourgeois et la bourgeoisie en France* (Paris, 1987), while a key group in late twentieth-century France is studied by Luc Boltanski, *The Making of a Class: Cadres in French Society* (Cambridge, 1987). Georges Lavau, Gérard Grunberg, and Nonna Mayer, *L'Univers politique des classes moyennes* (Paris, 1983), discuss middle-class attitudes to politics. John Talbott, *The Politics of Educational Reform in France, 1918–1940* (Princeton, 1969), is informative on attitudes to education and for the history of education more generally one can still turn to Antoine Prost, *Histoire de l'enseignement en France, 1900–1967* (Paris, 1968). John Ardagh, *The New France: De Gaulle and after* (London,

1970, and subsequent editions) is an acute observer of social change, while Pierre Birnbaum, *The Heights of Power: An Essay on the Power Elite in France* (Chicago, 1982) is good on elites. On the evolution of social policy, Henri Hazfeld, *Du Paupérisme à la sécurité sociale, 1850–1940* (Paris, 1971) should be supplemented by Susan Pedersen, *Family, Dependence, and the Origins of the Welfare State: Britain and France 1914–1945* (Cambridge, 1993).

Women: distant vistas, changed lives

There is a voluminous literature on the history of women in France. Works cited here are mostly recent general surveys which carry full bibiographies of earlier and more specialized publications. The collective volumes edited by Georges Duby and Michelle Perrot, *The History of Women in the West* (Cambridge, Mass., 1994; see the volumes for the nineteenth and twentieth centuries) in practice contain many essays on France. Cf. Christine Fauré (ed.), *Encyclopédie politique et historique des femmes* (Paris, 1997). On historiography, see Michelle Perrot's collected articles, *Les Femmes ou les silences de l'histoire* (Paris, 1998); Françoise Thébaud, *Écrire l'histoire des femmes* (Fontenay-aux-Roses, 1998); Anne-Marie Sohn and Françoise Thélamon (eds.), *L'Histoire sans les femmes est-elle possible?* (Rouen, 1999), and Joan Wallach Scott, *Only Paradoxes to Offer: French Feminists and the Rights of Man* (Cambridge, Mass., 1996).

For the early period covered here, the most up-to-date and thorough history in English is James F. McMillan, *France and Women 1789–1914: Gender, Society and Politics* (London, 2000), which complements his earlier *Housewife or Harlot: The Place of Women in French Society 1870–1940* (Brighton, 1981). See also Anne-Marie Sohn, *Chrysalides: femmes dans la vie privée XIXe–XXe siècles* (Paris, 1996), and, on the First World War, Françoise Thébaud, *La Femme au temps de la guerre de 14* (Paris, 1984), and Margaret Darrow, *French Women and the First World War* (New York, 2001). Linda L. Clark, *The Rise of Professional Women in France* (Cambridge, 2000), is likewise relevant, and useful essays on both world wars are contained in Margaret R. Higonnet et al., *Behind the Lines: Gender and the Two World Wars* (New Haven, 1987). On the period between the wars, Mary-Louise Roberts, *A Civilization without Sexes? Reconstructing Gender in Post-War France 1917–1927* (Chicago, 1994), is an innovative cultural history. Paul Smith, *Feminism and the Third Republic: Women's Political and Civil Rights in France, 1918–1945* (Oxford, 1996), provides scholarly coverage of the parliamentary suffrage campaigns, which are set in a wider context in Steven Hause with Anne Kenney, *Women's Suffrage and Social Politics in the French Third Republic* (Princeton, 1984). Christine Bard, *Les Filles de Marianne: Histoire des féminismes 1914–1940* (Paris, 1995) is a thorough study of every kind of feminism; Siân Reynolds, *France between the Wars: Gender and Politics* (London, 1996), considers the alternative

242 | FURTHER READING

politics of the age. Useful essays covering the period will be found in Laura Frader and Sonya Rose (eds.), *Gender and Class in Modern Europe* (Ithaca, NY, 1996). Karen Offen, *European Feminisms 1700–1950: A Political History* (Cambridge, 2000) provides a comparative perspective.

On the Second World War, the works by Francine Muel-Dreyfus, *Vichy et l'éternel féminin*, and Miranda Pollard, *Reign of Virtue: Mobilizing Gender in Vichy France*, already cited, both analyse the gendered ideology of the Vichy régime; Hanna Diamond, *Women and the Second World War in France 1939– 1948* (Harlow, 2000), provides an up-to-date survey, analysis, and bibliography of women's survival, collaboration, and resistance. On the post-war period see Claire Duchen, *Women's Rights, Women's Lives in France 1944–1968* (London, 1994), and Sylvie Chaperon, *Les Années Beauvoir 1945–1970* (Paris, 2000). For women in politics in this period, there is the useful thesis by William Guéraiche, *Les Femmes et la République: essai sur la répartition du pouvoir de 1943 à 1979* (Paris, 1999). On the women's movement from the 1970s, see Claire Duchen, *Feminism in France from May 68 to Mitterrand* (London, 1986), and Francoise Picq, *Libération des femmes, les années-mouvement* (Paris, 1993). On more recent issues see Mariette Sineau and Jane Jenson, *Mitterrand et les Françaises: un rendezvous manqué* (Paris, 1995) and Janine Mossuz-Lavau, *Femmes, hommes, la parité* (Paris, 1998). Christine Bard (ed.), *Un siècle d'antiféminisme* (Paris, 1999) covers the whole period and contains a large section on resistance to change over the last thirty years. See also Margaret Maruani, *Travail et emploi des femmes* (Paris, 2000), and Michelle Perrot (ed.), *An 2000: quel bilan pour les femmes?* (Paris: La Documentation française, Problèmes politiques et sociaux, no. 835, 2000). Further surveys are contained in C. Bard, *Les Femmes dans la société française au XXe siècle* (Paris, 2001), and Gill Allwood and Khursheed Wadia, *Women and Politics in France 1958–2000* (London, 2000). On the Ministry, see Françoise Thébaud, 'Promouvoir les droits des femmes', in Serge Berstein et al. (eds.), *François Mitterrand, les années du changement* (Paris, 2001). The very recent period is tackled in Abigail Gregory and Ursula Tidd (eds.), *Women in Contemporary France* (Oxford, 2000). Finally, the revue *Clio: Histoire, Femmes et Sociétés*, published by the Presses Universitaires du Mirail in Toulouse since 1995, is a valuable source of information and scholarship.

Culture and the intellectuals

For the early years, Roger Shattuck, *The Banquet Years: The Origins of the Avant-Garde in France, 1885 to World War I* (London, 1969), is analytical and anecdotal; Charles Rearick, *Pleasures of the Belle Epoque: Entertainment and Festivity in Turn-of-the-Century France* (New Haven, 1985), is full of information. More specialized studies include Vanessa R. Schwartz, *Spectacular Realities: Early Mass Culture in Fin-de-Siècle Paris* (Berkeley, Calif., 1998), and

Mark Antliff, *Inventing Bergson: Cultural Politics and the Parisian Avant-Garde* (Princeton, 1993). Important for the First World War are Kenneth E. Silver, *Esprit de Corps: The Art of the Parisian Avant-Garde and the First World War, 1914–1925* (London, 1989), and Jay Winter, *Sites of Memory, Sites of Mourning: The Great War in European Cultural History* (Cambridge, 1995). Charles Rearick, *The French in Love and War: Popular Culture in the Era of the World Wars* (New Haven, 1997), despite its title is an excellent overview; Philippe Burrin, *Living with Defeat: France under the German Occupation, 1940–1944* (London, 1996), examines cultural life in context. On the post-war period, a useful if sometimes bland introduction is Malcolm Cook (ed.), *French Culture since 1945* (London, 1993), while David L. Looseley, in *The Politics of Fun: Cultural Policy and Debate in Contemporary France* (London, 1995), provides a balanced examination of modern state cultural policy. A withering gaze is cast on intellectuals by David Caute, *Communism and the French Intellectuals, 1914–1960* (London, 1964), Tony Judt, *Past Imperfect: French Intellectuals, 1944–1956* (Berkeley, Calif., 1992), and Sunil Khilnani, *Arguing Revolution: The Intellectual Left in Post-war France* (New Haven, 1993). Jeremy Jennings (ed.), *Intellectuals in Twentieth-Century France: Mandarins and Samurais* (London, 1993), contains some excellent essays. Valuable works of reference are Denis Hollier (ed.), *A New History of French Literature* (Cambridge, Mass., 1989), and Alex Hughes and Keith Reader (eds.), *Encyclopedia of Contemporary French Culture* (London, 1998). French readers naturally have an immense range both of broader and more specialist studies. Among the former, Pascal Ory and Jean-François Sirinelli, *Les Intellectuels en France de l'Affaire Dreyfus à nos jours* (Paris, 1992), is a lucid and penetrating survey; Jean-Pierre Rioux and Jean-François Sirinelli, *Histoire culturelle de la France; iv: Le Temps des masses: le vingtième siècle* (Paris, 1998), is a little uneven but comprehensive and lavishly illustrated. Géraldi Leroy and Julie Bertrand-Sabiani, *La Vie littéraire à la Belle Époque* (Paris, 1998), is an exemplary combination of scholarship and readability. On state policy, Pascal Ory, *La Belle Illusion: culture et politique sous le signe du Front Populaire, 1935–1938* (Paris, 1994), exhaustively examines a key period, while Marc Fumaroli, *L'État culturel: essaie sur une religion moderne* (Paris, 1992), is both polemic and history. Invaluable works of reference are Jacques Julliard and Michel Winock, *Dictionnaire des intellectuels français* (Paris, 1996), and Martine Bercot and André Guyaux, *Dictionnaire des lettres françaises: le XXe siècle* (Paris, 1998).

Religion, anticlericalism, and secularization

Gérard Cholvy and Yves-Marie Hilaire, *Histoire religieuse de la France contemporaine*, vols. ii: *1880–1930* and iii: *1930–1988* (Toulouse, 1986–8), provide a detailed chronological account of religious developments in the period as a whole—for which there is as yet no equivalent in English—and their findings are succinctly summarized and updated in Gérard Cholvy, *La Religion en France de la fin du XVIII*ᵉ *à nos jours* (Paris, 1991). Kay Chadwick (ed.), *Catholicism, Politics and Society in Twentieth-Century France* (Liverpool, 2000), contains a very useful, if occasionally uneven, collection of essays that underline the main issues at stake during the various stages of the twentieth century, while Maurice Larkin, *Religion, Politics and Preferment in France since 1890: La Belle Époque and its legacy* (Cambridge, 1995), gives a brief outline of Catholic developments in the same period as background to the book's main theme of politico-religious discrimination in French public employment. For close comprehensive coverage of these years in English, however, the reader is obliged to piece together the accounts of shorter periods in the publications listed below—notably those by Gibson, McManners, Dansette, McMillan, Hall, and Bosworth. For individual surveys of the chequered fortunes of Protestants, Jews, and Islamists throughout the period, see André Encrevé, *Les Protestants en France de 1800 à nos jours: histoire d'une réintégration* (Paris, 1985), Francis Malino and Bernard Wasserstein, *The Jews in Modern France* (Hanover, NH, 1985), and Miriam Feldblum, *Reinstating Citizenship: The Politics of Nationality Reform and Immigration in Contemporary France* (Albany, NY, 1999). The historical evolution of the principles and practice of *laïcité* is clearly described and discussed in Jean-Marie Mayeur, *La Question laïque, XIX*ᵉ*–XX*ᵉ *siècle* (Paris, 1997), while the impact of social and political change on churchgoing is closely analysed in Fernand Boulard and Jean Rémy, *Pratique religieuse urbaine et régions culturelles* (Paris, 1968). The principal works in English that cover the broad current of religious developments between 1870 and 1914 are Ralph Gibson, *A Social History of French Catholicism, 1789–1914* (London, 1989), John McManners, *Church and State in France, 1870–1914* (London, 1972), and Adrien Dansette, *Religious History of Modern France*, vol. ii: *Under the Third Republic* (trans., Edinburgh, 1961), which terminates in 1930. The *lois laïques* of the 1880s on education are examined in Pierre Chevallier, *La Séparation de l'Église et de l'École: Jules Ferry et Léon XIII* (Paris, 1981), while the impact of those of two decades later is appraised in André Lanfrey, *Les Catholiques français et l'école (1902–1914)*, 2 vols. (Paris, 1990). The causes and consequences of the Separation of Church and state in 1905 are analysed in Maurice Larkin, *Church and State after the Dreyfus Affair: The Separation Issue in France* (London, 1974), which also contains a general assessment of Vatican diplomacy towards France under Leo XIII and Pius X. The Church's role during the First World War is discussed in Jacques Fontana, *Les Catholiques français pendant la Grande Guerre* (Paris, 1990) and, more briefly in English, in James F. McMillan, 'French Catholics: *rumeurs infâmes* and the Union Sacrée', in Francis Coetzee and Marilyn Shevin-Coetzee (eds.),

Authority, Identity and the Social History of the Great War (Oxford, 1995). For the interwar period, Harry W. Paul, *The Second Ralliement: The Rapprochement between Church and State in France in the Twentieth Century* (Washington, 1967), examines the *détente* of the 1920s, while the internal tensions of French Catholicism in the 1930s are treated in John Hellmann, *Emmanuel Mounier and the New Catholic Left, 1930–1950* (Toronto, 1981), R. W. Rauch, Jr., *Politics and Belief in Contemporary France: Emmanuel Mounier and Christian Democracy, 1932–1950* (The Hague, 1972), and O. L. Arnal, *Ambivalent Alliance: The Catholic Church and the Action Française, 1919–1939* (Pittsburgh, 1985). Accounts in English of other politico-religious aspects of the interwar years are mainly to be found in individual essays in works of compilation, notably James F. McMillan, 'France', in Tom Buchanan and Martin Conway (eds.), *Political Catholicism in Europe, 1919–1965* (Oxford, 1996), and 'Catholicism and Nationalism in France: The Case of the Fédération Nationale Catholique', in Frank Tallett and Nicholas Atkin, *Catholicism in Britain and France since 1789* (London, 1996)—and the interwar selection of essays in Chadwick (ed.) above. The Occupation years are comprehensively covered in Wilfred D. Halls, *Politics, Society and Christianity in Vichy France* (Oxford, 1995), while the post-war decades are usefully described in William Bosworth, *Catholicism and Crisis in Modern France: French Catholic Groups at the Threshold of the Fifth Republic* (Princeton, 1962), and in Ronald E. M Irving, *Christian Democracy in France* (London, 1973). Publications in English on particular aspects of these years include Jean-Marie Mayeur, 'De Gaulle as Politician and Christian', in Hugh Gough and John Horne (eds.), *De Gaulle and Twentieth-Century France* (London, 1994), and in O. L. Arnal, *Priests in Working-Class Blue: The History of the Worker Priests (1943–1954)* (New York, 1986). The substantial changes that have occurred in French religious life since the 1960s are perceptively examined in Danièle Hervieu-Léger, *Vers un nouveau christianisme?* (Paris, 1986), and in Jean-Marie Donegani, *La Liberté de choisir: pluralisme religieux et pluralisme politique dans le catholicisme français contemporain* (Paris, 1993). Brief discussions in English are provided by Colin Roberts, 'Secularisation and the (Re)formulation of French Catholic Identity', in Chadwick (ed.) above, and by Yves Lambert, 'From Parish to Transcendent Humanism in France', in James A. Beckford and Thomas Luckmann (eds.), *The Changing Face of Religion* (London, 1989).

Chronology

1880   (Mar.) decrees banning unauthorized religious orders; (May) public commemoration of the Commune at the Mur des Fédérés; (June) Chamber votes amnesty for the Communards; (July) inauguration of the Bastille Day holiday; (Dec.) See law on the secondary education of girls

1881   (May) establishment of protectorate over Tunis; (June) law on free primary education; (Aug.–Sept.) legislative elections

1882   (Mar.) law on compulsory primary education

1884   Divorce law

1885   (Mar.) resignation of Ferry; (Oct.) legislative elections

1887   Resignation of Grévy after Wilson scandal

1888   Electoral victories of Boulanger

1889   (Jan.) Boulanger elected in the Seine; (Feb.) electoral law changed from *scrutin de liste* to *scrutin d'arondissement*; (Apr.) flight of Boulanger; (June) Second International Congress for Women's Rights; (Sept.–Oct.) legislative elections

1890   Inauguration of the Ralliement

1894   (Jan.) Franco-Russian military convention; (June) President Carnot assassinated; (Dec.) Dreyfus tried and banished to Devil's Island

1895   Protectorate in Madagascar

1898   (Jan.) Zola's 'J'accuse' creates Dreyfus Affair; (May) legislative elections; (June) League of the Rights of Man founded; (Sept.) stand-off at Fashoda

1899   (Feb.) death of President Faure; (June) Waldeck-Rousseau prime minister; (Aug.–Sept.) second trial of Dreyfus at Rennes, followed by presidential pardon

1900   (Apr.) opening of Paris Exhibition; (Sept.) International Congress on the Condition and Rights of Women; (Dec.) agreement on Morocco and Libya with Italy

1901   Law on the authorization of religious congregations

1902   (May) legislative elections; (June) Combes prime minister

1904   (Apr.) Entente Cordiale with Britain; (July) law banning religious orders from teaching and severance of diplomatic relations with Rome

1905   (Mar.) first Moroccan crisis; (Dec.) law on the separation of Church and state

1906   (Mar.) Courrières mining disaster; (Oct.) Amiens Congress of CGT, Clemenceau prime minister

1908   Labour unrest, arrest of CGT leaders

1909   (July) Jouhaux secretary-general of CGT, Briand prime minister

1910   Legislative elections

1911   (June) Caillaux prime minister; (July) second Moroccan crisis

1912   (Jan.) Poincaré prime minister; (Mar.) French protectorate established in Morocco

1913   (Jan.) Poincaré prime minister; (Aug.) Three-year law on military service

1914   (Mar.) assassination of editor of Le Figaro by Mme. Caillaux; (June) assassination of Archduke Francis Ferdinand and his wife at Sarajevo; (Aug.) outbreak of the First World War; (Sept.) battle of the Marne

1915   Italy enters the First World War

1916   (Feb.–Dec.) Battle of Verdun; (July–Nov.) Battle of the Somme

1917   (Mar.) first Russian Revolution; (Apr.) entry of USA into First World War; (May) mutinies in the French army; (Nov.) Bolshevik seizure of power in Russia, Clemenceau prime minister in France

1918   (Jan.) President Wilson's Fourteen Points; (Mar.–July) German offensive; (July–Aug.) allied offensive; (Nov.) armistice

1919   (Jan.) opening of Paris Peace Conference; (Apr.) law introducing eight-hour working day; (May) debate on women's suffrage in Chamber of Deputies; (June) Treaty of Versailles; (Nov.) victory of Bloc National in legislative elections

1920   (July) law proscribing contraception and abortion; (Dec.) Congress of Tours

1922   (Jan.) Poincaré prime minister; (Nov.) Senate rejects women's suffrage bill

1923   (Jan.) Franco-Belgian occupation of the Ruhr; (Mar.) anti-abortion law

1924   (Jan.) alliance between France and Czechoslovakia; (Mar.) introduction of female baccalauréat; (May) victory of the Cartel des Gauches

1925   (Apr.) resignation of Herriot; (Oct.) Locarno conference; (Nov.) Briand prime minister

1926   (May) Moroccan revolt crushed; (June) treaty with Romania; (July) Poincaré prime minister

1927   Electoral law changed to scrutin d'arrondissement, with two ballots

1928   (Apr.) legislative elections; (Aug.) Kellogg–Briand Pact

1929 (May) Young Plan on reparations; (July) resignation of Poincaré; (Oct.) Wall Street crash; (Nov.) Tardieu prime minister; (Dec.) funds voted for construction of Maginot Line

1932 (May) assassination of President Doumer; (May) legislative elections

1933 Hitler becomes German Chancellor

1934 (Jan.) death of Stavisky; (Feb.) riots in Paris, resignation of Daladier and separate anti-fascist demonstrations by communists and socialists; (July) PCF–SFIO electoral pact; (Oct.) assassination of Foreign Minister Barthou

1935 (Jan.) Franco-Italian agreement between Laval and Mussolini; (Apr.) Stresa conference, Britain, France, and Italy; (May) Franco-Soviet pact; (Oct.) Italian invasion of Ethiopia

1936 (Mar.) German reoccupation of the Rhineland; (Apr.–May) Popular Front electoral victory and factory occupations; (June) Blum prime minister, Matignon Agreements, dissolution of right-wing leagues and introduction of paid holidays and forty-hour week; (July) outbreak of Spanish Civil War; (Sept.) devaluation of French franc; (Oct.) creation of PSF by Colonel de la Rocque

1937 (Feb.) 'pause' in Popular Front programme; (May) inauguration of Paris Exhibition; (June) Blum resigns; (Aug.) creation of the SNCF

1938 (Mar.–Apr.) second Blum government, succeeded by Daladier government; (Sept.) Munich conference

1939 (Mar.) Anglo-French agreement on Poland; (Aug.) Nazi–Soviet pact; (Sept.) German invasion of Poland and outbreak of Second World War

1940 (May–June) fall of France: German troops enter Paris, 14 June; (July) Pétain voted full powers by National Assembly at Vichy; (Aug.) creation of the Légion Française des Combattants; (Oct.) statute on the Jews and meeting of Hitler and Pétain at Montoire

1941 (June) Darlan replaces Laval as Vichy's number two; (June) German invasion of Soviet Union; (Dec.) Pearl Harbour and American entry into the war

1942 (June) Laval returns; (July) round-up of Parisian Jews at Vél-'d'hiv'; (Oct.) beginning of the battle of Stalingrad; (Nov.) Germans occupy southern France; (Dec.) assassination of Darlan

1943 Creation of the Milice; (Feb.) introduction of STO; (May) foundation of CNR; (June) arrest of Jean Moulin; (Dec.), beginnings of FFI

1944 (Jan.) Brazzaville conference; (Mar.) CNR Charter; (June) allied landings in Normandy; (Aug.) Liberation of Paris and de Gaulle's assumption of power; (Dec.) Franco-Soviet pact signed in Moscow

1945   (May) German collapse; (Oct.) constitutional referendum and elections for first Constituent Assembly; (Nov.) de Gaulle elected head of the Provisional Government

1946   (Jan.) resignation of de Gaulle; (May) rejection of first draft constitution by referendum; (June) elections to second Constitutional Assembly; (Oct.) second draft constitution approved by referendum; (Nov.) bombardment of Haiphong and outbreak of war in Indo-China

1947   (Jan.) Auriol elected president of the Fourth Republic; (Mar.) insurrection in Madagascar; (Apr.) foundation of RPF; (May) sacking of PCF ministers; (June) France accepts Marshall Aid; (Nov.) massive strike wave

1949   Signature of NATO Pact

1950   Coal and Steel Community established

1951   Legislative elections, shift to centre right

1952   Signature of EDC treaty

1953   (July) beginnings of Poujadist movement; (Dec.) Coty elected president

1954   (May) Dien Bien Phu; (June) Mendès-France prime minister; (Nov.) beginning of Algerian insurrection

1955   resignation of Mendès-France

1956   (Jan.) legislative elections, Mollet prime minister; (Nov.) Soviets suppress Hungarian uprising, Suez expedition

1957   Treaty of Rome

1958   (May) Algiers coup; (June) return of de Gaulle; (Sept.) referendum approves constitution of the Fifth Republic; (Nov.) legislative elections

1960   (Jan.–July) independence given to French colonies in sub-Saharan Africa; (Feb.) French explode atomic bomb in the Sahara

1961   (Apr.) putsch of generals in Algeria; (Oct.) police brutally repress Arab demonstrators in Paris

1962   (Mar.) Evian Agreements end Algerian war; (Apr.) Pompidou prime minister; (Oct.) referendum endorses direct elections to the presidency of the Republic; (Nov.) legislative elections

1963   (Jan.) de Gaulle vetoes British entry into Common Market, Franco-German treaty of cooperation

1965   de Gaulle re-elected president

1966   France quits integrated military command of NATO

1967 (Mar.) legislative elections; (July) de Gaulle's Montreal speech; (Dec.) Neuwirth law on contraception

1968 (May) massive protest movement of students and workers; (June) legislative elections, resounding Gaullist victory; (July) Couve de Murville replaces Pompidou as prime minister; (Aug.) Soviet invasion of Czechoslovakia

1969 (Apr.) resignation of de Gaulle; (June) Pompidou elected president

1971 Founding congress of new socialist party at Épinay

1972 Socialists and PCF draw up a common programme

1973 Oil crisis

1974 (Apr.) death of Pompidou; (May) Giscard d'Estaing elected president, Jacques Chirac prime minister

1975 Law liberalizing abortion

1976 (Aug.) resignation of Chirac, Raymond Barre prime minister; (Dec.) foundation of RPR

1977 Collapse of left-wing unity

1978 (Feb.) foundation of UDF; (March), legislative elections, defeat of the left

1979 (Mar.) France joins EMS; (June) European elections

1981 (Apr.–May) François Mitterrand elected president; (June) legislative elections, victory of the left: Mauroy government includes four communists

1982 Law on decentralization

1983 U-turn in socialist economic policy

1984 (Jan.) foundation of Green party; (June) European elections; (July) Laurent Fabius prime minister, communists leave government

1985 Sinking of the *Rainbow Warrior*

1986 Legislative elections lead to victory of the right and 'cohabitation': Chirac prime minister

1987 Trial of Klaus Barbie

1988 (Apr.–May) Mitterrand re-elected president: Rocard prime minister; (June) legislative elections, socialists return to power

1989 (June) European elections; (Oct.) Muslim headscarf affair; (Nov.) fall of Berlin Wall

1991 (May) Edith Cresson first woman prime minister; (Dec.) treaty of Maastricht

1992 (Apr.) Bérégovoy replaces Cresson as prime minister; (Sept.) referendum on Maastricht Treaty

1993 (Mar.) legislative elections: right victorious, second cohabitation,

Balladur prime minister; (May) suicide of Bérégovoy and revision of French laws on nationality

1994 (Mar.–Apr.) trial of Paul Touvier; (June) European elections; (Sept.) the *affaire* Mitterrand

1995 (Apr.–May) Chirac elected president

1996 Death of Mitterrand

1997 Legislative elections, victory of the left and third cohabitation under Chirac and Lionel Jospin

1998 (Apr.) Maurice Papon convicted of 'complicity in crimes against humanity'; (May) law on 35-hour working week (effective 2000); (July) France wins football World Cup; (Oct.) homosexual couples recognized in law

1999 Law on gender parity in politics

2001 11 September, suicide bombing of World Trade Center, New York

2002 (Apr.–May) presidential elections, Chirac re-elected after sensational Front National showing in first ballot; (June) legislative elections, return of the right, Jean-Pierre Raffarin prime minister

Maps

Map 1 Departments of France
Source: Richard Vinen, *France 1934–1970* (Macmillan, 1996)

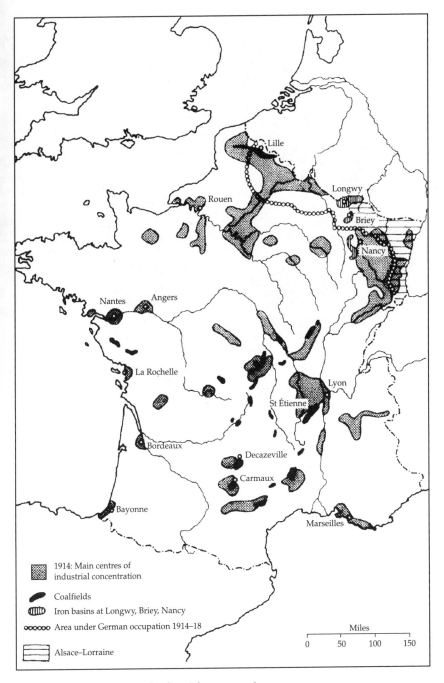

Map 2 1914: Main centres of industrial concentration
Source: J. P. T. Bury, *France 1814–1940* (Methuen, 1985)

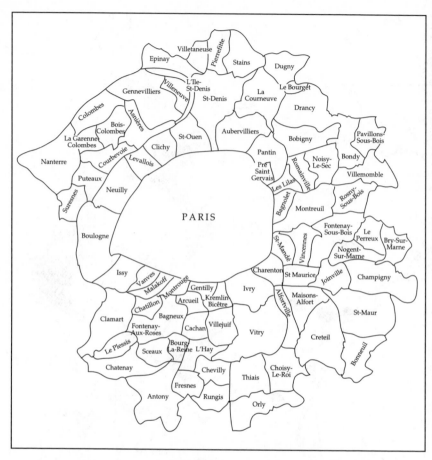

Map 3 Paris and the Department of the Seine in 1920, showing the 'Red Belt'
Source: Tyler Stovall, *The Rise of the Paris Red Belt* (University of California Press, Berkeley, 1990)

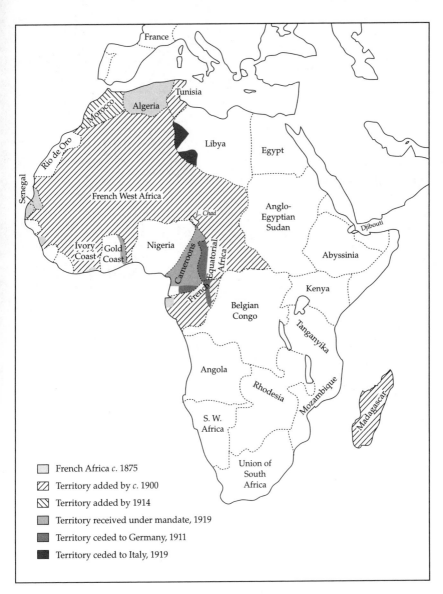

Map 4 French Africa
Source: J. P. T Bury, *France 1814–1940* (Methuen, 1995)

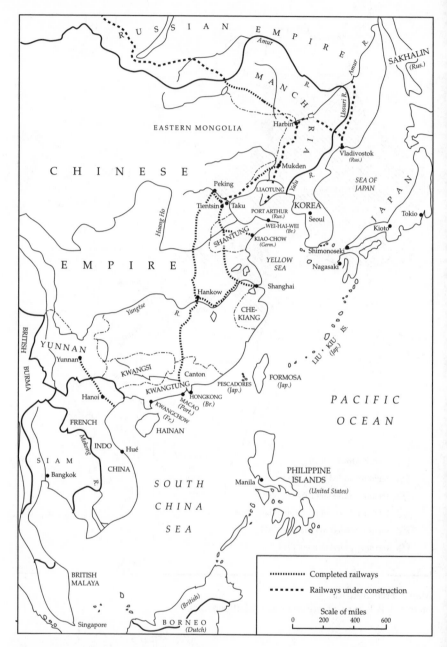

Map 5 Imperialism in the Far East, 1900
Source: Carlton J. H. Hayes, *A Generation of Materialism* (Harper and Row, 1941)

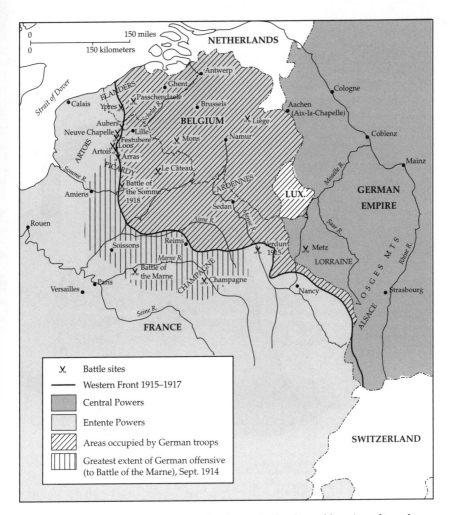

Map 6 The Western Front, 1914–1917, showing major battles and location of trenches at the end of 1915 and at the end of 1917

Source: John Merriman, *A History of Modern Europe: From the Renaissance to the Present*, vol. 2 (W. W. Norton, 1996)

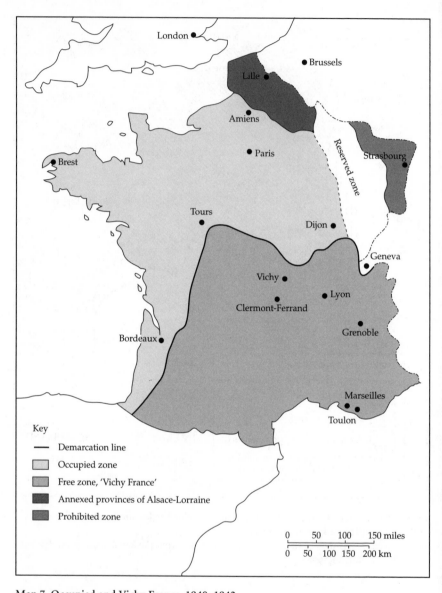

Map 7 Occupied and Vichy France, 1940–1942
Source: Philippe Burrin, *Living with Defeat: France under the German Occupation, 1940–1944* (Edward Arnold, 1996)

Index